Impossibility Results
for Distributed Computing

Synthesis Lectures on Distributed Computing Theory

Editor
Nancy Lynch, *Massachusetts Institute of Technology*

Synthesis Lectures on Distributed Computing Theory is edited by Nancy Lynch of the Massachusetts Institute of Technology. The series will publish 50- to 150-page publications on topics pertaining to distributed computing theory. The scope will largely follow the purview of premier information and computer science conferences, such as ACM PODC, DISC, SPAA, OPODIS, CONCUR, DialM-POMC, ICDCS, SODA, Sirocco, SSS, and related conferences. Potential topics include, but not are limited to: distributed algorithms and lower bounds, algorithm design methods, formal modeling and verification of distributed algorithms, and concurrent data structures.

Impossibility Results for Distributed Computing
Hagit Attiya and Faith Ellen
2014

Distributed Graph Coloring: Fundamentals and Recent Developments
Leonid Barenboim and Michael Elkin
2013

Distributed Computing by Oblivious Mobile Robots
Paola Flocchini, Giuseppe Prencipe, and Nicola Santoro
2012

Quorum Systems: With Applications to Storage and Consensus
Marko Vukolic
2012

Link Reversal Algorithms
Jennifer L. Welch and Jennifer E. Walter
2011

Cooperative Task-Oriented Computing: Algorithms and Complexity
Chryssis Georgiou and Alexander A. Shvartsman
2011

New Models for Population Protocols
Othon Michail, Ioannis Chatzigiannakis, and Paul G. Spirakis
2011

The Theory of Timed I/O Automata, Second Edition
Dilsun K. Kaynar, Nancy Lynch, Roberto Segala, and Frits Vaandrager
2010

Principles of Transactional Memory
Rachid Guerraoui and Michal Kapalka
2010

Fault-tolerant Agreement in Synchronous Message-passing Systems
Michel Raynal
2010

Communication and Agreement Abstractions for Fault-Tolerant Asynchronous
Distributed Systems
Michel Raynal
2010

The Mobile Agent Rendezvous Problem in the Ring
Evangelos Kranakis, Danny Krizanc, and Euripides Markou
2010

Impossibility Results for Distributed Computing
Hagit Attiya and Faith Ellen

ISBN: 978-3-031-00882-5   paperback
ISBN: 978-3-031-02010-0   ebook

DOI 10.1007/978-3-031-02010-0

A Publication in the Springer series
SYNTHESIS LECTURES ON DISTRIBUTED COMPUTING THEORY

Lecture #12
Series Editor: Nancy Lynch, *Massachusetts Institute of Technology*
Series ISSN
Synthesis Lectures on Distributed Computing Theory
Print 2155-1626   Electronic 2155-1634

Impossibility Results
for Distributed Computing

Hagit Attiya
Technion–Israel Institute of Technology

Faith Ellen
University of Toronto

SYNTHESIS LECTURES ON DISTRIBUTED COMPUTING THEORY #12

ABSTRACT

To understand the power of distributed systems, it is necessary to understand their inherent limitations: what problems cannot be solved in particular systems, or without sufficient resources (such as time or space).

This book presents key techniques for proving such impossibility results and applies them to a variety of different problems in a variety of different system models. Insights gained from these results are highlighted, aspects of a problem that make it difficult are isolated, features of an architecture that make it inadequate for solving certain problems efficiently are identified, and different system models are compared.

KEYWORDS

lower bounds, indistinguishability, shifting, scaling, scenario arguments, information theory arguments, covering, valency, reductions, simulations, implementations, consensus, set consensus, approximate agreement, clock synchronization, mutual exclusion, snapshots, timestamps

Hagit Attiya dedicates this book to the memory of her parents,
Malka and David Attiya, who instilled in her a passion for learning.

Faith Ellen dedicates this book to the memory of her father,
Leonard Whyne, who always encouraged her interest in mathematics.

Contents

Acknowledgments

This book originated from lecture notes for graduate courses given at the Technion and the University of Toronto. We are grateful to the students and postdoctoral fellows, Armando Castañeda, Xiwen Chen, Mika Göös, Marek Janicki, Serhei Makarov, Avery Miller, Rotem Oshman, and Ami Paz, who read parts of earlier drafts and pointed out small mistakes or parts they found difficult to understand. We would like to thank our reviewers, Keren Censor Hillel and James Aspnes, for their insightful comments on the manuscript. We particularly value Keren's help with Section 7.5. Hagit would like to thank her family for their love and support. Finally, we appreciate the encouragement and patience of our editors, Nancy Lynch and Diane Cerra.

Hagit Attiya is supported by the Yad-Handiv Foundation and by the Israel Science Foundation (grant number 1227/10). Faith Ellen is supported by the Natural Science and Engineering Research Council of Canada and, while at the Technion, by a fellowship from the Lady Davis Foundation.

Hagit Attiya and Faith Ellen
January 2014

CHAPTER 1

Introduction

1.1 UNSOLVABILITY RESULTS AND LOWER BOUNDS

This book studies computation in distributed systems, specifically *unsolvability* results, which show that certain problems cannot be solved, and *lower bound* results, which show that certain problems cannot be computed when insufficient resources are available. In general, such impossibility results depend on assumptions about the system, for example, how processes communicate with one another or what kinds of failures can occur. They also depend on the types of algorithms allowed, for example, whether randomization can be used.

For solvable problems, we study their complexity under a number of different measures, most notably, time, number of steps, number of messages and their size, number of shared variables, their type and size, and contention. Our goal is to find lower bounds on one or more of these resources or tradeoffs among them.

Note that, unlike the situation when we study algorithms, bigger lower bounds are better. Impossibility results for weaker problems are better because they automatically imply the same results for stronger problems. Similarly, it is better to prove impossibility results for stronger models, for example, with more powerful primitives, more synchrony, a source of randomness, or less faulty behaviour.

1.2 WHY STUDY IMPOSSIBILITY RESULTS?

Lower bounds and unsolvability results help us understand the nature of distributed computing:

- What makes certain problems hard? What parts of the problem requirements cause the difficulty? How do two different problems relate to one another?

- What makes certain systems powerful? What are the crucial limitations of real systems? How do two different systems (or, more precisely, formal models of those systems) relate to one another?

Lower bounds also tell us when to stop looking for better solutions, namely, when they match an existing upper bound. (Unfortunately, this does not happen very often.) Impossibility results that assume restricted types of algorithms, for example, deterministic algorithms or algorithms that do not distinguish between different processes, indicate which approaches will not work.

If a problem needs to be solved despite an unsolvability result, the proof may indicate how to adjust either the problem statement (making it weaker) or the system model (making it stronger). In this manner, lower bounds have influenced real systems, by showing the system must satisfy certain assumptions, if important problems must be solved. For example, the unsolvability of consensus in asynchronous shared memory systems where processes communicate through registers has led to manufacturers including more powerful primitives such as compare&swap into their architectures.

Trying to prove a lower bound can suggest new and different algorithmic approaches for solving a problem. It can be fruitful to alternately work on getting a lower bound and getting a better algorithm, using the difficulties encountered in one to provide insight for the other.

Finally, lower bounds are fun to prove!

1.3   STRUCTURE OF THE BOOK

This book considers a variety of problems and models for distributed systems, emphasizing techniques, rather than results. (Surveys of lower bound results appear in Nancy Lynch, "A hundred impossibility proofs for distributed computing," *PODC*, 1989 [59], and in Faith Fich and Eric Ruppert, "Hundreds of impossibility results for distributed computing," *Distributed Computing*, 2003 [39].) After explaining a technique, we present several applications of it, going from simpler ones to more complicated ones. We have not always chosen the most important or most complicated results. Instead, we prefer proofs that expose the really important aspects of the techniques. We do not described topology-based techniques for studying distributed computing, as they require significant additional background. This topic is covered in the book *Distributed Computing through Combinatorial Topology* by Maurice Herlihy, Dmitry Kozlov, and Sergio Rajsbaum 2013 [48].

For each result, we begin by carefully specifying the model and the problem. Unless stated otherwise, we assume all models are deterministic. We assume the reader is familiar with standard models of distributed computing, for example, as defined in Hagit Attiya and Jennifer Welch's book *Distributed Computing: Fundamentals, Simulations, and Advanced Topics*, 2004 [22]. Throughout the book, we use $p_0, \ldots, p_{n-1}$ to denote the processes of the model in which we are working. To distinguish operations we are trying to implement from those that we are using for an implementation, we denote the former with initial capital letters, for example, WRITE and GetTS, and we denote the latter with lower case letters, for example, write. We call the latter *primitives*.

CHAPTER 2

Indistinguishability

Most impossibility results in distributed computing follow from a lack of knowledge or uncertainty about the system. At any point in time, the state of a process, including the value of its input variables, is the knowledge the process has about the system. To solve many distributed computing problems, processes need to learn information about the states of other processes. Proofs of unsolvability results show that this knowledge cannot be obtained; proofs of lower bounds show that this knowledge cannot be obtained with limited resources.

Lack of knowledge stems from uncertainty about many aspects of the system, including the inputs of other processes (since different processes may get different inputs), asynchrony (how many steps other processes have taken, what messages have been sent and received), and failures (crashes, omissions, and malicious processes). How do we say that a process doesn't know something? If its local knowledge is compatible with two different executions, then it doesn't know which of the two executions has occurred. A key method for capturing lack of knowledge is by arguing about the indistinguishability of certain executions or configurations.

A *configuration* describes the system at some point in time. It consists of the states of all processes and the state of the environment (for example, the values of all shared variables, or the contents of all message channels). Two configurations, C and C', are *indistinguishable* to a process p_i, if it has the same state in both configurations. In other words, p_i does not know whether it is in C or C'. This is denoted $C \overset{p_i}{\sim} C'$. If P is a set of processes and $C \overset{p_i}{\sim} C'$ for all $p_i \in P$, we write $C \overset{P}{\sim} C'$. Note that, in some of the distributed computing literature, the definition of $C \overset{p_i}{\sim} C'$ also requires that the state of the environment is the same in C and C'. We prefer to address the state of the environment separately, because we often consider configurations that differ in parts of the environment that will not affect p_i.

At any configuration, there is a fixed set of events that can occur, each of which affects one process. Some examples of events are message m is delivered to process p_i on channel c, process p_i writes value v to register r, and process p_i reads value v from register r. An *execution* is a sequence of alternating configurations and events, starting with a configuration, such that each event can occur at the configuration which precedes it and which results in the configuration that follows it. If an execution is finite, it ends with a configuration. A *solo execution* is an execution in which every event is performed by the same process. An execution is p_i-*free* if it contains no event performed by process p_i. An execution is P-*free* if it is p_i-free for every process p_i in the set of processes P.

The *history* associated with an execution is its sequence of events. A sequence of events σ *can occur starting at* a configuration C if there is an execution that begins with C whose history is σ. If σ is finite, we use $C\sigma$ to denote the last configuration in this execution. No event of a *P-free history* is performed by a process in P. All events of a *P-only history* are performed by processes in P. A *solo history* is a $\{p\}$-only history for some process p. We sometimes partition a history into a set of n *local histories*, one for each process, consisting of the events which affect that process.

Whether σ can occur starting at C depends on the state of the environment in C. Specifically, in shared memory systems, it depends on the values of the shared objects accessed by σ and, in message passing systems, it depends on the contents of the message channels on which messages are delivered in σ. If the last configuration of execution α is the same as the first configuration of execution α', then $\alpha\alpha'$ denotes the execution consisting of α followed by all but the first configuration of α'.

Two executions, α and α', starting from configurations C and C', respectively, are *indistinguishable* to a set of processes P if $C \overset{P}{\sim} C'$ and each process $p_i \in P$ has the same local history in both executions. This is denoted $\alpha \overset{P}{\sim} \alpha'$.

If two configurations, C and C', are indistinguishable to a set of processes and the same finite sequence of events, σ, can occur starting at each, then the two resulting configurations, $C\sigma$ and $C'\sigma$, will also be indistinguishable to these processes. The following lemma and its corollary are useful for identifying such situations. They are straightforward to prove by induction.

Lemma 2.1 Let σ be a sequence of events by some set of processes P that can occur starting from configuration C. If $C \overset{P}{\sim} C'$ and the part of the environment accessed by σ has the same value in C and C', then σ can occur starting from C' and, if σ is finite, $C\sigma \overset{P}{\sim} C'\sigma$.

Corollary 2.2 *Let α be an execution starting from some configuration C, all of whose events are by processes in some set P. If $C \overset{P}{\sim} C'$ and the part of the environment accessed by α has the same value in C and C', then there is an execution α' by the processes in P starting from C' such that $\alpha \overset{P}{\sim} \alpha'$.*

If some process cannot distinguish between two executions of an algorithm, but it must produce different outputs in each, then the algorithm is incorrect. It is often useful to think of these bad executions as being produced by an *adversary*, which controls, depending on the circumstances, the inputs processes receive, the order in which they take steps, when to deliver messages and the way failures occur (i.e., what kind of failures, by what processes, and when). The adversary tries to limit the amount of knowledge processes have, either forever, or for as long as possible, by keeping the execution indistinguishable from other executions in which the results should be different.

An algorithm is *wait-free* if each process that doesn't fail completes its task after taking some finite number of steps, no matter how the adversary does its scheduling. A weaker condition is *solo termination*, also known as *obstruction freedom*, in which a process completes its task, provided it is given sufficiently many consecutive steps by the adversary. Thus, lower bounds assuming solo termination also apply to wait-free algorithms.

In the remainder of this chapter, we present three fairly simple proofs of impossibility results that rely on indistinguishability, followed by two which are more involved. Section 2.1 gives a lower bound on the tradeoff between the worst case time to perform READ and the worst case time to perform WRITE in any implementation of a register in a message passing system. In Section 2.2, we present a lower bound on the size of shared memory necessary for first-come first-served mutual exclusion. Section 2.3 contains a lower bound on the worst-case step complexity of approximate agreement. A lower bound on the number of rounds to solve consensus, as a function of the number of process failures that might occur, is presented in Section 2.4. Finally, in Section 2.5, we show that the possibility of asynchrony, even if it doesn't occur, can make a problem take more rounds in a message passing environment.

2.1 A TIME TRADEOFF BETWEEN READ AND WRITE IN THE IMPLEMENTATION OF A REGISTER

Consider the problem of implementing a register in a message passing system. A solution to this problem allows one to convert algorithms designed for a shared memory system to be used in a message passing system. Understanding the complexity of this problem tells us how much overhead is incurred in doing so. It also allows us to transfer lower bounds proved in a message passing system to shared memory.

An implementation of a register contains an algorithm READ for each process that may read from the register and an algorithm WRITE(v) for each process that may write to the register. The input parameter v may have any value that can be stored in the register. A very weak requirement for these algorithms is that, in any execution in which no WRITE overlaps any other operation, each READ must return the last value written before it began.

We consider a message passing model in which processes communicate by sending messages directly to one another through a complete network. We assume that the system is semisynchronous: each step by a process can take up to 1 unit of time to be executed and messages can take up to d units of time to be delivered. In addition, we assume that no processes fail and communication is reliable.

For any implementation, let R denote the worst case time to perform a READ and let W denote the worst case time to perform a WRITE. We use an indistinguishability argument to prove the following tradeoff.

Theorem 2.3 $R + W \geq d$.

Proof. Suppose not. Consider an execution α_1 in which process p_1 performs WRITE(1) starting at time 0, process p_0 performs READ starting at time W, and all messages sent have delay d. Then, by time $W + R < d$, process p_0 has returned its response, but it has not received any messages.

Let α_2 be the execution that is the same as α_1, except that p_1 performs WRITE(2) instead of WRITE(1). These two executions are indistinguishable to p_0 during the first $W + R$ units of time, so it must return the same result for its READ in both executions. Thus, in at least one of these two executions, it returns an incorrect response.   □

This result is from a 1988 Princeton University technical report entitled "PRAM: A scalable shared memory," by Richard Lipton and Jonathan Sandberg [56].

2.2   A SPACE LOWER BOUND FOR FIRST-COME FIRST-SERVED MUTUAL EXCLUSION

In the mutual exclusion problem, processes may need temporary exclusive access to a shared resource. A process which has this access is said to be in the *critical section*. To get the resource, a process performs an *entry protocol*. When a process has finished with the resource, it performs an *exit protocol*. A process that does not currently care about the resource is said to be in the *remainder section*.

A mutual exclusion algorithm consists of code for the entry and exit protocols for each process. It must satisfy the following properties.

- *Mutual Exclusion*: two or more processes are never simultaneously in the critical section.

- *Deadlock Freedom*: starting from any configuration in which some process is performing the entry protocol and no process is in the critical section, some process eventually enters the critical section.

- *Unobstructed Exit*: a process can always perform the exit protocol using only a finite number of its own steps.

A mutual exclusion algorithm is *first-come first-served* if each entry protocol begins with a section of code, called a *doorway*, and processes enter the critical section in the order that they perform the doorway. More precisely, for any two processes $p_i \neq p_j$, if p_i completes the doorway of some instance of the entry protocol before p_j begins some other instance of the entry protocol, then p_i completes its instance of the entry protocol and enters the critical section before p_j does. The doorway has the property that it can always be performed by a process using only a finite number of its own steps.

In this section, we consider asynchronous shared memory models which support arbitrary objects. There are no process failures. Moreover, when a process is in the critical section, it eventually finishes using the resource (and performs the exit protocol). We use an indistinguishability argument to prove a lower bound of $\log_2(n)$ bits on the space needed to solve first-come first-served mutual exclusion.

Theorem 2.4   *Any first-come first-served mutual exclusion algorithm has at least n possible values for its shared memory.*

Proof. Consider any mutual exclusion algorithm in which the shared memory has less than n possible values. We show that an adversarial scheduler can construct an execution starting from the initial configuration in which the first-come first-served property is violated.

Let C_0 be an initial configuration in which all processes are in the remainder section. For $i = 0, \ldots, n-1$, starting from configuration C_i, consider the finite history in which process p_i takes steps until it completes its doorway. Let C_{i+1} be the resulting configuration and let v_{i+1} be the value of the shared memory in this configuration.

By the pigeonhole principle, there exist i and j, $1 \leq i < j \leq n$ such that $v_i = v_j$. Let $P = \{p_0, \ldots, p_{i-1}\}$. Starting from C_i, consider a scheduler that repeatedly schedules the processes in P in round-robin order. By deadlock freedom, eventually some process in P enters the critical section. When a process enters the critical section, it begins the exit protocol at its next turn. By unobstructed exit, it eventually completes the exit protocol. After entering the remainder section, it performs the entry protocol again, beginning at its next turn. This happens repeatedly. Eventually some process $p_k \in P$ enters the critical section a second time. Let σ denote the finite sequence of events performed starting from C_i until this occurs.

Since $C_i \overset{P}{\sim} C_j$ and $v_i = v_j$, it follows from Lemma 2.1 that σ can be performed starting from C_j. Consider the execution from C_0 to C_j followed by the sequence of events σ. In this execution, process p_{j-1} completes its doorway before process p_k begins its doorway for the second time. However, process p_k enters the critical section twice, whereas process p_{j-1} does not enter the critical section at all. This violates the first-come first-served property. $\square$

This lower bound is due to James Burns, Paul Jackson, Nancy Lynch, Michael Fischer, and Gary Peterson, from their paper, "Data Requirements for Implementation of N-Process Mutual Exclusion Using a Single Shared Variable," which appeared in *Journal of the ACM* in 1982 [29].

2.3 A LOWER BOUND ON THE STEP COMPLEXITY OF APPROXIMATE AGREEMENT

In the *approximate agreement* problem, processes have to output values that are close to one another. Formally, each process p_i has a private input value x_i and, if it doesn't fail, has to output a value y_i. The processes all know an accuracy parameter $\epsilon > 0$. The output values must satisfy the following two properties.

- *ϵ-Agreement*: All output values are within ϵ of each other.

- *Validity*: All output values are between the smallest and largest input values,
  i.e., $\min\{x_0, \ldots, x_{n-1}\} \leq y_i \leq \max\{x_0, \ldots, x_{n-1}\}$ for all $i \in \{0, \ldots, n-1\}$.

In particular, if all the input values are the same, all the output values must equal this input value. One place this problem arises is in clock synchronization when processes attempt to maintain clock values that are close to one another.

We consider an asynchronous shared memory model with no process failures and only single-writer registers.

Theorem 2.5 *For $x_0, \ldots, x_{n-1} \in \{0, 1\}$ and $\epsilon < 1$, any algorithm for approximate agreement that satisfies solo termination has worst case step complexity at least n.*

Proof. The proof is by contradiction. Consider any approximate agreement algorithm. Let C_0 be the initial configuration in which the input values of all processes are 0 and let p_i be any process. By solo termination, there is a terminating solo execution α by process p_i starting from C_0. By validity, p_i must output 0 in α. Suppose this execution takes fewer than n steps. Then, during α, either (1) process p_i doesn't read the single-writer register r_j of some process $p_j \neq p_i$ or (2) it reads the single-writer register of every other process, but doesn't write to its own single-writer register r_i. In case (2), let p_j be any process other than p_i.

Next, let C_1 be the initial configuration in which the input values of all processes are 1. By solo termination and validity, there is a solo execution β by process p_j starting from C_1 in which p_j outputs 1.

Let C be any initial configuration in which p_i has input value 0 and p_j has input value 1, so $C_0 \overset{p_i}{\sim} C$ and $C_1 \overset{p_j}{\sim} C$. Each single-writer register has the same initial value in every initial configuration. Then, by Corollary 2.2, there exists solo executions α' by process p_i and β' by process p_j starting from C such that $\alpha \overset{p_i}{\sim} \alpha'$ and $\beta \overset{p_j}{\sim} \beta'$. In particular, p_i outputs 0 in α' and p_j outputs 1 in β'.

In case (1), let C' be the configuration at the end of β'. Since process p_i takes no steps during β', $C \overset{p_i}{\sim} C'$. Every single-writer register, except r_j, has the same value in C and C' and process p_i does not read from r_j during α. Corollary 2.2 implies there exists a solo execution α'' by process p_i starting from C' such that $\alpha' \overset{p_i}{\sim} \alpha''$. Hence, process p_i outputs 0 in execution α''.

In case (2), let C'' be the configuration at the end of α'. Since process p_j takes no steps during α', $C \overset{p_j}{\sim} C''$. No process writes during α', so every register has the same value in C and C''. Corollary 2.2 implies there exists a solo execution β'' by process p_j starting from C'' such that $\beta' \overset{p_j}{\sim} \beta''$. Hence, process p_j outputs 0 in execution β''.

In executions $\beta'\alpha''$ and $\alpha'\beta''$ process p_i outputs 0 and process p_j outputs 1. Thus, in both cases, ϵ-agreement is violated. This contradicts the correctness of the algorithm. $\square$

A wait-free approximate agreement algorithm using multi-writer registers with step complexity in $O(\log(1/\epsilon))$ is presented in the paper "Faster Approximate Agreement with Multi-Writer Registers," by Erik Schenk, which appeared in *FOCS*, 1995 [63]. When $x_0, \ldots, x_{n-1} \in \{0, 1\}$ and $\epsilon = \frac{1}{2}$, it has $O(1)$ step complexity. (See Section 9.3.) Together with Theorem 2.5, this implies that single-writer registers are less powerful than multi-writer registers.

Theorem 2.6 *Any implementation of a multi-writer register shared by n processes using only single-writer registers that satisfies solo termination has $\Omega(n)$ worst case step complexity.*

Thus, lower bounds on a particular problem can be used to prove that one model is more powerful than another model. Theorem 2.6 can also be proved directly, using an argument similar to that in the proof of Theorem 2.5.

In "Atomic Shared Register Access by Asynchronous Hardware," by Paul Vitányi and Baruch Awerbuch, which appeared in *FOCS*, 1986 [65], there is a wait-free implementation of a multi-writer register with $O(n)$ step complexity. By Theorem 2.6, this is optimal.

2.4   CHAIN ARGUMENTS FOR CONSENSUS

In a *chain argument*, the idea is to construct a chain or sequence of executions such that each pair of consecutive executions in the chain is indistinguishable to at least one process. If, in each execution, all processes must have the same result as one another, it follows that the processes have the same result in all executions in the chain. This leads to a contradiction if the result at one end of the chain must differ from the result at the other end.

For any two executions, α and α', we write $\alpha \sim \alpha'$ if there is a process p_i such that $\alpha \overset{p_i}{\sim} \alpha'$. Let $\approx$ denote the transitive closure of $\sim$. In other words, $\alpha \approx \alpha'$ if and only if there is a chain of executions $\alpha = \alpha_0, \alpha_1, \ldots, \alpha_k = \alpha'$ such that α_{i-1} and α_i are indistinguishable to at least one process, for $i = 1, \ldots, k$, i.e., for each i, there exists a process p_j such that $\alpha_{i-1} \overset{p_j}{\sim} \alpha_i$.

Consensus is one of the most widely studied problems in the theory of distributed computing and is used as a building block in many algorithms. In this problem, all processes that do not fail in an execution must output the same value. A trivial solution is to have each process simply output the value 0. The problem becomes more interesting if each process has a private input value and is required to output this value when every other process has the same input value.

Formally, each process p_i has a private input value x_i and, if it doesn't fail, it has to output a value y_i. The output values must satisfy the following two properties:

- *Agreement*: All output values are the same.

- *Validity*: Every output value is one of the input values.

Binary consensus is a restricted version of the consensus problem, where all input values are in $\{0, 1\}$.

We say that an execution of a consensus algorithm *decides* a value v if some process outputs v during the execution. If α and α' are executions that decide v and v', respectively, and $\alpha \approx \alpha'$, it follows that $v = v'$.

We begin with an important observation about binary consensus algorithms, which is proved by a simple chain argument. It applies to both synchronous and asynchronous models in which processes can fail. We will use this observation in this section and, again, in Chapter 7.

Lemma 2.7 *Any binary consensus algorithm has an initial configuration from which there are two executions that decide different values. In one of these executions, no processes fail. In the other, one process crashes before taking any steps, but no other processes fail.*

Proof. For $i = 0, \ldots, n$, let C_i denote the initial configuration in which the first i processes, $p_0, \ldots, p_{i-1}$, have input 1 and the rest have input 0, i.e.,

$$x_j = \begin{cases} 1 & \text{for } j < i \\ 0 & \text{for } j \geq i. \end{cases}$$

Let v_i be the value decided by some execution α_i, starting from C_i, in which no processes fail. In configuration C_0, all processes have input 0, so by validity, $v_0 = 0$. Similarly, in configuration C_n, all processes have input 1, so $v_n = 1$.

Since $v_0 \neq v_n$, there exists $j \in \{0, \ldots, n-1\}$ such that $v_j \neq v_{j+1}$. Let α be an execution starting from C_j in which process p_j crashes before taking any steps and no other process fails. If α does not decide v_j, then the claim is true for executions α_j and α, which both start from C_j. So, suppose that α decides v_j.

Configurations C_j and C_{j+1} are the same, except for the state of process p_j. By Corollary 2.2, there is an execution α' by the processes excluding p_j starting from C_{j+1} such that $\alpha \overset{p}{\sim} \alpha'$ for all $p \neq p_j$. Hence none of these processes crashes in α', α' decides v_j, and the claim is true for executions α_{j+1} and α', which both start from C_{j+1}. $\square$

For the rest of this section, we consider a synchronous message passing model in which processes can only fail by crashing. In each round, every process that has not terminated and does not crash sends a message to every other process and then receives all the messages that were sent to it in that round, ordered by the identifiers of the processes that sent them. At most one process crashes in each round. In a round in which a process crashes, it sends messages to an arbitrary prefix (chosen by an adversary) of the sequence of other processes, ordered by their identifiers. A process that crashes sends no messages in any subsequent round.

Now, we will prove a lower bound on the number of rounds needed to solve consensus in this model. The key to the proof is the following technical lemma, which uses a more complicated chain argument. The chain of executions that it constructs is very long.

Lemma 2.8 *Consider any f-round execution α of a consensus algorithm for $n \geq f + 2$ processes. Let γ be the f-round execution that is the same as α during its first r rounds and has no crashes after round r, for some $0 \leq r \leq f$. Then $\alpha \approx \gamma$.*

Proof. The proof is by backwards induction on r. If $r = f$, then $\alpha = \gamma$, so $\alpha \approx \gamma$. Suppose $0 \leq r < f$ and assume the claim is true for $r + 1$.

Let β be the f-round execution that is the same as α during its first $r + 1$ rounds and has no crashes after round $r + 1$. By the induction hypothesis, $\alpha \approx \beta$. Thus, it suffices to show $\beta \approx \gamma$. This is illustrated in Figure 2.1, where a round that contains no crashes is indicated by an empty box and a round that may contain a crash is indicated by a shaded box.

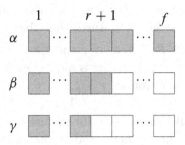

Figure 2.1: Some of the executions considered in the proof of Lemma 2.8.

If no process crashes during round $r + 1$ of execution β, then $\beta = \gamma$ and, hence, $\beta \approx \gamma$. So, suppose there is a process p_i that crashes during round $r + 1$. By assumption, no other process crashes during round $r + 1$.

Let P denote the set of processes that do not fail during β. From the model, we know that $|P| \geq n - f \geq 2$. Let Q be the subset of processes in P to which p_i does *not* send a message during round $r + 1$. These are the processes that can distinguish β from γ at the end of round $r + 1$. If $Q = \phi$, let $t = 0$. Otherwise, let $t = |Q|$ and let $q_1, \ldots, q_t$ be the processes in Q in increasing order by identifier.

We construct a chain of executions between β and γ. Let $\beta_0 = \beta$ and, for $1 \leq k \leq t$, let β_k be the f-round execution that has no crashes after round $r + 1$ and is the same as β during its first $r + 1$ rounds, except that p_i also sends messages to $q_1, \ldots, q_k$ during round $r + 1$. See Figure 2.2.

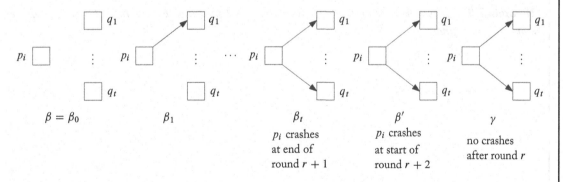

Figure 2.2: The behaviour of process p_i in round $r + 1$ of the executions in the chain from β to γ.

First suppose that $f = r + 1$. For $1 \leq k \leq t$, the only difference between β_{k-1} and β_k is whether p_i sends a message to q_k in round $r + 1$. Therefore $\beta_{k-1} \overset{p}{\sim} \beta_k$ for all processes $p \in P - \{q_k\}$. Since $|P| \geq 2$, there is at least one process in this set, so $\beta_{k-1} \approx \beta_k$. Hence

$\beta \approx \beta_t$. In β_t, process p_i crashes in the last round, after sending messages to all processes in P, so no process in P can learn whether p_i crashed. Note that γ is the same as β_t, except that p_i does not crash, so $\beta_t \overset{P}{\sim} \gamma$. Since $P \neq \phi$, $\beta_t \approx \gamma$ and, thus, $\beta \approx \gamma$.

Now suppose that $f > r + 1$. This case is more complicated because processes in P can communicate with one another in rounds $r + 2, \ldots, f$. We inductively construct a chain of executions between β_{k-1} and β_k, for $1 \leq k \leq t$. Let δ_k be the f-round execution that has no crashes after round $r + 2$, is the same as β_k for its first $r + 1$ rounds, and, at the beginning of round $r + 2$, process q_k crashes without sending messages to any other process. Similarly, let δ'_k be the f-round execution that has no crashes after round $r + 2$, is the same as β_{k-1} during its first $r + 1$ rounds, and, at the beginning of round $r + 2$, process q_k crashes without sending messages to any other process. It follows from the induction hypothesis that $\beta_k \approx \delta_k$ and $\beta_{k-1} \approx \delta'_k$. See Figure 2.3.

Note that, up to the end of round $r + 1$, δ_k and δ'_k are indistinguishable to all processes in $P - \{q_k\}$. In both these executions, q_k is the only process that crashes in round $r + 2$, it sends no messages in round $r + 2$, and there are no crashes after round $r + 2$. It follows that $\delta_k \overset{P}{\sim} \delta'_k$ for all $p \in P - \{q_k\}$. Since $|P| \geq n - f \geq 2$, there is at least one process in this set, so $\delta_k \approx \delta'_k$. Thus $\beta_{k-1} \approx \beta_k$ and, hence, $\beta \approx \beta_t$.

In execution β_t, process p_i crashes at the end of round $r + 1$, after sending messages to all other processes, and no processes crash in subsequent rounds. Let β' be the execution that is the same as β_t, except that p_i crashes at the beginning of round $r + 2$, before sending messages to any other processes. Then $\beta_t \overset{P}{\sim} \beta'$. Hence $\beta_t \approx \beta'$. Since β' has no crashes during round $r + 1$, the first $r + 1$ rounds of β' and γ are the same. By the induction hypothesis, $\beta' \approx \gamma$, so $\beta \approx \gamma$.

Therefore the claim is true for round r and, thus, by induction, for $0 \leq r \leq f$. $\square$

Theorem 2.9 *Any consensus algorithm with $n \geq f + 2$ processes that tolerates f crashes requires more than f rounds.*

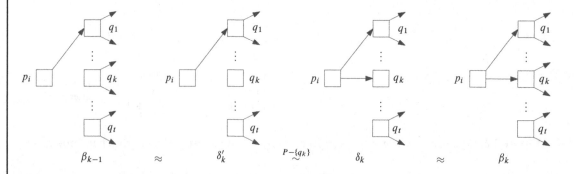

Figure 2.3: The behaviour of process q_k in round $r + 2$ of the executions in the chain from β_{k-1} to β_k.

Proof. Suppose there is a consensus algorithm with $n \geq f + 2$ processes that tolerates f crashes and uses at most f rounds. By Lemma 2.7, there is an initial configuration from which there are two executions α and γ that decide different values and in which no processes crashes, except for one process that crashes at the beginning of the first round of α. Lemma 2.8 with $r = 0$ implies that $\alpha \approx \gamma$. Hence these executions decide the same value. This is a contradiction. $\square$

The proof of Lemma 2.7 is due to Michael Fischer, Nancy Lynch, and Michael Paterson, from their paper, "Impossibility of Distributed Consensus with One Faulty Processor," *Journal of the ACM,* 1985 [41]. Theorem 2.9 appeared in Cynthia Dwork and Yoram Moses, "Knowledge and Common Knowledge in a Byzantine Environment: Crash Failures," *Information and Computation,* 1990 [34].

2.5 CAUSALITY ARGUMENTS

Consider an execution α in a message passing system and let $\overset{\alpha}{\Longrightarrow}$ be the smallest partial order on the events of the execution such that $e \overset{\alpha}{\Longrightarrow} e'$ if e and e' are events of the same process and e occurs before e' in α, or e is a send of a message and e' is the receipt of that message.

Similarly, in a shared memory system, let $\overset{\alpha}{\Longrightarrow}$ be the smallest partial order on the events of the execution α such that $e \overset{\alpha}{\Longrightarrow} e'$ if e occurs before e' in α and either e and e' are events of the same process or e and e' access the same shared variable (and e is a nontrivial operation).

If $e \overset{\alpha}{\Longrightarrow} e'$, we say that e *causally precedes* e'. Since $\overset{\alpha}{\Longrightarrow}$ is a partial order, it is both reflexive and transitive. This partial order can be used to describe a set of executions that are indistinguishable from α to all processes. Let $P = \{p_0, \dots, p_{n-1}\}$ denote the set of all processes.

Lemma 2.10 *If α is an execution and σ is a reordering of the events in α that is consistent with $\overset{\alpha}{\Longrightarrow}$, then there exists an execution α' with history σ such that $\alpha' \overset{P}{\sim} \alpha$.*

In a causality argument, the key is to show there are certain pairs of events in an execution such that neither event causally precedes the other and, hence, there is no flow of information from one to the other. Then, in an asynchronous execution, the two events can be ordered arbitrarily relative to one another. This allows indistinguishable executions to be constructed.

To show that the synchronous message passing model without faults is more powerful than the asynchronous message passing model without faults, it suffices to find a problem that is easy to solve in the former, but hard to solve in the latter. One such problem is *barrier synchronization*. In this problem, the goal of each process is to perform a particular step and then learn when all the other processes have performed their particular steps. The ability to solve barrier synchronization enables any synchronous algorithm to be simulated in a round-by-round manner in an asynchronous system: When a process learns that all processes have performed a step, it can proceed with its next step. However, repeatedly solving barrier synchronization is not necessary for more general simulations. For example, in many iterative numerical approximation algorithms, only a small amount of interleaving of the updates to various elements ensures convergence.

The *s-session* problem is essentially the implicit repetition of s consecutive instances of barrier synchronization. The goal of the problem is to ensure that a sufficient amount of interleaving of the steps of all processes has occurred. Specifically, processes must be able to determine that at least s rounds have occurred, although they do not have to know when each round has ended. When a process has determined that at least s rounds have occurred, it outputs DONE. When $s = 1$, the s-session problem is simply barrier synchronization. In a synchronous system, it is trivial to solve the s-session problem: each process can output DONE after it has performed s steps.

We consider algorithms that solve the problem in an asynchronous message passing model. In this model, a round ends (and a new round begins) as soon as every process has taken at least one step (in the round). We consider synchronous executions of such algorithms: every process performs exactly one step per round and each message sent in a round is delivered at the beginning of the next round. Thus, in a synchronous execution, sending a message from one process to another process distance d away takes at least $d + 1$ rounds. We will count the number of rounds until there is a process that outputs DONE.

Theorem 2.11   *In a communication network of diameter D, any synchronous execution of an asynchronous algorithm for the s-session problem in which some process outputs DONE has more than $(s-1)D$ rounds.*

Proof. Fix any communication network of diameter D. Suppose, for contradiction, that there is a synchronous execution α with at most $(s-1)D$ rounds in which some process outputs DONE. Let $\alpha = \alpha_1 \cdots \alpha_t \beta$, where

- $t \leq s-1$,

- α_i consists of D rounds of α, for $1 \leq i < t$,

- α_t consists of between 0 and $D-1$ rounds of α,

- β is a single round, and

- there is a process p_ℓ whose only event in β is to output DONE.

Let p_j and p_k be any two processes in the network that are distance D apart. If t is odd, then we will assume, without loss of generality, that $k \neq \ell$. Similarly, if t is even, then we will assume that $j \neq \ell$. Let e be the first event by p_j in α_1 and let e' be the last event by p_k in α_1. If $e \overset{\alpha_1}{\Longrightarrow} e'$, there is a chain of messages from p_j to p_k contained in α_1. But this is impossible, since the distance from p_j to p_k is D, so a message sent by p_j in some round of α_1 does not reach p_k until after α_1 is over. Hence, there is a reordering of the history of α_1 consistent with $\overset{\alpha_1}{\Longrightarrow}$ in which e' precedes e. In other words, there is a p_j-free history γ_1 and a p_k-free history

δ_1 such that $\gamma_1\delta_1$ is a reordering of the history of α_1 consistent with $\stackrel{\alpha_1}{\Longrightarrow}$. This is illustrated in Figure 2.4.

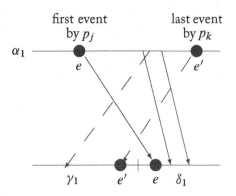

first event
by p_j

last event
by p_k

α_1

e

e'

γ_1 e' e δ_1

Figure 2.4: A reordering of the history of α_1 consistent with $\stackrel{\alpha_1}{\Longrightarrow}$.

Similarly, for each odd i, there is a p_j-free history γ_i and a p_k-free history δ_i such that $\gamma_i\delta_i$ is a reordering of the history of α_i consistent with $\stackrel{\alpha_i}{\Longrightarrow}$ and, for each even i, there is a p_k-free history γ_i and a p_j-free history δ_i such that $\gamma_i\delta_i$ is a reordering of the history of α_i consistent with $\stackrel{\alpha_i}{\Longrightarrow}$.

Let σ be the history obtained from the history of β by moving the event of process p_ℓ to the beginning. Then σ is consistent with $\stackrel{\beta}{\Longrightarrow}$. Since $\alpha = \alpha_1\cdots\alpha_t\beta$, it follows that $\gamma_1\delta_1\gamma_2\delta_2\cdots\gamma_t\delta_t\sigma$ is consistent with $\stackrel{\alpha}{\Longrightarrow}$. Lemma 2.10 implies there is an execution α' with this history that is indistinguishable from α to all processes. Since γ_1 is p_j-free, it is not a complete round, so the first round must end after γ_1. Since $\delta_1\gamma_2$ is p_k-free, the second round must end after $\gamma_1\delta_1\gamma_2$. Likewise, round t must end after $\gamma_1\delta_1\gamma_2\delta_2\cdots\gamma_t$ and the remainder of δ_t, if any, after the end of round t is not a complete round. Thus $\gamma_1\delta_1\gamma_2\delta_2\cdots\gamma_t\delta_t$ contains at most $t \leq s-1$ complete rounds. This says that fewer than s rounds have been completed before the first step of σ, in which process p_ℓ outputs DONE. Thus the algorithm is incorrect. $\qquad\square$

This proof is adapted from Hagit Attiya and Marios Mavronicolas, "Efficiency of Semisynchronous versus Asynchronous Networks," *Mathematical Systems Theory*, 1994 [17]. A similar proof, together with a simple information theory argument, can be used to show an $(s-1)\lfloor\log_c n\rfloor$ lower bound for the s-session problem in an asynchronous shared memory system where, at any point in an execution, at most c processes can be about access the same object. It appears in the paper "Efficiency of Synchronous versus Asynchronous Distributed Systems," by Eshrat Arjomandi, Michael Fischer, and Nancy Lynch, in *Journal of the ACM*, 1983 [6].

CHAPTER 3

Shifting and Scaling

In this chapter, we consider distributed systems in which the uncertainty is very limited. Specifically, we consider message-passing systems in which the clocks of all processes run at the same rate. The uncertainty in the system arises only from message delays and from differences in the initial values of process variables. Even so, it is possible to derive interesting lower bounds.

We present two lower bound techniques, *shifting* and *scaling*, that manipulate the relative timing of events at processes. We apply shifting, discussed in Section 3.1, to derive lower bounds for two important, but unrelated, problems: implementing a multi-writer register and clock synchronization, in Sections 3.2 and 3.3, respectively. Scaling, which is presented in Section 3.4, is used to obtain a lower bound for another clock synchronization problem in Section 3.5.

3.1   SHIFTING ARGUMENTS

Consider a distributed system in which every process has an accurate local clock, which all run at the same rate, but are not necessarily aligned with one another. In particular, there is no global clock that allows processes to synchronize with one another. One simple way to perturb executions of such a system in an indistinguishable manner is to *shift* the events of processes: the relative times at which events occur at a process remain unchanged, but the relative times at which events occur at two different processes may be changed by a fixed amount. Specifically, we associate a real time with each event and define shift($\alpha; p_i, u_i$) to be the execution in which each event of p_i occurs u_i units of time later than in the execution α. The local times of the events of p_i are the same in both executions. The real times and local times of all events of other processes are also the same in both executions. Hence, to all processes, the shifted execution and the original execution are indistinguishable.

Observation 3.1   For all executions α and all processes p_i, α and shift($\alpha; p_i, u_i$) are indistinguishable to all processes.

To denote multiple processes that are shifted by possibly different amounts, we use, for example, shift($\alpha; p_i, u_i; p_j, u_j$) = shift(shift($\alpha; p_i, u_i); p_j, u_j$). To shift events earlier by u_i units, we shift them later by $-u_i$ units.

In a message passing system, message delays may change as a result of shifts, even though the local times at which sends and receives occur at each process remain the same. This is illustrated in Figure 3.1.

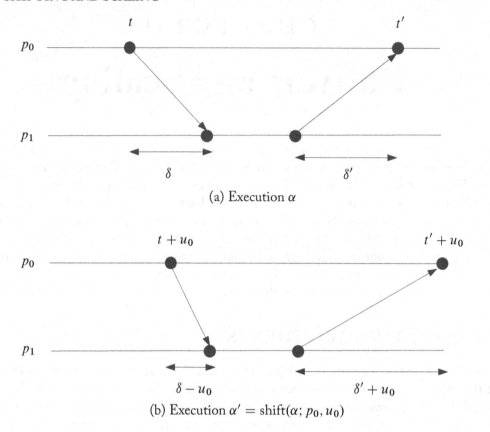

(a) Execution α

(b) Execution $\alpha' = \text{shift}(\alpha; p_0, u_0)$

Figure 3.1: Shifting the events of process p_0 later by u_0 units of time.

For the shifted execution to be *admissible*, it is necessary that every message is sent before it is received. Thus, the delays of the messages that a process sends and receives limit how much its events can be shifted. If the model imposes upper or lower bounds on message delay, these bounds also have to be satisfied in the shifted execution for it to be admissible.

Observation 3.2   If a message from process p_i to process p_j has delay δ, the events of process p_i are shifted by u_i, and the events of process p_j are shifted by u_j, then, after the shifts, the delay of the message is $\delta - u_i + u_j$.

Throughout our discussion of shifting arguments, we consider a message passing system in a complete network, where no messages are lost, no processes fail, and all processes take steps at the same rate. Between every pair of processes, d is an upper bound on message delay and $d - u$ is a lower bound on message delay. Here $u \leq d$ captures the *uncertainty* about message delay.

3.2   TIME LOWER BOUNDS FOR IMPLEMENTING A MULTI-WRITER REGISTER

We consider the problem, introduced in Section 2.1, of implementing a multi-writer register.

The period of time between when a READ or WRITE operation begins and when it completes is called its *execution interval*. We assume that each process has at most one READ or WRITE in progress at any time. This means that the execution intervals of its operation instances cannot overlap.

An execution of an implementation of a register is *sequential* if it has no overlapping execution intervals. Such an execution is *legal* if it obeys the semantics of a register: a READ returns the last value written.

We say that an implementation of a shared register is *sequentially consistent* if for every execution, there is a legal sequential execution such that each process performs the same sequence of READ operations (with the same results) and WRITE operations (of the same values) in both executions. Moreover, if every pair of operations (by different processes) whose execution intervals do not overlap in the original execution have the same relative order in the sequential execution, we say the implementation is *linearizable*.

We will show separate lower bounds on W, the worst case time to perform a WRITE, and R, the worst case time to perform a READ in any linearizable implementation.

Theorem 3.3   *In any linearizable implementation of a multi-writer register by three or more processes, $W \geq u/2$.*

Proof. Suppose there is a linearizable implementation in which $W < \frac{u}{2}$. Using a shifting argument, we show how an adversary can construct an admissible sequential execution of the implementation that is not legal.

First, consider the admissible sequential execution, α, depicted in Figure 3.2(a). In this execution, process p_0 invokes WRITE(1) at time 0 and this operation completes at some time before $\frac{u}{2}$. The invocation of WRITE(2) by process p_1 occurs at time $\frac{u}{2}$ and it completes prior to time u. The invocation of READ by process p_2 occurs at time u and it returns the value 2. In execution α, all messages from p_0 to p_1 have delay d and all messages from p_1 to p_0 have delay $d - u$. All other messages (to or from p_2) have delay $d - \frac{u}{2}$, so a shift of the events of either p_0 or p_1 by $\frac{u}{2}$, either later or earlier, will not violate the message delay bounds.

Let $\alpha' = \text{shift}(\alpha; p_0, \frac{u}{2}; p_1, -\frac{u}{2})$. The events of p_0 are shifted $\frac{u}{2}$ later and the events of p_1 are shifted $\frac{u}{2}$ earlier. This execution is illustrated in Figure 3.2(b).

All of the messages in α' obey the delay bounds: By Observation 3.2, the messages from p_0 to p_1 have delay $d - \frac{u}{2} - \frac{u}{2} = d - u$, the messages from p_1 to p_0 have delay $(d - u) + \frac{u}{2} + \frac{u}{2} = d$, and all other messages have delay $d - \frac{u}{2} \pm \frac{u}{2} \in \{d - u, d\}$. Thus, α' is admissible.

By Observation 3.1, none of the processes can distinguish between the shifted execution α' and the original execution α. Thus p_2 also returns 2 in α'. Note that α' is a sequential execution, but it is not legal. Hence the implementation is not correct. $\square$

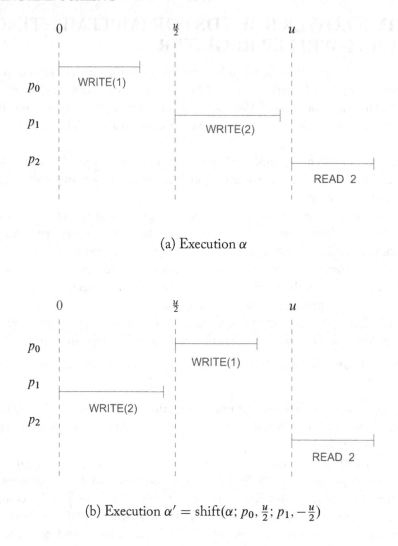

(a) Execution α

(b) Execution $\alpha' = \text{shift}(\alpha; p_0, \frac{u}{2}; p_1, -\frac{u}{2})$

Figure 3.2: The executions considered in the proof of Theorem 3.3.

The proof of the lower bound for READ operations is similar. It also applies to linearizable implementations of a single-writer register.

Theorem 3.4   *In any linearizable implementation of a register by three or more processes, $R \geq u/4$.*

Proof. Suppose there is a linearizable implementation in which $R < \frac{u}{4}$. Consider the execution, β, depicted in Figure 3.3(a), in which the register has initial value 0, the invocations of READ by process p_0 occur at even multiples of $\frac{u}{4}$, and the invocations of READ by process p_1 occur at odd

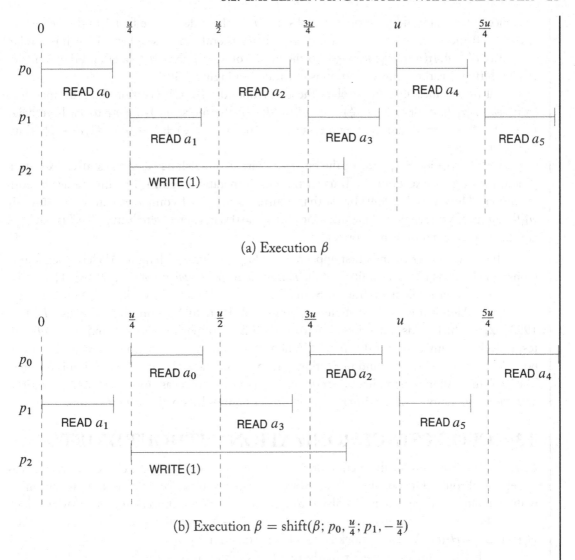

(a) Execution β

(b) Execution $\beta = \text{shift}(\beta; p_0, \frac{u}{4}; p_1, -\frac{u}{4})$

Figure 3.3: The executions considered in the proof of Theorem 3.4.

multiples of $\frac{u}{4}$. Note that none of these READ operations overlap. The invocation of WRITE(1) by process p_2 occurs at time $\frac{u}{4}$. All messages have delay $d - \frac{u}{2}$, to give the adversary the maximum amount of flexibility.

The first READ must return 0 and every read that begins after the WRITE is complete must return 1. Linearizability implies that the sequence of values returned, $a_0, a_1, \ldots$ consists of a sequence of 0's followed by a sequence of 1's. Let i be the index of the first 1 in this sequence, so $a_{i-1} = 0$ and $a_i = 1$. We consider the case when i is odd. The case when i is even is similar.

Let β' = shift$(\beta; p_0, \frac{u}{4}; p_1, -\frac{u}{4})$, so the events of p_0 are shifted $\frac{u}{4}$ later and the events of p_1 are shifted $\frac{u}{4}$ earlier. This execution is illustrated in Figure 3.3(b).

All of the messages in β' obey the delay bounds: By Observation 3.2, the messages from p_0 to p_1 have delay $(d - \frac{u}{2}) - \frac{u}{4} - \frac{u}{4} = d - u$, the messages from p_1 to p_0 have delay $(d - \frac{u}{2}) + \frac{u}{4} + \frac{u}{4} = d$, and all other messages have delay $(d - \frac{u}{2}) \pm \frac{u}{4} \in \{d - \frac{3u}{4}, d - \frac{u}{4}\}$. Thus, β' is admissible.

By Observation 3.1, none of the processes can distinguish between the shifted execution β' and the original execution β. Thus all the READ operations return the same values in both executions. However, the READ by p_0 that returns value $a_i = 1$ completes before the READ by p_1 that returns value $a_{i-1} = 0$ begins. Since the value 0 is never written during β', β' is not legal and the implementation is not correct. □

These two lower bounds first appeared in Hagit Attiya and Jennifer Welch, "Sequential Consistency versus Linearizability," *ACM Transactions on Computer Systems*, 1994 [21].

There is an implementation in Soma Chaudhuri, Rainer Gawlick, and Nancy Lynch, "Designing Algorithms for Distributed Systems with Partially Synchronized Clocks," *PODC*, 1993 [32] in which reads and writes have worst case time complexities $bd + u$ and $(1 - b)d + u$, respectively, for any constant $0 \leq b \leq 1$. When there is no uncertainty, i.e., $u = 0$, this upper bound matches the lower bound in Section 2.1, so, in this case, the implementation is optimal. The implementation also implies upper bounds of u on the worst case times for READ operations and WRITE operations, which differ from our lower bounds by small constant factors.

3.3 CLOCK SYNCHRONIZATION WITHOUT DRIFT

Clock synchronization is an abstraction of the problem of maintaining the clocks of processes as closely synchronized as possible. A hardware clock is a way of formalizing how much information about real time is made available to a process. For each process p_i, its hardware clock (i.e., its local time) is an increasing function $H_i : \mathbb{R} \to \mathbb{R}$ of real time. Thus, if $\Delta > 0$, then $H_i(t + \Delta) > H_i(t)$. A perfect clock is the identity function.

In this section, we consider hardware clocks whose rate is the same as real time, i.e., $H_i(t) = H_i(0) + t$ for some constant $H_i(0)$. Such clocks are said to have *no drift*. The hardware clocks of different processes p_i are not necessarily synchronized: the values $H_i(0)$ can be arbitrarily far apart.

In this case, the clock synchronization problem is for each process p_i to compute an adjustment adj_i so that the *adjusted clocks* $A_i(t) = adj_i + H_i(t)$ of all processes are close together. The *skew* of a clock synchronization algorithm is $\max\{A_i(t) - A_j(t)\}$, where the maximum is taken over all pairs of process indices i, j, over all times t, and over all admissible executions.

If there is no uncertainty in message delay, i.e., $u = 0$, then clock synchronization is trivial to solve: All processes simply adopt the time, say, of process p_0, which they can determine when they receive a message from p_0 that contains the time at which it was sent. So, we assume that $u > 0$.

We will use a shifting argument combined with a chain argument to prove a lower bound on the skew of any clock synchronization algorithm.

Theorem 3.5   *The skew of any clock synchronization algorithm is at least $\frac{n-1}{n} u$ in a system of n processes with message delay uncertainty u, even if the hardware clocks of all processes have no drift.*

Proof. We start with the two process case. Fix a clock synchronization algorithm. Suppose it has skew ϵ.

Consider an admissible execution α, where $H_0(t)$ is the hardware clock of process p_0, $H_1(t)$ is the hardware clock of process p_1, messages from p_0 to p_1 have delay $d - u$, and messages from p_1 to p_0 have delay d. Let A_0 and A_1 be the adjusted clocks of p_0 and p_1 in execution α.

Let $\alpha' = \text{shift}(\alpha; p_1, u)$ be the execution obtained from α in which the events of p_1 are shifted u time units later. By Observation 3.2, messages from p_0 to p_1 in α' have delay d and messages from p_1 to p_0 in α' have delay $d - u$. Thus α' is admissible.

By Observation 3.1, executions α and α' are indistinguishable to both processes. Thus they make the same adjustments to their clocks in both executions, i.e., $adj'_0 = adj_0$ and $adj'_1 = adj_1$. Moreover, for each process, its events appear to occur at the same local time in both executions, i.e., $H'_0(t) = H_0(t)$ and $H'_1(t + u) = H_1(t)$. Since the hardware clocks have no drift, $H'_1(t + u) = H'_1(t) + u$. Hence the adjusted clocks of p_0 and p_1 in execution α' are

$$A'_0(t) = A_0(t)$$

and

$$A'_1(t) = adj_1 + H'_1(t) = adj_1 + H'_1(t + u) - u = adj_1 + H_1(t) - u = A_1(t) - u.$$

This is illustrated in Figure 3.4.

The skew of the clock synchronization algorithm is ϵ, so $A'_0(t) - A'_1(t) \le \epsilon$ and $A_1(t) - A_0(t) \le \epsilon$. It follows that

$$A'_0(t) \le A'_1(t) + \epsilon = A_1(t) - u + \epsilon \le A_0(t) + \epsilon - u + \epsilon = A'_0(t) + 2\epsilon - u.$$

Hence, $\epsilon \ge u/2$.

Now, we extend the argument to an arbitrary number of processes, $n \ge 2$. Fix a clock synchronization algorithm and consider an admissible execution α, in which, for all $i < j$, messages from p_i to p_j have delay $d - u$ and messages from p_j to p_i have delay d. Let A_i denote the adjusted clock of process p_i in execution α, for $i = 0, \ldots, n - 1$. Then the skew, ϵ, is at least $A_{n-1}(t) - A_0(t)$, i.e., $A_{n-1}(t) - A_0(t) \le \epsilon$.

Let $1 \le k \le n - 1$ and let $\alpha' = \text{shift}(\alpha; p_k, u; \ldots; p_{n-1}, u)$ be the execution obtained from α in which the events of $p_k, \ldots, p_{n-1}$ are shifted u time units later. For $i < k$ and $j \ge k$,

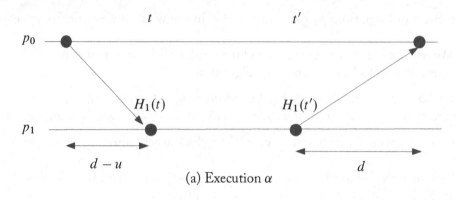

(a) Execution α

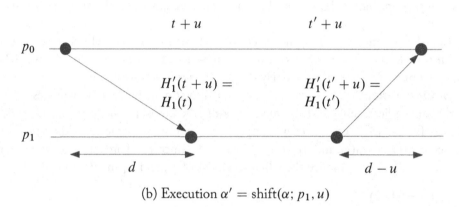

(b) Execution $\alpha' = \text{shift}(\alpha; p_1, u)$

Figure 3.4: The executions considered in the proof of Theorem 3.5.

messages from p_i to p_j have delay d in α' and messages from p_j to p_i have delay $d - u$. The delays of all other messages are the same in α and α'. Thus α' is admissible. Moreover, the adjusted clocks of p_i and p_j in execution α' are $A_i'(t) = A_i(t)$ and $A_j'(t) = A_j(t) - u$.

The skew of the clock synchronization algorithm is ϵ, so $A_k'(t) - A_{k-1}'(t) \leq \epsilon$. Hence,

$$A_{k-1}(t) = A_{k-1}'(t) \leq A_k'(t) + \epsilon = A_k(t) - u + \epsilon.$$

By induction, it follows that $A_0(t) \leq A_k(t) + k(\epsilon - u)$ for all $k = 0, \ldots, n - 1$. In particular,

$$A_0(t) \leq A_{n-1}(t) + (n - 1)(\epsilon - u) \leq A_0(t) + \epsilon + (n - 1)(\epsilon - u).$$

Therefore, $\epsilon \geq \frac{n-1}{n}u$. $\square$

This lower bound is due to Jennifer Lundelius and Nancy Lynch, "An Upper and Lower Bound for Clock Synchronization," *Information and Control*, 1984 [58]. They also prove a matching upper bound.

3.4   SCALING ARGUMENTS

Scaling, also called *stretching*, is a generalization of shifting in which the timing of process events is changed by a multiplicative factor, rather than an additive factor.

For any execution α and any positive real number s, define $\alpha' = \text{scale}(\alpha; s)$ to be the execution obtained from α by multiplying the real time at which each event occurs by s, while leaving its local time unchanged. Note that this keeps the relative rate of all processes the same. (It is also possible to multiply the times at which events occur at different processes by different amounts, which changes their relative rates, but we shall not do so here.) A message that has delay δ in α, has delay $s \cdot \delta$ in α'. An event that occurs at real time t in α occurs at real time $s \cdot t$ in α'. Thus, if H_i and H_i' are the hardware clocks of process p_i in α and α', respectively, then $H_i(t) = H_i'(s \cdot t)$ for all times t.

Observation 3.6   The executions α and $\text{scale}(\alpha; s)$ are indistinguishable to all processes, for all $s \in \mathbb{R}^+$.

3.5   CLOCK SYNCHRONIZATION WITH DRIFT

We consider hardware clocks with *drift* $\rho > 0$. This means the rate of the hardware clock of each process differs from the rate of real time by at most a factor $(1 + \rho)$, i.e.,

$$\frac{\Delta}{1 + \rho} \le H_i(t + \Delta) - H_i(t) \le (1 + \rho)\Delta$$

for every process p_i and every real number $\Delta > 0$.

As before, we consider a message passing system in a complete network, where no messages are lost, no processes fail, d is an upper bound on message delay and u is an upper bound on the uncertainty in message delay. In each execution, the hardware clocks of all processes run at the same rate, but this rate can be different in different executions.

The goal of clock synchronization in this model is for each process, p_i to compute an adjusted clock $A_i : \mathbb{R} \to \mathbb{R}$ so that all adjusted clocks are close to one another, i.e., the skew, $\max\{A_i(t) - A_j(t)\}$, is small, where the maximum is taken over all pairs of process indices i, j, over all times t, and over all admissible executions.

There is a very simple algorithm that achieves this goal: each process fixes its adjusted clock to the same constant value, for example $A_i(t) = 0$ for all processes p_i. For this algorithm, the skew is 0.

This is an example of a *counterexample algorithm*. Such algorithms may not be practically useful, but they say that we cannot get a good lower bound for the problem in the given model.

One way to refine the problem is to require that the drift of the adjusted clocks be some constant $\gamma \ge 0$, i.e.,

$$\frac{\Delta}{1 + \gamma} \le A_i(t + \Delta) - A_i(t) \le (1 + \gamma)\Delta$$

for every process p_i and every real number $\Delta > 0$.

Theorem 3.7 *If $u \geq d\left(1 - \frac{1}{(1+\rho)^2}\right)$, then for any clock synchronization algorithm, the drift of the adjusted clocks is at least as large as the drift of the hardware clocks.*

Proof. Consider any clock synchronization algorithm that produces adjusted clocks with drift at most γ. Let α be an admissible execution in which $H_i(t) = (1 + \rho)t$ for all processes p_i and the delay of every message is $d/(1 + \rho)^2 \geq d - u$, the lower bound on message delay.

Consider the execution $\alpha' = \text{scale}(\alpha; (1 + \rho)^2)$. The delay of every message is d, so α' is admissible. For all times $t \geq 0$, $H_i'((1 + \rho)^2 t) = H_i(t)$. Thus, for all times $t' \geq 0$, $H_i'(t') = H_i(t'/(1 + \rho)^2)) = t'/(1 + \rho)$ and the drift of the hardware clocks in executions α and α' are ρ.

Consider any process p_i. By Observation 3.6, executions α and α' are indistinguishable. Since $H_i'((1 + \rho)^2 t) = H_i(t)$, it follows that $A_i'((1 + \rho)^2 t) = A_i(t)$, for all $t \geq 0$. Furthermore, the drift of the adjusted clocks is at most γ in both α' and α, so $(1 + \rho)^2 t/(1 + \gamma) \leq A_i'((1 + \rho)^2 t) - A_i'(0) = A_i(t) - A_i(0) \leq (1 + \gamma)t$. Hence $(1 + \rho)^2 \leq (1 + \gamma)^2$, which implies that $\gamma \geq \rho$. $\square$

This lower bound is from T.K. Srikanth and Sam Toueg, "Optimal Clock Synchronization," *Journal of the ACM*, 1987 [64]. The trivial algorithm in which every process uses its hardware clock as its adjusted clock gives a matching upper bound.

CHAPTER 4

Scenario Arguments

A scenario argument is a method to find a bad execution for an algorithm by pasting together parts of several executions, starting from different, carefully selected initial configurations. An adversary chooses these executions so that each process finds certain pairs of executions indistinguishable. These arguments are typically employed when faulty processes can behave in an arbitrary manner. An execution of the algorithm in a hypothetical system architecture is used to describe the behaviour of faulty processes. This execution is not necessarily legal, since the algorithm is not guaranteed to work in this system. We call such an execution a *scenario*.

We present two lower bounds on the ratio between the number of nonfaulty processes and faulty processes, when failures are arbitrary. The first result, in Section 4.1, is for consensus, while the second, in Section 4.2, is for clock synchronization.

4.1 IMPOSSIBILITY OF CONSENSUS WITH ARBITRARY PROCESS FAILURES

We consider the consensus problem, defined in Section 2.4, in a synchronous message passing model. We assume the network is completely connected, so that every process can directly communicate with every other process. We also assume that at most f arbitrary (Byzantine) process failures can occur. Processes that fail can behave arbitrarily: They may send extra messages or messages with incorrect information, they may lie about messages they have received from other processes, they may send correct messages at the wrong time, and they may fail to send some messages they are supposed to.

The following impossibility result considers a system with three processes, one of which may fail in a Byzantine manner. We think about the behaviour of this faulty process as being under the control of an adversary. To tell the faulty process how to behave, namely, what messages to send and at what rounds to send them, the adversary runs the algorithm in a larger system with six processes. Although the algorithm is not designed for this larger system, this scenario is a convenient way for the adversary to specify what the processes should do.

Theorem 4.1 *Consensus is impossible for three processes, if one arbitrary process failure can occur.*

Proof. Suppose there is a consensus algorithm for three processes p_0, p_1, and p_2. Consider a system with six processes, $p_0, p_1, p_2, p'_0, p'_1, p'_2$, joined in a ring, where p'_i is a copy of p_i for $i = 0, 1, 2$. (See Figure 4.1.) From the point of view of each process, this system appears the same as the original system, since each process has the same neighbours in both. Let α be an execution of the algorithm in this system, where p_0, p_1, and p_2 have input 0 and p_0', p_1', and p_2' have input 1. Note that this execution does not necessarily solve consensus.

The output value of each process in scenario α can be determined by considering a legal execution which is indistinguishable from α to that process.

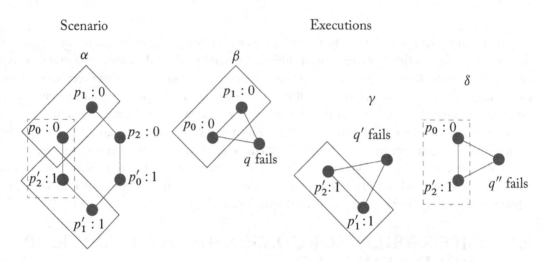

Figure 4.1: The scenario and legal executions considered in the proof of Theorem 4.1.

Let β be an execution of the algorithm in a system with three processes, p_0, p_1, and q, where each process starts with input 0. Process q fails in β. It sends the same messages to p_0 as p_2' sends to p_0 in α and sends the same messages to p_1 as p_2 sends to p_1 in α. Then, the steps performed by p_0 and p_1 in β are identical to the steps performed by p_0 and p_1 in α. Since p_0 and p_1 must output 0 in β, p_0 and p_1 must also output 0 in α.

Similarly, by considering an execution γ in a system with three processes, p_1', p_2', and q', where each process starts with input 1 and q' fails, one can show that p_1' and p_2' must output 1 in α.

Finally, consider the execution δ in a system with three processes, p_0, p_2', and q'', where p_0 has input 0, p_2' has input 1, and q'' fails, sending the same messages to p_0 as p_1 sends to p_0 in α and sending the same messages to p_2' as p_1' sends to p_2' in α. The steps performed by p_0 and p_2' in δ are the same as the steps they perform in α. Process p_0 must output 0 in δ, since p_0 outputs 0 in α, and p_2' must output 1 in δ, since p_2' outputs 1 in α. This contradicts the agreement property for the execution δ. □

The elegance of this argument lies in its ability to draw conclusions about the behaviour of processes without requiring any detailed analysis of exactly what those processes are doing.

This unsolvability result can be extended to synchronous message passing systems with $n \le 3f$ processes, of which at most f can have arbitrary failures, via a reduction from the case for three processes.

Theorem 4.2   *Consensus is impossible for $n \le 3f$ processes, if up to f arbitrary process failures can occur.*

Proof. To obtain a contradiction, suppose that there is a consensus algorithm for $n \le 3f$ processes, of which at most f can fail. From this algorithm we can get an algorithm for the case of three processes, p_0, p_1, and p_2, of which at most one can fail. Specifically, the processes p_0, p_1, and p_2 can together simulate these n processes, so that each simulates a disjoint set of at most f processes. In any execution, if one of p_0, p_1, or p_2 fails, then at most f of the simulated processes fail. Hence, there will be agreement among the values decided by the processes simulated by the processes that do not fail. This enables the processes that do not fail to agree. This contradicts Theorem 4.1.   □

The proofs of Theorems 4.1 and 4.2 are from Michael Fischer, Nancy Lynch, and Michael Merritt, "Easy Impossibility Proofs for Distributed Consensus Problems," *Distributed Computing*, 1986 [40]. There is an algorithm that solves consensus, tolerating $f \ge 1$ arbitrary process failures, provided the number of processes, n, is greater than $3f$, in Juan Garay and Yoram Moses, "Fully Polynomial Byzantine Agreement for $n > 3t$ Processors in $t + 1$ Rounds," *SIAM Journal on Computing*, 1998 [43]. Thus, the lower bounds are tight.

4.2   CLOCK SYNCHRONIZATION WITH ARBITRARY PROCESS FAILURES

The next result deals with the clock synchronization problem. Its proof combines scaling with a scenario argument. As in Section 4.1, the adversary considers a larger system to describe the behaviour of faulty processes. In this case, the size of the hypothetical system depends on the drifts of the hardware and software clocks.

The model is a message passing system in which the hardware clock of each process has drift $\rho > 0$, as in Section 3.5. The upper and lower bounds on message delay are d and $d/(1 + \rho)^2$, respectively. In addition, at most f processes can fail. In particular, they can send messages at arbitrary times, so the delay of messages to them or from them is irrelevant.

Our proof even holds in a stronger model, where the hardware clock of each process is initially correct, i.e., $H_i(0) = 0$ for all processes p_i. Thus, this additional knowledge cannot be used to get better algorithms.

Again, the problem is for processes to compute adjusted clocks with small skew. This time, we require that the adjusted clock of every process be within a constant factor of its hardware clock. Otherwise, clock synchronization can be solved without communication. For example, if the adjusted clock of each process is proportional to the logarithm of its hardware clock, the adjusted clocks will eventually become close to one another.

Theorem 4.3   *For any constants $\epsilon, \gamma \geq 0$, there is no clock synchronization algorithm for $n \leq 3f$ processes with skew at most ϵ and*

$$\frac{H_i(t)}{1 + \gamma} \leq A_i(t) \leq (1 + \gamma) H_i(t)$$

for all $t \geq 0$ and every process p_i.

Proof. First, consider the case with three processes, p_0, p_1, and p_2, at most one of which can be faulty. Suppose, for contradiction, that there exists such an algorithm.

Let $k \equiv 0 \bmod 3$ be sufficiently large. (We will see that $k > 1 + \log(1 + \gamma)/\log(1 + \rho)$ suffices.) Consider a system of k processes, $p_0, p_1, \ldots, p_{k-1}$, where, for $i \geq 3$, process p_i runs the same code as process $p_{(i \bmod 3)}$ and has the same initial state at time 0. For $1 \leq i \leq k - 2$, process p_i communicates directly only with processes p_{i-1} and p_{i+1}. Processes p_0 and p_{k-1} also communicate directly with one another. This is illustrated in Figure 4.2.

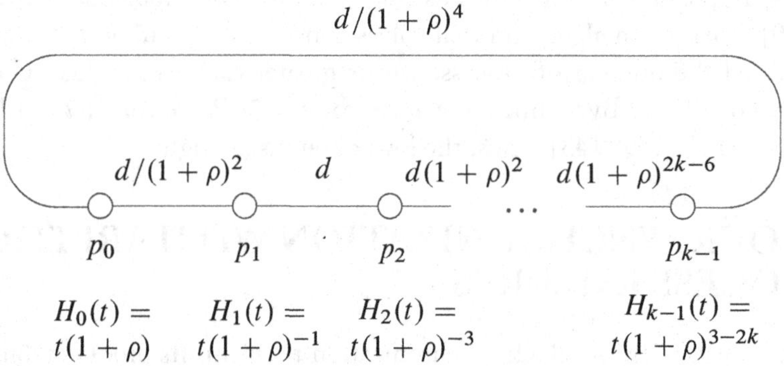

Figure 4.2: The scenario α.

Consider a scenario α of this system, where the hardware clock of process p_i is $H_i(t) = t(1 + \rho)^{1-2i}$ for $0 \leq i \leq k - 1$, the delay of every message between p_i and p_{i+1} is $d(1 + \rho)^{2i-2}$ for $0 \leq i \leq k - 2$, and the delay of every message between p_0 and p_{k-1} is $d/(1 + \rho)^4$. Note that this scenario is not an admissible execution of the algorithm. Let $A_i : \mathbb{R} \to \mathbb{R}$ be the adjusted clock, if any, produced by process p_i in α.

For $i = 0, \ldots, k - 2$, consider the execution α_i, depicted in Figure 4.3, in which processes p_i and p_{i+1} behave as in α, but process q, which is faulty, behaves like p_{i-1} (or p_{k-1}, if $i = 0$) to p_i and behaves like p_{i+2} (or p_0, if $i = k - 2$) to p_{i+1}. Scenario α and execution α_i are indistinguishable to both p_i and p_{i+1}, so they each produce the same adjusted clocks in α and α_i.

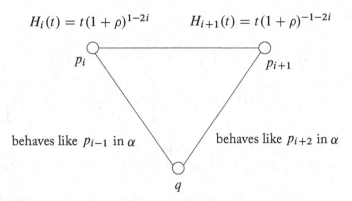

$$H_i(t) = t(1 + \rho)^{1-2i} \qquad H_{i+1}(t) = t(1 + \rho)^{-1-2i}$$

p_i

p_{i+1}

behaves like p_{i-1} in α

behaves like p_{i+2} in α

q

Figure 4.3: The execution α_i.

Since $H_0(t) = t(1 + \rho)$, $H_1(t) = t/(1 + \rho)$, and the message delay between p_0 and p_1 is $d/(1 + \rho)^2$, execution α_0 is admissible. Thus, the algorithm guarantees $A_0(t) - A_1(t) \leq \epsilon$ and $A_0(t) \geq H_0(t)/(1 + \gamma)$.

However, for $1 \leq i \leq k - 2$, the hardware clock of process p_{i+1} is too slow, so execution α_i is not admissible and we can't make any direct inferences about the behaviour of the adjusted clocks. Instead, we look at the scaled execution $\alpha_i' = scale(\alpha_i; (1 + \rho)^{-2i})$ in which time is shrunk (i.e., sped up) by a factor of $(1 + \rho)^{2i}$. The hardware clocks of p_i and p_{i+1} in execution α_i' are $H_i'(t) = t(1 + \rho)$ and $H_{i+1}'(t) = t/(1 + \rho)$, respectively. The message delay between p_i and p_{i+1} is $d/(1 + \rho)^2$. Thus, α_i' is an admissible execution and the algorithm guarantees that $A_i'(t') - A_{i+1}'(t') \leq \epsilon$ for all times t'.

By Observation 3.1, α_i' and α_i are indistinguishable to p_i and p_{i+1}. It follows that $H_i'(t(1 + \rho)^{-2i}) = H_i(t)$, $H_{i+1}'(t(1 + \rho)^{-2i}) = H_{i+1}(t)$, $A_i'(t(1 + \rho)^{-2i}) = A_i(t)$, and $A_{i+1}'(t(1 + \rho)^{-2i}) = A_{i+1}(t)$. Hence $A_i(t) - A_{i+1}(t) = A_i'(t(1 + \rho)^{-2i}) - A_{i+1}'(t(1 + \rho)^{-2i}) \leq \epsilon$ and $A_0(t) - A_{k-1}(t) = \sum_{i=0}^{k-2}(AC_i(t) - A_{i+1}(t)) \leq (k - 1)\epsilon$.

When $i = k - 2$, the algorithm also guarantees that $A_{k-1}'(t') \leq (1 + \gamma)H_{k-1}'(t')$ for all times t'. In particular, $A_{k-1}(t) = A_{k-1}'(t(1 + \rho)^{-2(k-2)}) \leq (1 + \gamma)H_{k-1}'(t(1 + \rho)^{-2i}) = (1 + \gamma)H_{k-1}(t)$. Furthermore, by definition, we have that $H_{k-1}(t) = t(1 + \rho)^{3-2k} = t(1 + \rho)(1 + \rho)^{2(1-k)} = H_0(t)(1 + \rho)^{2(1-k)}$. Hence,

$$
\begin{aligned}
(1 + \gamma)H_{k-1}(t) &\geq A_{k-1}(t) \\
&\geq A_0(t) - (k - 1)\epsilon \\
&\geq H_0(t)/(1 + \gamma) - (k - 1)\epsilon \\
&= \frac{(1 + \rho)^{2(k-1)}}{1 + \gamma}H_{k-1}(t) - (k - 1)\epsilon.
\end{aligned}
$$

This implies that

$$
\begin{aligned}
(k-1)\epsilon \quad &\geq \quad H_{k-1}(t)\left[\frac{(1+\rho)^{2(k-1)}}{1+\gamma} - (1+\gamma)\right] \\
&= \quad t(1+\rho)^{1-2(k-1)}\left[\frac{(1+\rho)^{2(k-1)}}{1+\gamma} - (1+\gamma)\right].
\end{aligned}
$$

Choosing $k > 1 + \log(1+\gamma)/\log(1+\rho)$ implies that $\frac{(1+\rho)^{2(k-1)}}{1+\gamma} - (1+\gamma) > 0$. Then the right hand side goes to ∞ as t goes to ∞, but the left hand side is constant. This is impossible.

   The general case follows using a reduction, as in the proof of Theorem 4.2. Suppose there is a clock synchronization algorithm for $n \leq 3f$ processes, $q_0, \ldots, q_{n-1}$, at most f of which can be faulty. We construct an algorithm for three processes, p_0, p_1, p_2, by having each process p_i simulate a disjoint set $S_i \subseteq \{q_0, \ldots, q_{n-1}\}$ of at most f processes, each with the same hardware clock as p_i. In advance, p_i chooses one of the processes in S_i and uses its adjusted clock as its own adjusted clock.

   Note that, if one of the three processes, p_i, is faulty, then at most f of the simulated processes are faulty, namely those in S_i. Thus, the other two processes in $\{p_0, p_1, p_2\}$ will have adjusted clocks satisfying the desired properties. This is a contradiction.   □

   This proof is by Michael Fischer, Nancy Lynch, and Michael Merritt, "Easy Impossibility Proofs for Distributed Consensus Problems," *Distributed Computing*, 1986 [40]. There is an algorithm in "Optimal clock synchronization," by T.K. Srikanth and Sam Toueg, *Journal of the ACM*, 1987 [64], that solves this version of clock synchronization for specific constants ϵ and γ, which are functions of d and ρ, and tolerates f Byzantine failures, provided $n \geq 3f + 1$.

CHAPTER 5

Information Theory Arguments

Information theory arguments rely on the fact that collecting information from many different processes takes a long time. They usually give bounds of the form $\Omega(\log n)$, where n is the number of processes in the system.

An information theory lower bound begins by carefully defining a measure of information, for example, the number of input values that influence the state of a process or the value of an object at a given point in time. Then a recurrence is used to describe how much the information can increase as a result of a single step.

Information theory arguments are mostly used to obtain lower bounds on the number of rounds in synchronous systems without process failures. These automatically imply lower bounds when processes can fail. In a synchronous system, each process takes one step per round until it completes or fails, so information theory arguments also give lower bounds for the number of steps taken by a process in an asynchronous system. But they are not generally useful for showing a problem is harder in an asynchronous system than in a synchronous system.

Throughout this chapter, our lower bounds do not assume any upper bounds on the sizes of the objects that are being used: the values that they contain can be arbitrarily large. This only makes the lower bounds stronger.

We begin this chapter with lower bounds for the simpler situation in which processes communicate using only single-writer registers. After developing an important technical lemma in Section 5.1, we apply it to obtain lower bounds for two problems: computing OR, in Section 5.2, and approximate agreement, in Section 5.3. Then we consider lower bounds when more powerful objects, including multi-writer registers, are available. In Section 5.4, we present another technical lemma, followed by two applications, to collect, in Section 5.5, and to atomic snapshots, in Section 5.6.

5.1 LOWER BOUNDS USING SINGLE-WRITER REGISTERS

In Sections 5.1, 5.2, and 5.3, we consider the synchronous shared memory model where processes communicate using single-writer registers and no processes fail. To minimize the flow of information in each round, an adversary will schedule the processes performing reads before the processes performing writes. The order in which processes read does not matter. Since no two processes write to the same register, the order in which processes write does not matter either.

A register is allowed to hold an arbitrarily large amount of information. Therefore, any number of single-writer registers that can be written to by the same process can be combined into one single-writer register with multiple components. Hence, there is no loss of generality in assuming that each process p_i has exactly one single-writer register r_i into which it may write. We may also restrict attention to full-information algorithms, in which each process writes its entire history whenever it writes to its single-writer register. Then $C \overset{p_i}{\sim} C'$ implies that r_i has the same value in both C and C'.

Consider any synchronous execution α. The set of processes whose inputs process p_i knows about at the end of round t can be described by the recurrence:

$$I(p_i, t) = \begin{cases} \{p_i\} & \text{if } t = 0, \\ I(p_i, t-1) \cup I(p_j, t-1) & \text{if the step by process } p_i \text{ in round } t \\ & \text{of } \alpha \text{ is a read from register } r_j, \\ I(p_i, t-1) & \text{otherwise.} \end{cases}$$

More generally, the cardinality of the set $I(p_i, t)$ is a measure of the amount of information process p_i has at the end of round t of execution α. Let $I(t) = \max\limits_{p_i}\{|I(p_i, t)|\}$. Then

$$\begin{aligned} I(0) &= 1, \text{ and} \\ I(t) &\leq 2I(t-1), \text{ for } t > 0. \end{aligned}$$

It is easy to prove by induction on t that $I(t) \leq 2^t$.

Let α_t denote the longest prefix of α in which no process has taken more than t steps. In other words, α_t consists of the first t rounds of α. In particular, α_0 is the empty execution starting from the initial configuration of α.

During α_t, process p_i only learns information about the input values of processes in $I(p_i, t)$. It does not learn any information about other input values. Formally, this means that p_i cannot distinguish α_t from the first t rounds of any other synchronous execution that has the same input values for all processes in $I(p_i, t)$.

Lemma 5.1 Let α be a synchronous execution starting from an initial configuration C. Let β be a synchronous execution starting from another configuration C'. For any process p_i and any nonnegative integer t, if $C \overset{p}{\sim} C'$ for all $p \in I(p_i, t)$, then $\alpha_t \overset{p_i}{\sim} \beta_t$.

Proof. The proof is by induction on t.

If $C \overset{p}{\sim} C'$ for all $p \in I(p_i, 0) = \{p_i\}$, then process p_i has the same state in C and C'. Since α_0 and β_0 are both empty executions, process p_i has the same local history in both. Thus $\alpha_0 \overset{p_i}{\sim} \beta_0$ and the claim is true for $t = 0$.

Let $t \geq 1$ and assume the claim is true for $t - 1$. Suppose that $C \overset{p}{\sim} C'$ for all $p \in I(p_i, t)$. Since $I(p_i, t-1) \subseteq I(p_i, t)$, it follows that $C \overset{p}{\sim} C'$ for all $p \in I(p_i, t-1)$. Hence, by the induction hypothesis, $\alpha_{t-1} \overset{p_i}{\sim} \beta_{t-1}$ and the local history of process p_i is the same in executions

α_{t-1} and β_{t-1} and p_i is in the same state at the end of both these executions. Thus, the step performed by process p_i in round t will be the same in executions α_t and β_t. For the local history of process p_i to be the same in executions α_t and β_t, it suffices to prove that this step, if it exists, has the same response in both executions.

Since writes always have the same response, it suffices to consider the case when the step by process p_i in round t is a read from the register, r_j, of some other process p_j. In this case, $I(p_j, t-1) \subseteq I(p_i, t)$. Hence, $C \overset{p}{\sim} C'$ for all $p \in I(p_j, t-1)$ and, by the induction hypothesis, $\alpha_{t-1} \overset{p_j}{\sim} \beta_{t-1}$. Therefore, the value of r_j is the same at the end of α_{t-1} and β_{t-1}. The reads in round t precede the writes in round t. It follows that process p_i reads the same value from r_j during round t in α_t and β_t. Therefore, the claim is true for t and, hence, by induction, for all $t \geq 0$. □

5.2 THE ROUND COMPLEXITY OF OR

We apply Lemma 5.1 to get a lower bound on the worst-case number of rounds to compute OR. In this problem, each process p_i has an input value $x_i \in \{0, 1\}$ and must output $x_0 \vee \cdots \vee x_{n-1}$. For a process to output 1, it only has to know that some input value is 1. However, to output 0, it has to know that all input values are 0. We focus on this case. Let C_0 denote the initial configuration in which all input values are 0.

Theorem 5.2 *Any synchronous algorithm for computing OR among n processes that only communicate using single-writer registers has an execution in which each process takes at least $\log_2 n$ steps.*

Proof. The proof is by contradiction. Let α denote any execution starting from C_0. Suppose there is a process p_i that outputs the OR in execution α within $t < \log_2 n$ steps. Since all the input values are 0, process p_i must output value 0 in α.

Since $|I(p_i, t)| \leq 2^t < n$, there is some process $p_j \notin I(p_i, t)$. Let C' denote the initial configuration in which $x_j = 1$, but all other input values are 0. Then $C_0 \overset{p}{\sim} C'$ for all $p \in I(p_i, t)$. Let β be an execution starting from C'. Lemma 5.1 implies that $\alpha_t \overset{p_i}{\sim} \beta_t$. Since process p_i outputs value 0 in α_t, it also outputs value 0 in β_t. But this is incorrect, since the OR of the input values in this execution is 1. □

If no processes fail, the OR can be computed in $O(\log n)$ rounds, using a binary tree to collect information.

Can we get a better (i.e., bigger) lower bound if all processes do not necessarily start at the same time? If the input values are private and all 0, then no process can output (the value 0) until after all of the processes have started, because, until then, it is possible that one of the input values is 1. This can be an arbitrarily long time.

So, suppose that the input value of each process p_i is initially in its single-writer register r_i. In this case, a process executing by itself from the initial configuration in which all of the input values are 0 would have to read the single-writer register of every other process. Thus, it must perform at least $n - 1$ steps.

If processes communicate using multi-writer registers, OR is easy to compute in a synchronous system in which processes don't fail: Assume that register r initially contains the value 0. In round 1, each process p_i with $x_i = 1$ writes 1 to r. In round 2, each process reads r and returns the value it contains. Thus, the lower bound on the number of rounds to compute OR using single-writer registers doesn't extend to multi-writer registers. Moreover, this implies that any synchronous simulation of multi-writer registers using only single-writer registers will have an execution in which some operation takes $\Omega(\log n)$ rounds to be performed.

Theorem 5.2 is a simplification of the $\log_2 n$ lower bound on the number of rounds to compute OR on an oblivious exclusive-write PRAM by Stephen Cook, Cynthia Dwork, and Rüdiger Reischuk in "Upper and Lower Time Bounds for Parallel Random Access Machines without Simultaneous Writes," *SIAM Journal on Computing*, 1986 [33]. They also prove similar $\Omega(\log n)$ lower bounds for OR on more general exclusive-write PRAMs.

5.3 THE ROUND COMPLEXITY OF APPROXIMATE AGREEMENT

Next, we consider the approximate agreement problem, which was defined in Section 2.3. If all processes are guaranteed to start in the same round, approximate agreement can be solved in two rounds, even for $\epsilon = 0$. In round 1, process p_0 writes its input x_0 to its register r_0 and outputs x_0. In round 2, all other processes read x_0 from r_0 and output x_0. So, the model considered in this section allows processes to start at different times (although, once a process has begun, it takes one step per round until it finishes). However, we will still prove a lower bound on the worst case number of steps taken by processes in executions in which all processes start at the same time. The lower bound holds even for a very restricted set of possible input values.

Theorem 5.3   *For any $\epsilon < 1$, any algorithm for approximate agreement among n processes that only communicate using single-writer registers has a synchronous execution in which no process outputs a value before round $\lceil \log_2 n \rceil$, even if all of the inputs $x_0, \ldots, x_{n-1}$ are restricted to be in $\{0, 1\}$.*

Proof. The proof is by contradiction. Let C_0 denote the initial configuration in which all input values are 0. Let α denote any synchronous execution starting from C_0. Let p_i be the first process that outputs a value in execution α. Suppose this happens during round $t < \lceil \log_2 n \rceil$. By validity, process p_i must output value 0 in α, since $\min\{x_1, \ldots, x_n\} = \max\{x_1, \ldots, x_n\} = 0$ in configuration C_0.

Since $|I(p_i, t)| \leq I(t) \leq 2^t < n$, there is some process $p_j \notin I(p_i, t)$. Let C_1 denote the initial configuration in which all input values are 1. Let γ denote the solo execution by process p_j starting from C_1 that continues until p_j halts. By validity, process p_j outputs value 1 during γ.

Let C denote the initial configuration in which $x_j = 1$ and all other input values are 0 and let γ' be the solo execution by process p_j starting from C. Since process p_j has the same state in C_1 and C and each register has the same value in C_1 and C, it follows that $\gamma \overset{p_j}{\sim} \gamma'$. Thus, process p_j outputs value 1 during γ'.

Let C' be the configuration at the end of γ'. Then $C_0 \overset{p}{\sim} C'$ for all $p \in I(p_i, t)$, since these processes take no steps in γ'. Let β be an execution starting from C'. Note that process p_j takes no steps in β, since it has halted in configuration C'. Lemma 5.1 implies that $\beta_t \overset{p_i}{\sim} \alpha_t$. Since process p_i outputs value 0 during α_t and takes no steps in γ', it also outputs value 0 during β_t and $\gamma'\beta_t$. But p_j outputs value 1 during γ' and, hence, during $\gamma'\beta$. This contradicts ϵ-agreement, since $\epsilon < 1$.   □

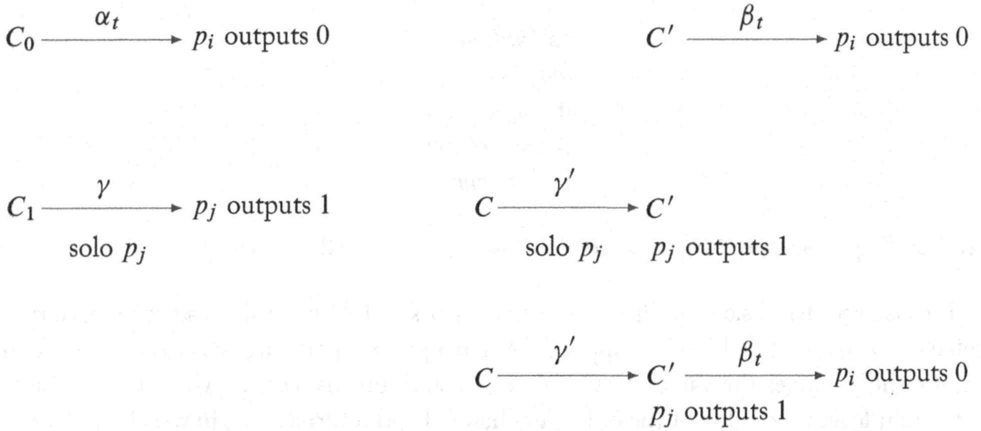

Figure 5.1: The executions considered in the proof of Theorem 5.3.

Since an asynchronous system is more general than a synchronous system in which processes can start at different times, $\log_2 n$ is also a lower bound on the worst case number of rounds taken by a process to solve approximate agreement in an asynchronous system.

The lower bound presented in this section is from Hagit Attiya, Nancy Lynch, and Nir Shavit, "Are Wait-free Algorithms Fast?," *Journal of the ACM*, 1994 [16]. In the same paper, they also show this bound is tight (to within a constant factor), even in an asynchronous system. Moreover, their algorithm tolerates process crashes, allows arbitrary inputs, and works for any value of ϵ.

For synchronous systems, the worst case step complexity of an algorithm is the same as its round complexity. However, for asynchronous systems, the worst case step complexity can be much larger, as the $\Omega(n)$ lower bound on step complexity for approximate agreement in Section 2.3 shows.

5.4   LOWER BOUNDS USING MORE POWERFUL OBJECTS

Proving information theory lower bounds is more difficult when multi-writer registers are available or when other primitives, such as compare&swap, load-linked, and store-conditional, can be applied to objects in shared memory.

The compare&swap primitive (which we abbreviate as cas) applied to an object r atomically reads the value of r, compares it to the value of the parameter *old*, and, if they are the same, writes the value of the parameter *new* to r. It returns the value r had immediately before the cas was applied. We say that a cas is *successful* if its comparison was successful, i.e., if it returns the value *old*. Formally, cas can be specified by the code in Figure 5.2, where r is the object to which it is being applied. If *old* = *new*, we say that the cas is *degenerate*.

cas(*old*, *new*)
temp ← r
if *temp* = *old*
then r ← *new*
return *temp*

Figure 5.2: Sequential specification of compare&swap (cas) applied to object r.

The load-linked and store-conditional primitives work as follows. Like read, load-linked returns the value of the object to which it is applied. When a process performs store-conditional(v) on an object, it either changes the value of the object to v and returns *true*, in which case we say it is *successful*, or it leaves the value of the object unchanged and returns *false*, in which case we say it is *unsuccessful*. The store-conditional performed by a process on an object is successful if and only if no write, successful store-conditional, or successful cas has been performed on the object since the process last performed load-linked on the object.

For the rest of this chapter, we consider the synchronous shared memory model in which no processes fail and processes communicate using the primitives read, write, cas, load-linked, store-conditional applied to any object. Once a process starts a computation, it performs exactly one of these primitives every round until it finishes. In the lower bound proofs, we restrict attention to certain synchronous executions. Specifically, in every round, all instances of read and load-linked are performed before any instances of cas, all instances of cas are performed before any writes, and all writes are performed before any instances of store-conditional. Amongst the cas operations, the degenerate ones are scheduled first, followed by those whose old value is different from the value, v, in the object at the end of the previous round, followed by those whose old value is v. Note that, in each round, at most one successful non-degenerate cas or successful store-conditional is applied to each object.

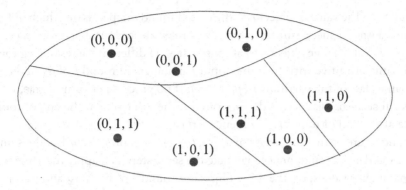

Figure 5.3: A partition of the set $\{0, 1\}^3$.

Consider any synchronous algorithm and let α_x denote a synchronous execution of this algorithm on the vector of inputs $x \in \{0, 1\}^n$. Let $\alpha_{x,t}$ denote the prefix of α_x containing its first t rounds. When only single-writer registers are available, Lemma 5.1 implies that, if $x_j = x'_j$ for all $p_j \in I(p_i, t)$, then $\alpha_{x,t} \overset{p_i}{\sim} \alpha_{x',t}$.

In the case of more general objects, we also want to understand what different inputs lead to executions that are indistinguishable to a process. For every process p_i and every round t, we partition the set $\{0, 1\}^n$ into equivalence classes such that $x, x' \in \{0, 1\}^n$ are in the same class if and only if the executions $\alpha_{x,t}$ and $\alpha_{x',t}$ are indistinguishable to process p_i, i.e., $\alpha_{x,t} \overset{p_i}{\sim} \alpha_{x',t}$. Let $P(p_i, t)$ denote this partition and let

$$P(t) = \max_{p_i}\{ \text{ number of classes in } P(p_i, t) \}.$$

Note that, for every process p_i, the partition $P(p_i, 0)$ has two classes, since $\alpha_{x,0} \overset{p_i}{\sim} \alpha_{x',0}$ if and only if $x_i = x'_i$. Hence $P(0) = 2$.

Similarly, for every object r and every round t, partition the set $\{0, 1\}^n$ into equivalence classes such that $x, x' \in \{0, 1\}^n$ are in the same class if and only if the value of r is the same after executions $\alpha_{x,t}$ and $\alpha_{x',t}$. Let $V(r, t)$ denote this partition and let

$$V(t) = \max_{r}\{ \text{ number of classes in } V(r, t) \}.$$

Since every object has its initial value at the end of $\alpha_{x,0}$ for each $x \in \{0, 1\}^n$, it follows that $V(0) = 1$.

Lemma 5.4 $P(t), V(t) \le 2^{2^t} n^{2^t - 1}$ for all nonnegative integers t.

Proof. Let $t > 0$. The value of object r at the end of round t depends on which of the n processes last performs a write, a successful cas, or a successful store-conditional on r during round t, if any. Each process p_i can change object r to at most $P(t-1)$ different values during round t, since it applies the same primitive with the same input parameters in round t of α_x and $\alpha_{x'}$, if x and x' are in the same class of the partition $P(p_i, t-1)$. If no process performs a write, a successful cas, or a successful store-conditional on r during round t, the value of r at the end of round t depends on its value at the end of round $t-1$. Hence $V(t) \leq n \cdot P(t-1) + V(t-1)$.

If x and x' are in the same class of $P(p_i, t-1)$, then process p_i has the same state at the end of $\alpha_{x,t-1}$ and $\alpha_{x',t-1}$ and, hence, will take the same step (i.e., apply the same primitive, with the same parameter values, on the same object) in round t of both α_x and $\alpha_{x'}$. If this step is a write, then p_i will have the same state at the end of $\alpha_{x,t}$ and $\alpha_{x',t}$, so $\alpha_{x,t} \overset{p_i}{\sim} \alpha_{x',t}$. In this case, x and x' remain in the same class of $P(p_i, t)$. If this step applies store-conditional, then p_i will get one of two possible responses, *true* or *false* and this class of $P(p_i, t-1)$ is split into at most two different classes in $P(p_i, t)$. If this step is a read or load-linked, then x and x' remain in the same class of $P(p_i, t)$ only if the object they access has the same value at the end of round $t-1$ in α_x and $\alpha_{x'}$. Thus, in this case, a class in $P(p_i, t-1)$ is split into at most $V(t-1)$ different classes. Otherwise, this step applies cas to some object. Then the value returned is either one of the at most $V(t-1)$ values in the object at the beginning of the round or one of the at most $P(t-1)$ different values each of the other $n-1$ processes could have changed it to. In this case, a class in $P(p_i, t-1)$ is split into at most $V(t-1) + (n-1)P(t-1)$ different classes. Hence, in all cases, $P(t) \leq P(t-1) \cdot [V(t-1) + (n-1)P(t-1)]$.

It follows by induction that $P(t), V(t) \leq 2^{2^t} n^{2^t - 1}$ for all $t \geq 0$. $\qquad\square$

The lemma can be extended to objects that also support k-cas. This primitive atomically compares the current values of k objects to *old* parameters and, if they are the same, assigns the values of *new* parameters to the objects. It returns a Boolean value, indicating whether it was successful. If, instead, the k-cas returns the values of the k objects accessed, then the lower bound becomes $\Omega(\log_k n)$. See Hagit Attiya and Danny Hendler, "Time and Space Lower Bounds for Implementations Using k-CAS," *IEEE Transactions on Parallel and Distributed Systems*, 2010 [14].

5.5 THE ROUND COMPLEXITY OF COLLECT

In the *collect* problem, each process p_i has an input value $x_i \in \{0, 1\}$ and must output the vector $x = (x_0, \ldots, x_{n-1})$ of all the input values. All processes are assumed to start the computation at the same time.

Theorem 5.5 *Any n-process synchronous algorithm for collect requires $\Omega(\log n)$ rounds in the worst case.*

Proof. If the algorithm performs t rounds in the worst case, then $P(t) = 2^n$, since, on each vector of inputs, the processes must produce a different output and, hence, each vector of inputs must be in a separate class of the partition $P(p, t)$, for every process p. Therefore, by Lemma 5.4, $(2n)^{2^t} \geq P(t) \geq 2^n$, so $t \geq \log_2 n - \log_2 \log_2(2n)$. This implies that $t \in \Omega(\log n)$. $\qquad\square$

This lower bound, for the case of multi-writer registers, is due to Paul Beame, "Limits on the Power of Concurrent-Write Parallel Machines," *Information and Computation*, 1988 [24]. A matching upper bound can be obtained by collecting the information using a binary tree. In his paper "A Time Complexity Lower Bound for Randomized Implementations of Some Shared Objects," which appeared in *PODC*, 1998 [52], Prasad Jayanti proves an equivalent lower bound for the load-linked, store-conditional, validate, swap, and move primitives.

5.6 A STEP COMPLEXITY TRADEOFF FOR SYNCHRONOUS SNAPSHOTS

In this section, we use Lemma 5.4 to get a tradeoff between the step complexities of two different operations of an implemented object. As in Section 5.3, processes may start at different rounds.

A *(multi-writer) snapshot* object consists of $m \geq 2$ components and supports two operations: Update(i, v), which sets the value of component i to v, and Scan, which returns the current value of all m components. Initially, all components are 0. A *single-writer* snapshot is an n-component snapshot in which only process p_i can perform Update on component i. Thus, in single-writer snapshots, no Update operations to the same component overlap one another. For our lower bound, it suffices to consider restricted executions of a single-writer snapshot object in which processes $p_1, \ldots, p_{n-1}$ may each perform a single Update and then process p_0 performs a single Scan. In particular, the Updates overlap, but the Scan does not overlap any Update. Thus, the value of component i returned by the Scan is either the value of the Update performed by p_i, or the initial value of component i, if p_i did not perform an Update. In these restricted executions, the Scan performed by p_0 is like solving collect, except that the other processes can coalesce information for p_0 before it starts.

Theorem 5.6 *Consider any implementation of a single-writer snapshot shared by n processes. If U is the worst case step complexity of Update and S is the worst case step complexity of Scan, then $U + \log_2 S \in \Omega(\log n)$.*

Proof. For every vector $x \in \{0, 1\}^{n-1}$, let C_x be the initial configuration where, for each $i \in \{1, \ldots, n-1\}$, process p_i has input x_i. Let α_x denote the U round execution starting from C_x in which process p_i performs Update$(i, 1)$ starting at round 1 for all $i \in \{1, \ldots, n-1\}$ with $x_i = 1$. Let σ_x denote the solo Scan performed by p_0 starting in round $U + 1$ at configuration $C_x \alpha_x$. Note that, by assumption, all Updates are finished by the end of round U.

For each $t' \leq S$, let $\sigma_{x,t'}$ denote the prefix of σ_x containing its first t' rounds. Also let $P'(p_0, t')$ denote the partition of $\{0, 1\}^{n-1}$ into equivalence classes, where $x, x' \in \{0, 1\}^{n-1}$ are in the same class if and only if the executions $\alpha_x \sigma_{x,t'}$ and $\alpha_{x'} \sigma_{x',t'}$ are indistinguishable to process p_0. Let $P'(t')$ denote the number of classes in $P'(p_0, t')$. Since p_0 has no input and takes no steps in the first U rounds, $P'(0) = 1$.

Now let $0 < t' \leq S$ and suppose that x and x' are in the same class of the partition $P'(p_0, t' - 1)$. Then process p_0 has the same state at the end of $\alpha_x \sigma_{x,t'-1}$ and $\alpha_{x'} \sigma_{x',t'-1}$ and, hence, will perform the same step in round $U + t'$ of both $\alpha_x \sigma_x$ and $\alpha_{x'} \sigma_{x'}$.

If this step is a write or store-conditional to an object or a read, load-linked, or cas of an object to which p_0 has previously performed read, load-linked, write, or cas, then p_0 will have the same state at the end of $\alpha_x \sigma_{x,t'}$ and $\alpha_{x'} \sigma_{x',t'}$. In other words, $\alpha_x \sigma_{x,t'} \stackrel{p_0}{\sim} \alpha_{x'} \sigma_{x',t'}$. In this case, x and x' are also in the same class of the partition $P'(p_0, t')$.

Otherwise, this step is a read, cas, or load-linked of an object r that p_0 has not already accessed. Since r has not changed since round U, it can have at most $V(U)$ different values. If r had the same value at the end of α_x and $\alpha_{x'}$, then the vectors x and x' are in the same class of $P'(p_0, t')$. Thus, each class of $P'(p_0, t' - 1)$ contains at most $V(U)$ different classes of $P'(p_0, t')$. Hence, the number of classes in $P'(p_0, t')$ is bounded above by $V(U)$ times the number of classes in $P'(p_0, t' - 1)$. In other words,

$$P'(t') \leq P'(t' - 1) \cdot V(U).$$

It follows by induction that $P'(t') \leq (V(U))^{t'}$.

The Scan by process p_0 completes by the end of round $U + S$. Thus $\sigma_x = \sigma_{x,S}$ for all $x \in \{0,1\}^{n-1}$. If $x' \neq x$, then the result returned by p_0's Scan must be different in the executions $\alpha_{x'} \sigma_{x'}$ and $\alpha_x \sigma_x$. Thus x' and x are in different classes of $P'(p_0, S)$. Hence $P'(S) = 2^{n-1}$.

By Lemma 5.4, $V(U) \leq (2n)^{2^U}$. It follows that $2^{n-1} = P'(S) \leq (V(U))^S \leq (2n)^{S 2^U}$. This implies that $U + \log_2 S \geq \log_2(n-1) - \log_2 \log_2(2n) \in \Omega(\log n)$. $\qquad\square$

When S denotes the number of objects used by the implementation, instead of the worst case step complexity of Scan, it is still the case that $U + \log_2 S \in \Omega(\log n)$. This is because a step by process p_0 only increases the number of classes in the partition if it is a read, load-linked, or cas of an object that p_0 has not already accessed. Since there are only S objects, this can happen at most S times. Each time, the number of classes increases by at most a factor of $V(U)$, so $2^{n-1} \leq (V(U))^S$.

The lower bound in Theorem 5.6, for the case of multi-writer registers, is from Alex Brodsky and Faith Ellen Fich, "Efficient Synchronous Snapshots," *PODC*, 2004 [28]. This paper also constructs a family of linearizable (multi-writer) snapshot implementations from multi-writer registers whose step complexities of Scan and Update match the lower bound to within a constant factor. Hence the complexities of implementing a restricted single-writer snapshot (in which only a single fixed process is allowed to perform Scan and only Scan operations that do not overlap Update operations are permitted) and a (multi-writer) snapshot are the same in this model. Moreover, allowing cas, load-linked, and store-conditional primitives in addition to read and write does not decrease the complexity of implementing a synchronous snapshot object.

CHAPTER 6

Covering Arguments

A process is *poised* at an object if it will apply a primitive to the object when it is next allocated a step by the scheduler. If the value of the object resulting from applying this primitive does not depend on its current value, then the information stored in the object will be obliterated. In this case, we say that the primitive is *historyless* and the process *covers* the object.

A *covering argument* is useful for proving lower bounds for asynchronous shared memory systems. The goal is to construct a configuration in which a large set of objects are covered. The size of the objects does not matter: They can be arbitrarily large. The construction is usually inductive, with the number of covered objects increasing as the argument progresses. The processes covering these objects can be used to hide information that other processes may have stored there and wished to communicate. If these objects are the only objects that the other processes have modified, then the steps of these other processes can be hidden, in the sense that if they are removed from the execution, the resulting execution is indistinguishable to the remaining processes.

For example, suppose that processes communicate through m multi-writer registers. Note that write is a historyless primitive. Consider a history, β, starting from some configuration C, in which m processes, $p_{i_1}, \ldots, p_{i_m}$, each write a value to a different register, one after the other. This is called a block write. Let γ be another history starting from C by a subset of processes Q disjoint from $\{p_{i_1}, \ldots, p_{i_m}\}$. Then the executions starting from C with histories β and $\gamma\beta$ are indistinguishable to all processes not in Q. Moreover, each register has the same value in configurations $C\beta$ and $C\gamma\beta$. Thus, γ is hidden from the processes not in Q, no matter what they do in the future.

Another example of a historyless primitive is swap. It has a single input parameter v. When applied to an object, it sets the value of the object to v and returns the value the object had beforehand. A consecutive sequence of swaps applied by different processes to different objects is called a block swap. When a set of processes performs a block write to a set of objects, they get no information about the previous values of those objects. In contrast, when a set of processes performs a block swap to a set of objects, they (collectively) learn the previous values of these objects. Hence, to hide the information that was stored there, the adversary does not let these processes take any further steps.

Any historyless primitive that sets the value of an object to v (regardless of its previous value) can be simulated by swap(v). Thus, for proving lower bounds on implementations using historyless primitives, it suffices to restrict attention to swap.

A primitive is *trivial* if it can never change the value of an object. The most common example of a trivial primitive is read. We say that an object is *historyless* if it only supports historyless and trivial primitives.

Covering arguments were introduced by James Burns and Nancy Lynch, in their paper "Bounds on Shared Memory for Mutual Exclusion," *Information and Computation,* 1993 [30], to prove a lower bound on the number of registers needed to solve mutual exclusion. This result will be presented in Section 6.1. In subsequent sections, we present a variety of other covering arguments: lower bounds on the number of multi-writer registers needed to implement timestamps, in Section 6.2; space and step complexity lower bounds for the implementation of a counter using swap, in Section 6.3; and a lower bound on the number of multi-writer registers needed to implement a multi-writer snapshot object and a step complexity lower bound for any space optimal implementation, both in Section 6.4.

In Section 6.5, we prove a lower bound on the worst case number of stalls incurred by ReadCounter in any implementation of a counter using read-modify-write primitives. We do this by constructing a configuration in which there are a large number of processes poised to apply nontrivial primitives to objects that will be accessed by the ReadCounter. In this case, our goal is to increase contention, rather than to hide information.

6.1 A SPACE LOWER BOUND FOR MUTUAL EXCLUSION

Our first covering argument shows that any algorithm for mutual exclusion, with $n \geq 2$ processes, uses at least n registers. Recall that the mutual exclusion problem was defined in Section 2.2. We consider an asynchronous shared memory model that contains only multi-writer registers. While a process is in the remainder section, we do not consider it to be covering any of the registers.

First, we look at a solo execution by a process that takes it from the remainder section to the critical section. We show that along the way, there is a configuration in which one more register is covered.

Lemma 6.1 *Suppose that C is a configuration in which process p_i is in its remainder section. Let α be a finite history by process p_i starting from configuration C such that p_i is in the critical section in configuration $C\alpha$. Let R be the set of registers which are covered in configuration C. Then, during α, process p_i writes to some register that is not in R.*

Proof. By contradiction. Suppose that during α, process p_i only writes to registers in R. Let β be a block write to R starting from configuration C. Then the value of every register is the same in configurations $C\beta$ and $C\alpha\beta$ and $C\beta \overset{q}{\sim} C\alpha\beta$, for all $q \neq p_i$. Note that p_i is still in the remainder section in configuration $C\beta$.

Starting from $C\beta$, we show that there exists a finite p_i-free history γ such that a process is in the critical section in configuration $C\beta\gamma$. If some process is in the critical section in $C\beta$, then it suffices to let γ be empty. If not, but there is some process in the trying section, then deadlock

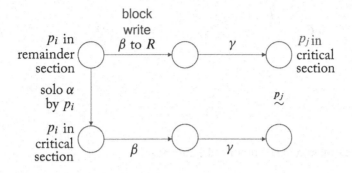

Figure 6.1: The situation in Lemma 6.1.

freedom implies the existence of γ. If there is no process in the trying or critical sections, but there is some process other than p_i in the remainder section, the adversary can first let some such process enter the trying section. Finally, if all processes other than p_i are in the exit section, the adversary can choose one of them and first allocate steps to it until it is in the remainder section. This is because a process that is in the exit section will always leave it within a bounded number of steps.

Let $p_j \neq p_i$ be a process in the critical section in configuration $C\beta\gamma$. Since $C\beta \overset{q}{\sim} C\alpha\beta$ for all $q \neq p_i$, it follows by Lemma 2.1 that $C\beta\gamma \overset{p_j}{\sim} C\alpha\beta\gamma$. This is illustrated in Figure 6.1. Note that both p_i and p_j are in their critical sections in configuration $C\alpha\beta\gamma$. This violates mutual exclusion.   □

A configuration C is *reachable* from configuration Q if there is a finite history α such that $C = Q\alpha$. A configuration is *quiescent* if every process is in the remainder section, i.e., there is no process that has entered the trying section, but has not subsequently finished the exit section. From any quiescent configuration, we show how to construct a sequence of reachable configurations with successively more covered registers. Furthermore, each of these configurations will be indistinguishable from a quiescent configuration to successively fewer processes.

Lemma 6.2 *From any quiescent configuration, for $k = 1, \ldots, n$, there are reachable configurations, C and D, such that D is quiescent, each register has the same value in C and D, $p_0, \ldots, p_{k-1}$ cover k different registers in C, and $C \overset{q}{\sim} D$ for all $q \in \{p_k, \ldots, p_{n-1}\}$.*

Proof. The proof is by induction on k.

First consider $k = 1$. From any quiescent configuration Q, deadlock freedom implies that there is a solo execution by process p_0 that results in a configuration in which p_0 is in the critical section. Let α be the history of that execution.

There are no registers covered in Q, so, by Lemma 6.1, during α, process p_0 writes to some register. Let α' be the longest prefix of α that contains no writes. Then p_0 covers a register

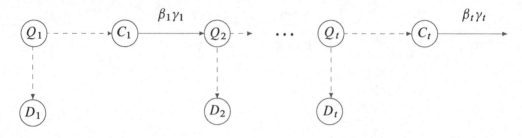

Figure 6.2: The situation in the proof of Lemma 6.2.

in $Q\alpha'$ and $Q\alpha' \overset{q}{\sim} Q$ for all $q \in \{p_1, \ldots, p_{n-1}\}$. Hence, the claim is true with $C = Q\alpha'$ and $D = Q$.

Now assume the claim is true for k, where $1 \le k < n$. By the induction hypothesis, from any quiescent configuration Q_t, there are configurations C_t and D_t that satisfy the claim. Let β_t be a block write by $\{p_0, \ldots, p_{k-1}\}$ starting from C_t. Since C_t and D_t are indistinguishable to the rest of the processes and D_t is quiescent, $p_k, \ldots, p_{n-1}$ are all in the remainder section in C_t. Thus, deadlock freedom implies that there is a finite history γ_t by the processes in $\{p_0, \ldots, p_{k-1}\}$ starting from $C_t\beta_t$ such that $Q_{t+1} = C_t\beta_t\gamma_t$ is quiescent.

From any quiescent configuration Q, consider the sequence of configurations $Q = Q_1, Q_2, \ldots$, as shown in Figure 6.2. By the pigeonhole principle, there exist $1 \le t < t' \le \binom{r}{k} + 1$ such that β_t and $\beta_{t'}$ are block writes to the same set of k registers R.

Configuration D_t is quiescent. Hence, deadlock freedom implies that there is a solo execution by process p_k, starting from D_t, that takes p_k to the critical section. Let α be the history of that execution. Since $C_t \overset{p_k}{\sim} D_t$ and each register has the same value in C_t and D_t, it follows by Lemma 2.1 that α can occur starting from C_t and p_k is in the critical section in $C_t\alpha$.

By Lemma 6.1, during α, process p_k writes to some register not in R. Let α' be the shortest prefix of α such that, in configuration $C_t\alpha'$, process p_k covers some register not in R. Since all writes in α' are to registers in R and β_t is a block write to R, each register has the same value in $C_t\beta_t$ and $C_t\alpha'\beta_t$. Since $C_t\beta_t \overset{q}{\sim} C_t\alpha'\beta_t$ for all $q \ne p_k$, Lemma 2.1 implies that $\gamma_t \cdots \beta_{t'-1}\gamma_{t'-1}$ can occur starting from $C_t\alpha'\beta_t$ and $C = C_t\alpha'\beta_t\gamma_t \cdots \beta_{t'-1}\gamma_{t'-1} \overset{q}{\sim} C_{t'}$ for all $q \ne p_k$. This is illustrated in Figure 6.3. Since $C_{t'} \overset{q}{\sim} D_{t'}$, for all $q \in \{p_k, \ldots, p_{n-1}\}$, it follows that $C \overset{q}{\sim} D_{t'}$ for all $q \in \{p_{k+1}, \ldots, p_{n-1}\}$.

Furthermore, each register has the same value in C, $C_{t'}$, and $D_{t'}$. Since p_k takes no steps during $\beta_t\gamma_t \cdots \beta_{t'-1}\gamma_{t'-1}$, it covers the same register in configuration C. Thus, $p_0, \ldots, p_{k-1}, p_k$ cover $k+1$ different registers in C. Therefore the claim is true for $k+1$ with $D = D_{t'}$. Hence, by induction, it is true for $k = 1, \ldots, n$. $\qquad\square$

The lower bound follows easily from this lemma with $k = n$, using the fact that the initial configuration is quiescent.

Theorem 6.3   *Any mutual exclusion algorithm for $n \ge 2$ processes must use at least n registers.*

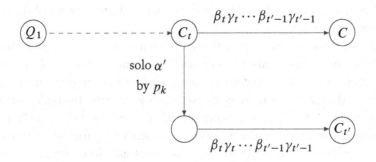

Figure 6.3: Two indistinguishable executions used in the proof of Lemma 6.2.

6.2   THE SPACE COMPLEXITY OF TIMESTAMPS

Timestamps provide information about the temporal ordering of events in an execution. Formally, a *timestamp* system consists of a partially ordered set $(U, <)$ of timestamps and an operation GetTS with range U that satisfies the following validity condition: If one GetTS operation is completed before another GetTS operation begins and these operations return t_1 and t_2, respectively, then $t_1 < t_2$. If two GetTS operations overlap, then t_1 can be less than, greater than, or incomparable to t_2.

The model we consider is asynchronous shared memory in which n processes communicate via multi-writer registers. We show that n is a lower bound on the number of registers needed for implementing a certain class of timestamp systems.

Theorem 6.4   *Any n-process implementation of* GetTS *with range* $\mathbb{N}$, *under its usual ordering, that satisfies solo termination requires at least n registers.*

Proof. We prove by induction that, for $i = 0, \ldots, n$, there is a reachable configuration C_i in which a set P_i of i processes cover a set R_i of i different registers. The theorem follows from this claim with $i = n$.

When $i = 0$, let C_0 be the initial configuration and let $P_0 = R_0 = \phi$. Now, let $1 \le i \le n$ and suppose that there is a reachable configuration C_{i-1} in which a set P_{i-1} of $i - 1$ processes cover a set R_{i-1} of $i - 1$ different registers. If $i > 1$, let $p \in P_{i-1}$; otherwise, let p be any process.

Consider an execution that starts from configuration C_{i-1} with a block write β by the processes in P_{i-1} to the registers of R_{i-1}, followed by a solo execution γ by p in which p completes its pending operation, if any, and then performs GetTS. By solo termination, this operation eventually completes and returns some timestamp t.

Let q be a process not in $P_{i-1} \cup \{p\}$. We now show that a solo execution by q, starting from C_{i-1}, in which it repeatedly performs GetTS, must eventually write to a register not in R_{i-1}. Note that, by solo termination, each instance of GetTS in this solo execution will eventually terminate. Let t_j be the timestamp returned by the j'th instance of GetTS by q in this solo execution. Then $t_j < t_{j+1}$ for all $j \geq 1$. There are only a finite number of timestamps less than t, so there exists j such that $t_j \not< t$.

To derive a contradiction, suppose that q does not write to any register outside R_{i-1} during the solo execution of its first j instances of GetTS, starting from C_{i-1}. Let α be the history of this solo execution. Since each register has the same value in configurations $C_{i-1}\beta$ and $C_{i-1}\alpha\beta$, if follows by Corollary 2.2 that there is an execution γ' starting from $C_{i-1}\alpha\beta$ such that γ and γ' are indistinguishable to p. Then p returns t as the result of its last GetTS in γ'. When α is performed starting from C_{i-1}, the j'th instance of GetTS by q finishes before the last instance of GetTS by p in γ' begins. Thus $t_j < t$, which is a contradiction. Hence q must write to some register outside R_{i-1} during α.

Let α' be the shortest prefix of α such that, in $C_{i-1}\alpha$, process q covers some register $r \notin R_{i-1}$. Let $C_i = C_{i-1}\alpha'$, let $P_i = P_{i-1} \cup \{q\}$, and let $R_i = R_{i-1} \cup \{r\}$. Then the claim is true for i and, hence, by induction, for n. □

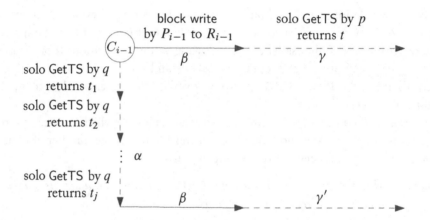

Figure 6.4: The executions used in the proof of Theorem 6.4.

The fact that the universe of possible timestamps is $\mathbb{N}$ under its usual ordering is only used to argue that there are only a finite number of timestamps less than t. The proof we presented actually holds when $(U, <)$ is any *nowhere dense* partially ordered set. This means that, for every two elements $x, y \in U$, there are only a finite number of elements $z \in U$ such that $x < z < y$. Some examples of nowhere dense partially ordered sets are $\mathbb{N}$ under its usual ordering, the set of all finite sets, ordered by set inclusion, and the set of integer vectors of length $k \geq 2$, under component-wise ordering, i.e., $x \leq y$ if and only if $x_i \leq y_i$ for all components i. Some examples of partially ordered sets that are NOT nowhere dense are $\mathbb{Q}$ under its usual ordering, $\mathbb{R}$ under its usual ordering, and the set of integer vectors of length $k \geq 2$, ordered lexicographically.

Theorem 6.5 *Any implementation of GetTS for n processes, with a nowhere dense partially ordered range, that satisfies solo termination requires at least n registers.*

Leslie Lamport, in his paper, *A new solution of Dijkstra's concurrent programming problem*, CACM, 1974 [55], gives a timestamp system with range $\mathbb{N}$ that uses n single-writer registers: Each process p_i stores its current timestamp in its single-writer register r_i and gets a new timestamp by reading all of the single-writer registers and adding one to the largest timestamp that it saw. Initially each register contains 0. The code for process p_i is:

$t \leftarrow 1 + \max\{r_0, \ldots, r_{n-1}\}$
$r_i \leftarrow t$
return t

Theorem 6.5 shows that this implementation is optimal, even if multi-writer registers are available, provided the universe of possible timestamps is a nowhere dense partially ordered set. Is it possible to use fewer registers when the universe can be more general?

The following algorithm uses $n - 1$ single writer registers, instead of n. Its timestamps are pairs of integers, ordered lexicographically. The code for processes $p_0, \ldots, p_{n-2}$ is the same as in Lamport's algorithm, except that they return $(t, 0)$ instead of t. The code for process p_{n-1} is:

$t \leftarrow \max\{r_0, \ldots, r_{n-2}\}$
if $t > old$ then $c \leftarrow 1$
        else $c \leftarrow c + 1$
$old \leftarrow t$
return (t, c)

The code involves two persistent variables, *old* and c, which are both initially 0. The idea for this simple algorithm came from understanding the lower bound. It is not a particularly useful algorithm, but it does show the necessity of the assumption that the partially ordered set is nowhere dense.

Without the restriction that the set of possible timestamps is nowhere dense, it is still possible to get a linear lower bound on the number of registers, but the proof is more involved.

Consider any timestamp implementation from registers that satisfies solo termination. Suppose there is a configuration in which each register in some subset is covered by at least two processes. Then we can show that, from this configuration, it is possible to reach another configuration in which some register not in the subset is covered by an additional process.

Lemma 6.6   *Let B_1, B_2, Q_1, and Q_2 be disjoint sets of processes and let C be a reachable configuration in which B_1 and B_2 each cover the same set of registers R. For $i \in \{1, 2\}$, let β_i be the* block write *performed by B_i starting from configuration C. Then there exists $i \in \{1, 2\}$ such that every Q_i-only history starting from $C\beta_i$ containing a complete instance of* GetTS *writes to some register not in R.*

Proof. To obtain a contradiction, suppose that, for all $i \in \{1, 2\}$, there is a Q_i-only history α_i from $C\beta_i$ that contains a complete instance I_i of GetTS, returns the timestamp t_i, and only writes to registers in R. Without loss of generality, we may assume that the histories α_1 and α_2 are finite. Processes in Q_1 take no steps in $\beta_2\alpha_2\beta_1$, so $C\beta_1 \overset{Q_1}{\sim} C\beta_2\alpha_2\beta_1$. The block write β_1 ensures that the contents of all shared registers are the same in these two configurations. Moreover, $C\beta_1 \overset{B_1}{\sim} C\beta_2\alpha_2\beta_1$ since processes in B_1 take no steps in $\beta_2\alpha_2$ and processes learn nothing from performing writes. Then, Lemma 2.1 implies that α_1 can be performed starting from $C\beta_2\alpha_2\beta_1$ and $C\beta_1\alpha_1 \overset{B_1\cup Q_1}{\sim} C\beta_2\alpha_2\beta_1\alpha_1$. Similarly, α_2 can be performed starting from $C\beta_1\alpha_1\beta_2$ and $C\beta_2\alpha_2 \overset{B_2\cup Q_2}{\sim} C\beta_1\alpha_1\beta_2\alpha_2$.

Since only processes in $B_1 \cup Q_1$ take steps in $\beta_1\alpha_1$ and only processes in $B_2 \cup Q_2$ take steps in $\beta_2\alpha_2$, the configurations $C\beta_1\alpha_1\beta_2\alpha_2$ and $C\beta_2\alpha_2\beta_1\alpha_1$ are indistinguishable to all processes. In other words, starting from configuration C, the histories $\beta_1\alpha_1$ and $\beta_2\alpha_2$ can be performed in either order without changing the resulting state of any process.

This is a problem because each of these histories contains a complete GetTS operation and the results of these two operations must indicate which was performed earlier. Specifically, I_1 is completed before I_2 begins in $\beta_1\alpha_1\beta_2\alpha_2$, so $t_1 < t_2$. Similarly, $t_2 < t_1$, since I_2 is completed before I_1 begins in $\beta_2\alpha_2\beta_1\alpha_1$. This is a contradiction.   □

We say that a configuration is *quiescent* if no process has started an instance of an operation that it has not yet finished. This is analogous to the definition of quiescent used in Section 6.1. Suppose that, from every quiescent configuration, it is possible to reach a configuration in which k processes cover registers, but no register is covered by more than three processes. Then, using an argument similar to part of the proof of Lemma 6.2, we show that there is an execution containing arbitrarily many configurations in which k processes cover registers and no register is covered by more than three processes. It follows that it is possible to find two such configurations which are the same in terms of the number of processes covering each register.

Lemma 6.7   *Let Q be a set of processes. Suppose that, from every reachable quiescent configuration, there is a Q-only history that results in a configuration in which exactly k processes cover registers and no register is covered by more than three processes. Then, from any reachable quiescent configuration D, there is a Q-only history $\alpha\beta_1\beta_2\beta_3\gamma$ such that*

- *there are exactly k processes covering registers in $D\alpha$,*

- *no register is covered by more than three processes in $D\alpha$,*

- *β_1, β_2, and β_3 are block writes by disjoint sets of processes to the set of registers that are covered by three processes in $D\alpha$, and*

- *each register is covered by the same number of processes in $D\alpha\beta_1\beta_2\beta_3\gamma$ as it is in $D\alpha$.*

Proof. We inductively define a sequence $E_0, E_1, \ldots$ of configurations reachable from D. Since D is reachable and quiescent, there is a Q-only history δ_0 starting from D that results in a configuration E_0 in which exactly k processes cover registers and no register is covered by more than three processes.

For $i \geq 0$, let R_i denote the set of registers that are covered exactly three times in E_i and let $\beta_{1,i}, \beta_{2,i}$, and $\beta_{3,i}$ denote block writes to R_i starting from E_i by disjoint sets of processes. Let ρ_i denote a history starting from $E_i\beta_{1,i}\beta_{2,i}\beta_{3,i}$ in which each process in Q with a pending operation completes that operation, but no new operations are begun. Then $E_i \beta_{1,i} \beta_{2,i} \beta_{3,i} \rho_i$ is a quiescent configuration. Hence, there is a Q-only history δ_{i+1} starting from this configuration that results in a configuration E_{i+1} in which exactly k processes cover registers and no register is covered by more than three processes.

There are a finite number of registers and a finite number of processes. So, by the pigeonhole principle, there exist $0 \leq i < j$ such that each register is covered by the same number of processes in E_i as it is in E_j. Let

$$\begin{aligned}
\alpha &= \delta_0 \beta_{1,0} \beta_{2,0} \beta_{3,0} \rho_1 \delta_1 \beta_{1,1} \beta_{2,1} \beta_{3,1} \rho_2 \cdots \delta_i, \\
\beta_1 &= \beta_{1,i}, \\
\beta_2 &= \beta_{2,i}, \\
\beta_3 &= \beta_{3,i}, \text{ and} \\
\gamma &= \rho_i \delta_{i+1} \beta_{1,i+1} \beta_{2,i+1} \beta_{3,i+1} \rho_{i+1} \delta_{i+2} \beta_{1,i+2} \beta_{2,i+2} \beta_{3,i+2} \rho_{i+2} \cdots \delta_j.
\end{aligned}$$

Then each register is covered by the same number of processes in $D\alpha\beta_1\beta_2\beta_3\gamma = E_j$ as it is in $D\alpha = E_i$, there are exactly k processes covering registers in $D\alpha$, no register is covered by more than three processes in $D\alpha$, R_i is the set of registers covered by three processes in $D\alpha$, and β_1, β_2, and β_3 are block writes to R_i by disjoint sets of processes. $\qquad\square$

Starting from a reachable configuration in which no register is covered by more than three registers, we use Lemmas 6.6 and 6.7 to obtain another configuration in which no register is covered by more than three registers, but the number of processes covering registers has increased. This allows us to obtain the desired lower bound.

Theorem 6.8 *Any n-process implementation of a timestamp from registers that satisfies solo-termination requires at least $\lceil (n-1)/6 \rceil$ registers.*

Proof. We prove inductively that, for $0 \leq k \leq \lfloor n/2 \rfloor$, from any reachable quiescent configuration D, there is a $\{p_0, \ldots, p_{2k-1}\}$-only history that results in a configuration in which exactly k processes cover registers and no register is covered by more than three processes. Then, for $k = \lfloor n/2 \rfloor$, there are at least $\lceil k/3 \rceil = \lceil (n-1)/6 \rceil$ covered registers.

For $k = 0$, the empty history satisfies the claim.

Let $0 < k \leq \lfloor n/2 \rfloor$ and let D be a reachable quiescent configuration. By the induction hypothesis, from every reachable quiescent configuration, there is a $\{p_0, \ldots, p_{2k-3}\}$-only history that results in a configuration in which exactly $k-1$ processes cover registers and no register is covered by more than three processes. Then, Lemma 6.7 implies that there is a $\{p_0, \ldots, p_{2k-3}\}$-only history $\alpha\beta_1\beta_2\beta_3\gamma$ starting from D such that there are exactly $k-1$ processes covering registers in $D\alpha$, no register is covered by more than three processes in $D\alpha$, β_1, β_2, and β_3 are block writes by disjoint sets of processes to the set of registers R that are covered by three processes in $D\alpha$, and each register is covered by the same number of processes in $D\alpha\beta_1\beta_2\beta_3\gamma$ as it is in $D\alpha$.

For $i \in \{1, 2\}$, let δ_i be a p_{2k-i}-only history starting from $D\alpha\beta_i$ in which p_{2k-i} performs a complete instance of GetTS. By Lemma 6.6, there exists $i \in \{1, 2\}$ such that p_{2k-i} writes to some register not in R during δ_i. Let λ be the longest prefix of δ_i in which p_{2k-i} only writes to registers in R and let $r \notin R$ be the register that p_{2k-i} covers in $D\alpha\beta_i\lambda$.

Note that $D\alpha\beta_1\beta_2\beta_3$ and $D\alpha\beta_2\beta_1\beta_3$ are indistinguishable to all processes and they are both indistinguishable from $D\alpha\beta_i\lambda\beta_{3-i}\beta_3$ to all processes except p_{2k-i}. Moreover, the block write β_3 overwrites all registers written during β_1, β_2, and λ, so each register has the same value in all three of these configurations.

Since γ is a $\{p_0, \ldots, p_{2k-3}\}$-only history, Lemma 2.1 implies that γ can also occur starting from $D\alpha\beta_2\beta_1\beta_3$ and $D\alpha\beta_i\lambda\beta_{3-i}\beta_3$ and the resulting configurations, $D\alpha\beta_1\beta_2\beta_3\gamma$, $D\alpha\beta_2\beta_1\beta_3\gamma$, and $D\alpha\beta_i\lambda\beta_{3-i}\beta_3\gamma$, are indistinguishable to all processes except p_{2k-i}. Thus, each process other than p_{2k-i} covers the same register in these configurations and each register other than r is covered by at most three processes.

Register $r \notin R$ is covered by at most two processes in $D\alpha$ and, hence, in $D\alpha\beta_1\beta_2\beta_3\gamma$. Therefore, it is covered by at most three processes in $D\alpha\beta_i\lambda\beta_{3-i}\beta_3\gamma$.

Finally, there are exactly $k-1$ processes in $\{p_0, \ldots, p_{2k-3}\}$ that cover registers in $D\alpha$ and, hence, in $D\alpha\beta_1\beta_2\beta_3\gamma$ and in $D\alpha\beta_i\lambda\beta_{3-i}\beta_3\gamma$. Thus, including p_{2k-i}, there are exactly k processes that cover registers in $D\alpha\beta_i\lambda\beta_{3-i}\beta_3\gamma$. This proves the claim for k. □

Theorem 6.4, Theorem 6.5, the second algorithm, and Lemma 6.6 are from "The Space Complexity of Unbounded Timestamps," by Faith Ellen, Panagiota Fatourou, and Eric Ruppert, which appears in *Distributed Computing*, 2008 [36]. Lemma 6.7 and Theorem 6.8 are from "The Space Complexity of Long-lived and One-Shot Timestamp Implementations," by Maryam Helmi, Lisa Higham, Eduardo Pacheco, and Philipp Woelfel, which appears in *PODC*, 2011 [46].

6.3   SPACE AND STEP COMPLEXITY LOWER BOUNDS FOR THE IMPLEMENTATION OF A COUNTER USING SWAP OBJECTS

Next, we consider the problem of implementing a *counter*, an atomic object whose set of values are the nonnegative integers and which supports two operations: ReadCounter, which returns the current value of the object, and Increment, which increases the value of the object by 1. The initial value of a counter is 0.

The model we consider is asynchronous shared memory system in which n processes communicate using swap objects that support the swap and read primitives. We will prove the following lower bound:

Theorem 6.9   *Any n-process implementation of a counter using only swap objects requires at least $n-1$ swap objects and, in the worst case, a* ReadCounter *takes at least $n-1$ steps.*

Fix any implementation of a counter and fix a process p. In this proof, an adversary will construct an execution (starting from an initial configuration C_0) in which p accesses $n-1$

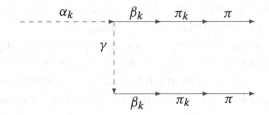

Figure 6.5: The histories used in the proof of Claim 6.10.

different swap objects while performing a ReadCounter. It will inductively construct a sequence of histories $\alpha_k \beta_k \pi_k$, for $k = 0, \ldots, n-1$ where

- $\alpha_k \beta_k$ is by set of k processes, not including p, in which each is performing Increment,

- β_k is a block swap of a set $\mathcal{H}_k$ of k swap objects, and

- π_k is the history of a prefix of a solo execution of a ReadCounter by p, in which $\mathcal{H}_k$ is the set of swap objects it accesses.

The base case, $k = 0$ is easy: Let α_0, β_0, and π_0, be empty histories and let $\mathcal{H}_k$ be the empty set of swap objects. So, let $0 \leq k < n-1$ and suppose the history $\alpha_k \beta_k \pi_k$ has been constructed. Let π be the extension of π_k in which p finishes the solo execution of its ReadCounter. Only $k < n-1$ processes take steps in $\alpha_k \beta_k$, so there is a process $q \neq p$ that takes no steps in $\alpha_k \beta_k$. Let γ be the history of a solo execution by q starting from $C_0 \alpha_k$ in which it performs $k+1$ complete Increments.

Claim 6.10   During $\pi_k \pi$, process p must access a swap object not in $\mathcal{H}_k$ that was modified by q.

Proof. Suppose not. Then the executions with histories $\alpha_k \gamma \beta_k \pi_k \pi$ and $\alpha_k \beta_k \pi_k \pi$ from C_0 are indistinguishable to p. This is because all the swap objects in $\mathcal{H}_k$ have the same values after the block swap, β_k, in both executions and, hence, all the swap objects that p accesses during $\pi_k \pi$ have the same values in both executions. It follows that p returns the same value for its ReadCounter in both executions.

Let c be the number of Increments completed in α_k. In β_k, one step is performed by each of k different processes, so there are at most k additional complete or incomplete Increments in $\alpha_k \beta_k$. Thus, the value that p returns for its ReadCounter in $\alpha_k \beta_k \pi_k \pi$ is at most $c + k$. In $\alpha_k \gamma$, there are $c + k + 1$ completed Increments, so the value that p returns for its ReadCounter in $\alpha_k \gamma \beta_k \pi_k \pi$ is at least $c + k + 1$. Therefore p returns different values for its ReadCounter in these two executions. This is a contradiction. $\square$

Let π_{k+1} be the shortest prefix of $\pi_k \pi$ in which p accesses a swap object H not in $\mathcal{H}_k$ and let $\mathcal{H}_{k+1} = \mathcal{H}_k \cup \{H\}$. Then π_{k+1} is the history of a prefix of a solo execution of a ReadCounter by p in which $\mathcal{H}_{k+1}$ is the set of swap objects it accesses. Note that π_k is a proper prefix of π_{k+1}, since p only accesses swap objects in $\mathcal{H}_k$ during π_k.

Let ψ be the first access of H by q in γ and let γ' be the prefix of γ up to, but not including ψ. Let $\alpha_{k+1} = \alpha_k \gamma'$ and let $\beta_{k+1} = \psi \beta_k$. Then $\alpha_{k+1}\beta_{k+1}$ is the history of an execution by a set of $k + 1$ processes, not including p, in which they are performing Increments, β_{k+1} is a block swap of $\mathcal{H}_{k+1}$, and the claim holds for $k + 1$. Hence, by induction, the claim holds for all k such that $0 \leq k \leq n - 1$.

Unfortunately, there is a mistake in this proof. The problem is that the first swap object $H \notin \mathcal{H}_k$ that p accesses in π might not be a swap object that q accesses. For example, p might access two swap objects not in $\mathcal{H}_k$, but only the second is also accessed by q.

An alternative is to define H to be the first swap object that q accesses which is not in $\mathcal{H}_k$. In this case, we can get an even simpler construction. Specifically, the history will be $\alpha_k \beta_k$, where

- $\alpha_k \beta_k$ is by a set of k processes, in which each is performing Increment, and

- β_k is a block swap of a set $\mathcal{H}_k$ of k swap objects.

Then, in the inductive step, it suffices to choose any distinct processes p and q that take no steps in $\alpha_k \beta_k$ and to let π be the history of a solo execution by p of a ReadCounter starting from $C_0 \alpha_k \beta_k$. The proof of the claim and the definitions of α_k and β_{k+1} remain the same. However, from this proof, we don't get a lower bound on the number of steps taken by a ReadCounter. We only get a lower bound of $n - 1$ on the number of swap objects needed by the implementation.

Instead, define H to be the first swap object that q accesses which is not in $\mathcal{H}_k$ and which is accessed by p in $\pi_k \pi$. Then let π_{k+1} be the shortest prefix of $\pi_k \pi$ in which p accesses $H \notin \mathcal{H}_k$. The problem now is that p may access other objects not in $\mathcal{H}_k$ before it accesses H. So, it is not necessarily the case that $\mathcal{H}_{k+1} = \mathcal{H}_k \cup \{H\}$ is the set of swap objects that p accesses in π_{k+1}. However, the equality is not important. It suffices that we inductively maintain that $\mathcal{H}_k$ is a *subset* of the processes that p accesses in π_k. Specifically, the inductively constructed histories are $\alpha_k \beta_k \pi_k$, where

- $\alpha_k \beta_k$ is an execution by a set of k processes, not including p, in which each is performing Increment,

- β_k is a block swap of a set $\mathcal{H}_k$ of k swap objects, and

- π_k is the history of a prefix of a solo execution of a ReadCounter by p, in which it accesses every swap object in $\mathcal{H}_k$.

Then the proof of Claim 6.10 still holds.

Finally, we have to be careful about the definition of π_{k+1}. It should *not* be the shortest prefix of $\pi_k \pi$ in which p accesses H. The problem is that p might access H near the beginning of π_k and, so, p might not access all the swap objects in $\mathcal{H}_k$ during π_{k+1}. A good way to define π_{k+1} is as the shortest prefix of $\pi_k \pi$ in which p accesses every swap object in $\mathcal{H}_{k+1}$. Then the inductive claim holds for $k + 1$.

This lower bound was first proved by Prasad Jayanti, King Tan, and Sam Toueg in their paper "Time and Space Lower Bounds for Nonblocking Implementations," which appeared in *SIAM Journal on Computing*, 2000 [53].

6.4   A LOWER BOUND ON STEP COMPLEXITY FOR SPACE-OPTIMAL IMPLEMENTATIONS OF A MULTI-WRITER SNAPSHOT

We consider wait-free implementations of an m-component snapshot object shared by $n > m$ processes, each of which can update any component. The definition of a snapshot object appears in Section 5.6. Our model is asynchronous shared memory, where processes communicate through multi-writer registers.

Fix any implementation of an m-component snapshot object shared by $n > m$ processes that communicate using at most m registers. We will prove that it uses at least m registers and, in the worst case, a Scan takes $\Omega(mn)$ steps. These lower bounds are tight.

We begin with the definition of a *fatal configuration*. It is fatal in the sense that, if an implementation ever reaches a fatal configuration, it is incorrect. Using this definition, we will prove the space lower bound and a number of structural properties of space optimal implementations. Then we will inductively construct a long Scan.

A configuration C is *k-fatal* if there exists a set, P, of $k \le m < n$ processes such that, in C, they cover k different registers and are performing Updates to fewer than k different components. A configuration is *fatal* if it is k-fatal for some $k \ge 1$.

Lemma 6.11   *No execution can reach a fatal configuration.*

Proof. Proof by contradiction. Consider the largest value of k for which there is a reachable k-fatal configuration C. Suppose that, in C, P is a set of k processes that covers a set, R, of k registers and the processes in P are performing Updates to a set, I, of fewer than k components. Without loss of generality, we may assume that all processes not in P are idle, because we can simply let each process not in P perform steps until it completes its operation.

Consider the execution starting from C in which the processes in P perform a block write β and then some process $p \in P$ performs a solo execution in which it completes its current operation and then performs a Scan. Let γ be the history of this solo execution. Pick any component $i \notin I$ and let v be the value of component i in the response from this Scan.

Pick a process $q \notin P$. There is such a process since there are n processes and $n > m \ge k$. Let δ be the history of the solo execution by q starting from C in which it Updates component i to a new value $v' \ne v$.

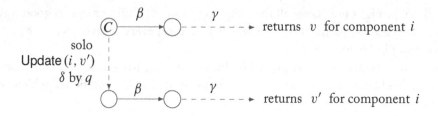

Figure 6.6: The histories used in the proof of Lemma 6.11.

Process q will eventually write to a register that is not in R. To see why, suppose that q only writes to registers in R during δ. Then $C\beta \overset{p}{\sim} C\delta\beta$, so by Lemma 2.1, γ can occur starting from $C\delta\beta$ and $C\beta\gamma \overset{p}{\sim} C\delta\beta\gamma$. Hence, p must return the same response from its Scan in both histories. In particular, it must return value v for component i in $\beta\gamma$. However, the Update by process q finishes before the Scan by p begins in $\delta\beta\gamma$ and there are no pending Updates to component i in configuration C, so process p must return value v' for component i in $\delta\beta\gamma$ starting from C. This is a contradiction.

Thus, there is a prefix δ' of δ such that q covers a register not in R in configuration $C\delta'$. This configuration is $(k + 1)$-fatal. This contradicts the maximality of k. $\qquad\square$

Now we present the structural lemmas.

Lemma 6.12   *Processes performing* Scan *operations do not write to registers.*

Proof. Otherwise, there is a configuration in which some process is performing a Scan and is covering a register. This configuration is 1-fatal. $\qquad\square$

Lemma 6.13   *Processes performing solo executions of* Update *operations to the same component starting from the same configuration, first write to the same register.*

Proof. Suppose there are solo executions of Update operations by p and q to the same component starting from the same configuration, C, that first write to different registers. Run p and q starting from C until just before their first writes. The resulting configuration is 2-fatal. $\qquad\square$

Lemma 6.14   *A process performing a solo execution of an* Update *operation to a particular component, i, starting from some configuration, C, first writes to the same register, no matter what new value it is using for its* Update.

Proof. Suppose that process p first writes to two different registers, r and r', when performing solo executions of Update(i, v) and Update(i, v'), respectively, starting from configuration C.

Let γ be the history of a solo execution by some other process q starting from C in which it finishes its pending operation, if any, and then performs an Update to component i until it first covers a register r''. Without loss of generality, suppose $r'' \neq r$. Let α denote the history of the longest prefix of p's solo execution of Update(i, v) starting from C in which p does not write.

Since $C\alpha$ is indistinguishable from C to process q, Lemma 2.1 implies that γ can occur starting from $C\alpha$. However, the resulting configuration $C\alpha\gamma$ is 2-fatal.   □

Let C_0 be the initial configuration in which all components have value $\bot$ and let r_i be the register to which a process first writes when performing a solo execution of Update to component i starting from configuration C_0.

Lemma 6.15   *Let α be the history of an execution starting from C_0 in which some process takes no steps. Then all Update operations to component i in α only write to r_i.*

Proof. Suppose that process p writes to a register $r \neq r_i$ during an Update operation to component i. Let α' denote a prefix of α such that, at the end of α', p is covering r while performing an Update to component i.

Let q be a process that takes no steps in α. By Lemma 6.13, a solo execution of an Update to component i by q starting from C_0 first writes to r_i. Let β be the history of the longest prefix of this solo execution in which q performs no writes.

Since C_0 and $C_0\beta$ are indistinguishable to process p, Lemma 2.1 implies that α' can occur starting from $C_0\beta$. However, the resulting configuration, $C_0\beta\alpha'$ is 2-fatal.   □

Lemma 6.16 $r_i \neq r_j$ for $i \neq j$.

Proof. Suppose there are solo executions of Update(i, v) by process p and Update(j, v') by process q starting from configuration C_0 that both write to the same register r. Note that both p and q are idle at C_0, so by Lemma 6.15, they only write to register r during these executions.

Let α denote the shortest prefix of the history of the solo execution of Update(i, v) by process p such that p covers register r in $C_0\alpha$ and let α' denote the history of the rest of this solo execution followed by a solo execution of a Scan by p. Let β denote the history of the solo execution of Update(j, v') by process q. Since C_0 and $C_0\alpha$ are indistinguishable to process q, Lemma 2.1 implies that β can occur starting from $C_0\alpha$. Likewise, α' begins with a write to register r and all writes in β are to register r, so $\alpha\beta\alpha'$ can also occur starting from C_0 and is indistinguishable from $\alpha\alpha'$ to p.

The Scan by p in history $\alpha\alpha'$ must return value $\bot$ for component j, since $\alpha\alpha'$ contains no Updates to component j. The Scan by p in execution $\alpha\beta\alpha'$ must return value v' for component j, because it starts after the Update to component j by q is finished. But this is impossible, since these two histories are indistinguishable to p.   □

From this lemma, we immediately get our space lower bound.

Theorem 6.17   *Any implementation of an $m < n$ component snapshot object shared by n processes requires at least m registers.*

Next, we prove our lower bound on the step complexity of Scan.

Theorem 6.18   *In any space-optimal implementation of an $m < n$ component snapshot object shared by n processes, a process requires $\Omega(mn)$ steps to perform a Scan in the worst case.*

We first outline the proof of this theorem. An adversary constructs a bad execution where a troublesome Scan by some process t performs $\Omega(n)$ batches of $m - 1$ reads. The adversary ensures that during this time, the snapshot always has at least one component that contains the value 1, which t has never seen. This implies that t cannot have terminated.

The bad execution employs $n - 4$ *visible processes*, $p_1, \ldots, p_{n-4}$, each of which has started an Update with value 0 to a carefully chosen component and is covering a register before t starts. To prevent t from seeing the hidden value 1, just before t reads from any register that might contain information about an Update with value 1, the adversary causes a visible process to write obsolete information to it. The bad execution also employs two *hidden processes*, q and q', performing Updates, so the snapshot object always contains at least one component with value 1, and Scans, to constrain the linearization points of the Updates by themselves and by the visible processes.

For each batch of reads of $m - 1$ different registers that t performs, the adversary uses one visible process to overwrite the last of these registers just before t reads it. Thus the adversary can schedule $\Omega(n)$ such batches. There is also one process that performs no steps in the bad execution. This is useful so that we can apply Lemma 6.15.

Proof. Formally, we construct a sequence of components, $i_1, \ldots, i_{n-4}$, and a sequence of histories, $\alpha_0, \ldots, \alpha_{n-4}$, that can occur starting from C_0 such that, for every k, where $0 \le k \le n - 4$,

- $\alpha_k = \beta_k \cdots \beta_1 \cdot \lambda_1 \cdot w_1 \cdots \lambda_k \cdot w_k$,

- w_j is the first write (to register r_{i_j}) by process p_j when it performs a solo execution of Update($i_j, 0$) starting from C_0 and β_j is the history of the portion of this execution preceding w_j,

- $\lambda_1 \cdots \lambda_k$ is the prefix of a single Scan performed by process t,

- process t reads from all registers except r_{i_j} during λ_j and is about to access r_{i_j} at the end of λ_j, and

- if t runs by itself starting from $C_0\alpha_k$, it will read every register before completing its Scan.

For the base case, $k = 0$, let α_0 be the empty history starting from C_0. Let λ be the solo history of a Scan by t starting from $C_0\alpha_0 = C_0$. Suppose t doesn't read some register r_ℓ during λ. Let γ be the solo history of Update($\ell, 1$) by process q starting from C_0. By Lemma 6.15, process q only writes to r_ℓ during γ, so $\gamma\lambda$ is a history that is indistinguishable from λ to process t. Hence, p must return the same value for component ℓ in both these histories. However in λ, process p has to return $\bot$ for component ℓ and in $\gamma\lambda$, process p has to return 1 for component ℓ. This is a contradiction.

Let $1 \le k \le n - 4$ and suppose the claim is true for $k - 1$. By the induction hypothesis, if t runs by itself starting from configuration $C_0\alpha_{k-1}$ will eventually read every register. Let λ_k be the longest solo history by t starting from $C_0\alpha_{k-1}$ in which t does not read from every register. Let r_{i_k} be the register that t is about to read at the end of λ_k.

Let w_k be the first write (to register r_{i_k}) by process p_k when it performs a solo execution of Update$(i_k, 0)$ starting from C_0 and let β_k be the history of the portion of this execution preceding w_k. Then

$$
\begin{aligned}
\alpha_k \quad = \quad & \beta_k \beta_{k-1} \cdots \beta_1 \cdot \\
& \lambda_1 \cdot w_1 \cdot \\
& \quad \vdots \\
& \lambda_{k-1} \cdot w_{k-1} \cdot \\
& \lambda_k \cdot w_k
\end{aligned}
$$

is a history that can occur starting from C_0. Let λ be the history of the solo execution by t starting from $C_0 \alpha_k$ until it finishes its Scan.

It remains to prove that t reads every register during λ. Suppose t doesn't read register r_ℓ during λ. We will construct a history α'' that is indistinguishable from $\alpha = \alpha_k \lambda$ to t, but in which t must return a different response. Specifically, we will show that in α'', process t has to return the value 1 for some component. However, in α, no Updates with value 1 are performed and no component has 1 as its initial value, so t can't return the same response.

We start by inserting $k + 1$ Updates with value 1 by the hidden process q, to components $i_1, \ldots, i_k, \ell$, into α. They are denoted $U_1(i_1, 1), \ldots, U_k(i_k, 1), U_{k+1}(\ell, 1)$. We also insert k Scans, $S_1, \ldots, S_k$, by process q into α. Let

$$
\begin{aligned}
\alpha' \quad = \quad & \beta_k \beta_{k-1} \cdots \beta_1 \cdot U_1(i_1, 1) \cdot \\
& \lambda_1 \cdot U_2(i_2, 1) \cdot w_1 \cdot S_1 \cdot \\
& \quad \vdots \\
& \lambda_{k-1} \cdot U_k(i_k, 1) \cdot w_{k-1} \cdot S_{k-1} \cdot \\
& \lambda_k \cdot U_{k+1}(\ell, 1) \cdot w_k \cdot S_k \cdot \\
& \lambda.
\end{aligned}
$$

All reads by the visible processes $p_1, \ldots, p_k$ occur in α' before q takes any steps, so α' and α are indistinguishable to them.

By Lemma 6.12, q doesn't write during its Scans. By Lemma 6.15, q only writes to r_{i_j} during $U_j(i_j, 1)$, for $j = 1, \ldots, k$. The register r_{i_j} is not read by t during λ_j and the contents of r_{i_j} are overwritten by the write w_j of visible process p_j. Therefore, t never reads any value written to r_{i_j} by q during $U_j(i_j, 1)$. Similarly, r_ℓ is the only register q writes to during $U_{k+1}(\ell, 1)$, and, by assumption, t does not read from r_ℓ during λ. Thus, process t does not read any value that q writes and α' is indistinguishable from α to t.

Next, we insert k Updates with value 0 by the other hidden process q', to components $i_1, \ldots, i_k$, into α'. They are denoted $U_1'(i_1, 0), \ldots, U_k'(i_k, 0)$. Let

$$
\begin{aligned}
\delta \;=\; & \beta_k \beta_{k-1} \cdots \beta_1 \cdot U_1(i_1, 1) \cdot \\
& \lambda_1 \cdot U_2(i_2, 1) \cdot U_1'(i_1, 0) \cdot w_1 \cdot S_1 \cdot \\
& \;\;\vdots \\
& \lambda_{k-1} \cdot U_k(i_k, 1) \cdot U_{k-1}'(i_{k-1}, 0) \cdot w_{k-1} \cdot S_{k-1} \cdot \\
& \lambda_k \cdot U_{k+1}(\ell, 1) \cdot U_k'(i_k, 0) \cdot w_k \cdot S_k \cdot \\
& \lambda .
\end{aligned}
$$

In δ, the operations by the hidden processes don't overlap with one another, so they must be linearized in the following order:

$$
\begin{aligned}
& U_1(i_1, 1), \\
& U_2(i_2, 1), U_1'(i_1, 0), S_1, \\
& U_3(i_3, 1), U_2'(i_2, 0), S_2, \\
& \quad\vdots \\
& U_k(i_k, 1), U_{k-1}'(i_{k-1}, 0), S_{k-1}, \\
& U_{k+1}(\ell, 1), U_k'(i_k, 0), S_k .
\end{aligned}
$$

The Updates by visible processes all use 0, so even if some of them are linearized between $U_j'(i_j, 0)$ and S_j, the Scan S_j must return 0 for component i_j in δ, for $j = 1, \ldots, k$.

Now consider the history

$$
\begin{aligned}
\alpha'' \;=\; & \beta_k \beta_{k-1} \cdots \beta_1 \cdot U_1(i_1, 1) \cdot \\
& \lambda_1 \cdot U_2(i_2, 1) \cdot U_1'(i_1, 1) \cdot w_1 \cdot S_1 \cdot \\
& \;\;\vdots \\
& \lambda_{k-1} \cdot U_k(i_k, 1) \cdot U_{k-1}'(i_{k-1}, 1) \cdot w_{k-1} \cdot S_{k-1} \cdot \\
& \lambda_k \cdot U_{k+1}(\ell, 1) \cdot U_k'(i_k, 1) \cdot w_k \cdot S_k \cdot \\
& \lambda .
\end{aligned}
$$

This history is the same as δ except that the Updates by process q' use 1 instead of 0. By Lemma 6.13, q' only writes to r_{i_j} during $U_j'(i_j, 0)$ and $U_j'(i_j, 1)$. But r_{i_j} is overwritten by w_j before r_{i_j} can be read by any other process. Therefore, to all other processes, α'' and δ are indistinguishable from α'. Hence, the Scan S_j must return 0 for component i_j in α'', for $j = 1, \ldots, k$.

As before, in α'', the operations by the hidden processes are linearized in the order

$$U_1(i_1, 1),$$
$$U_2(i_2, 1), U_1'(i_1, 1), S_1,$$
$$U_3(i_3, 1), U_2'(i_2, 1), S_2,$$
$$\vdots$$
$$U_k(i_k, 1), U_{k-1}'(i_{k-1}, 1), S_{k-1},$$
$$U_{k+1}(\ell, 1), U_k'(i_k, 1), S_k.$$

There are no Updates by hidden processes linearized between $U_j'(i_j, 1)$ and S_j. Since S_j returns 0 for component i_j, there must be at least one Update to component i_j by a visible process linearized between them, for $j = 1, \ldots, k$. Since there are k Scans by q and k Updates by visible processes, exactly one of these Updates must be linearized between $U_j'(i_j, 1)$ and S_j, for $j = 1, \ldots, k$.

Note that $i_j \neq i_{j-1}$. This is because t starts λ_j by reading $r_{i_{j-1}}$ and doesn't read r_{i_j} during λ_j. Similarly, $\ell \neq i_k$. Therefore, in the linearization of the operations in α'', every Update with value 0 is preceded by two Updates with value 1 to different components. Thus, after $U_1(i_1, 1)$, there will always be a component with value 1 in the resulting linearization. Hence, during α'', the troublesome Scan by t will have to return the value 1 in some component, no matter where it is linearized.

Since t does not return the value 1 in any component during α, and α and α'' are indistinguishable to t, we have a contradiction. Thus t reads every register during λ and the claim is true for k. □

The space and step complexity lower bounds apply to snapshot implementations from any historyless objects, provided that $m < n - 1$. The proof also shows that Scan has a very particular form in any efficient, space-optimal snapshot implementation.

The results in this section are from "Time Lower Bounds for Implementations of Multi-writer Snapshots," by Faith Ellen, Panagiota Fatourou, and Eric Ruppert, *Journal of the ACM*, 2007 [35].

When $m = n - 1$, Theorem 6.18 gives an $\Omega(n^2)$ lower bound on step complexity of Scan in any implementation of an $(n-1)$-component snapshot object from $n - 1$ registers. In contrast, there is an implementation of an n-component snapshot object using n registers with $O(n)$ step complexity for Scan. See Hagit Attiya and Ophir Rachman, "Atomic Snapshots in $O(n \log n)$ Operations," *SIAM Journal on Computing*, 1998 [19] and Amos Israeli, Amnon Shaham and Asaf Shirazi, "Linear-time Snapshot Implementations in Unbalanced Systems," *Mathematical Systems Theory*, 1995 [50].

6.5 A LOWER BOUND ON THE NUMBER OF STALLS INCURRED BY A COUNTER IMPLEMENTED USING ARBITRARY READ-MODIFY-WRITE PRIMITIVES

Here, we consider an asynchronous shared memory model in which processes can apply arbitrary read-modify-write primitives to base objects. A *read-modify-write* primitive has a fixed number of input variables. When it is applied to an object, the value of the object may be changed, based on the current value of the object and the values of these variables. A response is returned to the process that applied the primitive.

The time to perform an operation depends on the number of primitives a process applies to objects. But it can also be influenced by the amount of contention the process incurs at objects when other processes access them concurrently. A *stall* is a delay that results from waiting for another process that applies a nontrivial primitive to the same object. For example, suppose that in some configuration, there is some object at which no processes are poised. Let k processes each take steps that result in them being poised to apply a nontrivial primitive to this object. Then let each of them take another step. The i'th process to access the object incurs $i - 1$ stalls, for $1 \leq i \leq k$. In this section, we extend *cover* to mean poised to apply any nontrivial primitive, rather than just a nontrivial historyless primitive.

A process that accesses a shared counter provided by the hardware can incur $n - 1$ stalls if the other processes all want to increment the process incurs by implementing the counter the counter at the same time. Is it possible to reduce the maximum number of stalls using more shared objects, each shared by fewer processes, or by using more powerful shared objects? The following result says that it is not possible.

Theorem 6.19 *Any implementation of a counter shared by n processes has an execution in which some* ReadCounter *incurs at least n − 1 stalls.*

To prove this result, an adversarial scheduler constructs a bad execution in which some process p incurs $n - 1$ stalls while performing a single ReadCounter. This bad execution has a history of the form $\alpha\sigma_1 \cdots \sigma_r$. During α, all processes other than p take steps until they cover base objects that will later be accessed by p. Let $B_1, \ldots, B_r$ be the base objects covered by these processes at the end of α and, for $i = 1, \ldots, r$, let S_i be the set of those processes that cover B_i. Then $S_1 \cup \cdots \cup S_r$ is a disjoint union of all processes except p. During σ_i, process p takes steps until it is about to access B_i, then each process in S_i takes one step in which it accesses B_i, and, finally, p accesses B_i. Hence p incurs one stall in σ_i for each process in S_i. In total, p incurs $n - 1$ stalls in this execution.

A *k-stall execution* is an execution with a history $\alpha\sigma_1 \cdots \sigma_r$ where there are distinct base objects $B_1, \ldots, B_r$ and disjoint sets of processes $S_1, \ldots, S_r$ whose union has size k such that

- p is performing a single ReadCounter,

- all other processes only perform Increment,

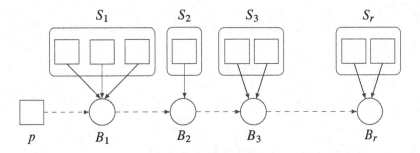

Figure 6.7: The configuration at the end of α in a k-stall execution.

- p takes no steps in α,

- at the end of α, each process in S_i covers B_i, for $i = 1, \ldots, r$,

- in σ_i, process p runs by itself until just before it first accesses B_i, then each of the processes in S_i accesses B_i, and, finally, p accesses B_i, and

- in every $(\{p\} \cup S_1 \cup \cdots \cup S_r)$-free extension τ of α by processes performing Increments, no process applies a nontrivial primitive to any base object accessed in $\sigma_1 \cdots \sigma_r$.

This is illustrated in Figure 6.7. Note that process p incurs k stalls in a k-stall execution. The empty execution is a 0-stall execution.

Using the following lemma, we can inductively construct an $(n - 1)$-stall execution. This proves Theorem 6.19.

Lemma 6.20 *If there is a k-stall execution, where $0 \leq k < n - 1$, then there is a $(k + m)$-stall execution, for some $m \geq 1$.*

Proof. Suppose there is a k-stall execution with history $\alpha\sigma_1 \cdots \sigma_r$. Let σ be the extension of $\alpha\sigma_1 \cdots \sigma_r$ in which p completes its ReadCounter. Let v be the value returned. Let τ be the extension of α in which some process $q \notin \{p\} \cup S_1 \cup \cdots \cup S_r$ performs n complete Increments.

From the definition of a k-stall execution, during τ, process q applies no nontrivial primitives to base objects accessed during $\sigma_1 \cdots \sigma_r$. Thus, by Lemma 2.1, $\sigma_1 \cdots \sigma_r$ can occur following $\alpha\tau$. If we let p finish its ReadCounter, then it must return a value larger than v. This is because, at the end of α, there are at most $n - 1$ processes with pending Increments. Thus, the number of Increments linearized by the end of α is at least $v - (n - 1)$ and the number of Increments linearized by the end of $\alpha\tau$ is at least $v + 1$.

During τ, process q must modify a base object accessed by p during σ; otherwise the executions with histories $\alpha\sigma_1 \cdots \sigma_r\sigma$ and $\alpha\tau\sigma_1 \cdots \sigma_r\sigma$ would be indistinguishable to p. Consider the set $\mathcal{E}$ of all extensions τ' of α by one or more processes not in $\{p\} \cup S_1 \cup \cdots \cup S_r$ which are performing Increments and such that, at the end of τ', at least one of these processes covers a base

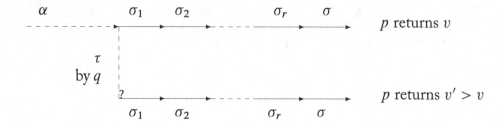

Figure 6.8: The histories used in the proof of Lemma 6.20.

object that is accessed by p during σ. The prefix of τ up to, but not including, its first application of a nontrivial primitive to a base object accessed by p during σ is an example of a history in $\mathcal{E}$.

Let B_{r+1} be the first base object accessed by p during σ that is covered at the end of one or more of these histories in $\mathcal{E}$. Since $\alpha\sigma_1 \cdots \sigma_r$ is the history of a k-stall execution, no history in $\mathcal{E}$ contains a nontrivial primitive applied to any base object accessed during $\sigma_1 \cdots \sigma_r$. Hence $B_{r+1} \notin \{B_1, \ldots, B_r\}$. Let σ' be the prefix of σ up to, but not including, p's first access of B_{r+1}.

Among all the histories in $\mathcal{E}$, let τ' be one such that, after $\alpha\tau'$, the largest number of processes cover B_{r+1}. Suppose there are m such processes. Call this set of processes S_{r+1}. Then, when each process in S_{r+1} is scheduled after τ', it first applies a nontrivial primitive to B_{r+1}. Let σ_{r+1} denote σ' followed by these m nontrivial primitives and then p's access of B_{r+1}. Let $\alpha' = \alpha\tau'$. By the choice of B_{r+1} and the definition of σ', τ' contains no nontrivial primitive applied to any base object accessed in σ'. By Lemma 2.1, $\sigma_1 \cdots \sigma_r\sigma_{r+1}$ can occur following α'.

From the definition of B_{r+1} and the maximality of m, it follows that no $(\{p\} \cup S_1 \cup \cdots \cup S_r \cup S_{r+1})$-free extension of α' contains a nontrivial primitive applied to any base object accessed in $\sigma_1 \cdots \sigma_r\sigma_{r+1}$. Thus $\alpha'\sigma_1 \cdots \sigma_r\sigma_{r+1}$ is the history of a $(k + m)$-stall execution. □

This result is from Faith Ellen, Danny Hendler, and Nir Shavit, "On the Inherent Sequentiality of Concurrent Objects," *SIAM Journal on Computing*, 2012 [37].

CHAPTER 7

Valency Arguments

In a valency argument, configurations are classified as either univalent or multivalent. Starting from a *univalent* configuration, all terminating executions (from some class) lead to the same result. In particular, all final configurations are univalent. Starting from a *multivalent* configuration, there are two or more different terminating executions (from the class) that each lead to a different result. When there are only two possible results, for example, in binary consensus, a multivalent configuration is called *bivalent*.

A valency argument typically has two parts. One part is proving that every algorithm has a multivalent initial configuration. This typically follows from the problem specifications. For example, Lemma 2.7 uses a chain argument to prove the existence of a bivalent initial configuration for any binary consensus algorithm.

The other part of a valency argument is proving that, from every multivalent configuration, there is a nonempty execution (from the class) that leads to a multivalent configuration. Together with the existence of a multivalent initial configuration, this implies the existence of an infinite execution containing only multivalent configurations. Since no final configuration is multivalent, the termination property is violated.

Valency arguments were introduced by Michael Fischer, Nancy Lynch, and Michael Paterson in their paper "Impossibility of Distributed Consensus with One Faulty Processor," *Journal of the ACM*, 1985 [41], to show that consensus is impossible in asynchronous message passing systems, even if at most one process can crash.

We begin, in Section 7.1, with a proof that wait-free binary consensus among two or more processes is unsolvable in asynchronous systems where processes communicate via registers. More generally, even if a process can atomically write to a number of registers, wait-free consensus remains unsolvable, if the number of processes is sufficiently large. Then, in Section 7.2, we give a lower bound on the number of rounds needed to solve binary consensus in synchronous message passing systems. We prove Fischer, Lynch, and Paterson's result, but using a simpler argument, in Section 7.3. In Section 7.4, we use a valency argument combined with a covering argument to prove a lower bound on the number of registers needed to solve randomized consensus, starting with the special case when processes are anonymous. Finally, we present a step complexity lower bound for randomized consensus, in Section 7.5.

7.1   THE UNSOLVABILITY OF CONSENSUS USING m-ASSIGNMENT

The *consensus number* of an object is the maximum number of processes for which wait-free consensus can be solved in an asynchronous system in which processes communicate using only copies of the object and registers. Thus, proving an upper bound on the consensus number of an object is equivalent to proving that consensus cannot be solved using only copies of the object and registers when the number of processes is sufficiently large.

The model we consider is asynchronous shared memory, where processes communicate via m-assignment objects. An m-assignment object consists of an array of registers that can be read one at a time and any m (or less) of which can be written to simultaneously:

$$r_{i_1}, \ldots, r_{i_m} \leftarrow v_1, \ldots, v_m.$$

When $m = 1$, processes write to one register at a time. In other words, a 1-assignment object is simply an array of registers that each support read and write.

A *critical configuration* is a multivalent configuration where one step by any process moves the system into a univalent configuration. We prove, by contradiction, that critical configurations cannot exist when there are only m-assignment objects. Different cases are considered, depending on what step each process is about to take. In each case, we identify two univalent configurations from which different values are decided. We identify a set of processes that cannot distinguish between these configurations and we identify a part of the environment that is the same in both configurations. Next, we choose a terminating execution by processes in this set that only accesses this part of the environment. Then, by Corollary 2.2, there is an execution starting from the second configuration which is indistinguishable from the first execution to all processes in the set. Thus, these processes decide the same value in both executions. This contradicts the assumption that these executions start from two univalent configurations from which different values are decided.

Hence, there are no critical configurations. By Lemma 2.7, there is an initial multivalent configuration. Thus, every multivalent configuration leads to another multivalent configuration. Since the algorithm cannot terminate in a multivalent configuration, this implies that the algorithm has an infinite execution.

Theorem 7.1   *It is impossible to solve wait-free binary consensus among n processes that communicate using m-assignment objects if $n \geq 2$ and $m = 1$ or $n \geq 2m - 1$ and $m \geq 2$.*

Proof. Suppose there is an implementation of wait-free binary consensus among n processes, where $m = 1$ and $n \geq 2$ or $m \geq 2$ and $n \geq 2m - 1 \geq 3$. Consider any critical configuration C. Let P_0 be the set of processes whose step from C takes the system to a univalent configuration from which only 0 is decided and let P_1 be the set of processes whose step from C takes the system to a univalent configuration from which only 1 is decided. Then P_0 and P_1 partition the set $\{p_0, \ldots, p_{n-1}\}$ of all processes. Since C is bivalent, neither P_0 nor P_1 is empty.

Suppose that some process p_i does a read starting from C. Let p_j be a process in the other part of the partition. Let C' be the configuration obtained from C by performing one step of p_j. Let C'' be the configuration obtained from C by performing one step of p_i and then one step of p_j. Since p_i and p_j are in different parts of the partition, different values are decided starting from C' and C''. However, $C' \overset{p_j}{\sim} C''$ and all registers have the same values in C' and C'', so p_j decides the same value in solo terminating executions starting from C' and C''. This is a contradiction.

Hence, in configuration C, each process is about to write to at most m different registers. Let R_i denote the set of at most m registers that p_i covers in C.

In configuration C, each process p_i covers some register that is not covered by any other process, i.e., $R_i \not\subseteq \bigcup \{R_k \mid k \neq i\}$. To see why, suppose that $R_i \subseteq \bigcup \{R_k \mid k \neq i\}$. Consider any process p_j in the other part of the partition. Let α be a history that consists of one step of p_j, in which it writes to the registers in R_j, followed by one step by p_k, for each $k \neq i, j$, in which it writes to the registers in R_k. Let σ be the history that consists of one step by p_i, in which it writes to the registers in R_i. Since p_i and p_j are in different parts of the partition, different values are decided starting from $C\alpha$ and $C\sigma\alpha$. However, $C\alpha \overset{p_j}{\sim} C\sigma\alpha$. Furthermore, all registers have the same values in $C\alpha$ and $C\sigma\alpha$, since all the registers to which p_i writes are overwritten during α. Therefore p_j decides the same value in solo terminating executions starting from $C\alpha$ and $C\sigma\alpha$. This is a contradiction.

Next, we show that, in configuration C, for each process $p_i \in P_0$ and each process $p_j \in P_1$, there is some register that is covered by both p_i and p_j, but is not covered by any other process, i.e., $R_i \cap R_j \not\subseteq \bigcup \{R_k \mid k \neq i, j\}$. To see why, suppose that $R_i \cap R_j \subseteq \bigcup \{R_k \mid k \neq i, j\}$. Let σ be the history that consists of one step of p_i, in which it writes to each register in R_i, and let τ be the history starting from C that consists of one step of p_j, in which it writes to each register in R_j. Then all executions starting from $C\sigma$ decide 0 and all executions starting from $C\tau$ decide 1. Let α be a history that consists of one step of every process p_k, for $k \neq i, j$. Since $R_i \cap R_j \subseteq \bigcup \{R_k \mid k \neq i, j\}$, every register written during both σ and τ is overwritten during α. Hence configurations $C\sigma\tau\alpha$ and $C\tau\sigma\alpha$ are identical. Thus, all terminating executions starting from $C\tau\sigma\alpha$ and $C\sigma\tau\alpha$ decide the same value. This is a contradiction.

Without loss of generality, suppose that $|P_1| \geq |P_0|$. Let p_i be a process in P_0. Then R_i contains at least $|P_1| + 1$ registers: one that is covered by p_i, but by no other process, and, for each $p_j \in P_1$, one that is covered by p_i and p_j, but by no other process. Since $|P_0 \cup P_1| = n$, it follows that $|P_1| \geq \lceil n/2 \rceil \geq m$ and, thus, $|R_i| \geq m + 1$. This is a contradiction because the model requires that $|R_i| \leq m$. $\square$

This result is due to Maurice Herlihy in his paper "Wait-free Synchronization," *ACM Transactions on Programming Languages and Systems*, 1991 [47]. That paper also gives a matching upper bound: a wait-free consensus algorithm for $2m - 2$ processes. Thus, the consensus number of the m-assignment object is $2m - 2$ and there are objects with arbitrarily large consensus number.

7.2 THE ROUND COMPLEXITY OF CONSENSUS

Valency arguments can also be used to obtain lower bounds on the number of rounds to solve consensus in synchronous models. Here, we consider the synchronous message passing model defined in Section 2.4 and give another proof of Theorem 2.9. Recall that we assume at most f processes crash in each execution. There is a similar proof for the shared memory model in which processes communicate via registers.

Theorem 7.2 *Any binary consensus algorithm in a synchronous message passing system with $n \geq f + 2$ processes that tolerates f crashes requires more than f rounds, even if at most one process crashes in each round.*

Proof. We restrict attention to the class of synchronous executions in which at most one process crashes in each round. By Lemma 2.7, there is an initial bivalent configuration. Therefore, it suffices to prove that, starting from any bivalent configuration in which fewer than f processes have crashed, there is a round in which at most one process crashes and which results in a bivalent configuration. Essentially, we show that the adversary may crash one process during each round to maintain bivalence. This can continue as long as enough processes remain for the adversary to crash.

Let C be a bivalent configuration in which fewer than f processes have crashed. Since $n \geq f + 2$, there are at least three processes that have not crashed. To obtain a contradiction, suppose that each round starting from C, in which at most one process crashes, results in a univalent configuration. Let α be the round starting from C in which no processes crash and let v be the value decided by all terminating executions in the class that start from configuration $C\alpha$. Since C is bivalent, the set of rounds starting from C in which one process crashes and from which all terminating executions in the class decide $1 - v$ is nonempty. Among all the rounds in this set, let β be one in which the process p_i that crashes sends the largest number of messages.

First, suppose that, in round β, process p_i sends a message to every other process p_j that has not crashed in C. Then $C\alpha \overset{p_j}{\sim} C\beta$. Consider any terminating execution in the class by the remaining processes starting from $C\alpha$. It decides v. By Lemma 2.1, the same sequence of events can occur starting from $C\beta$. This is impossible, since every execution in the class starting from $C\beta$ decides $1 - v$.

Therefore, there is some process p_k that has not crashed in C to which p_i does not send a message in β. Let γ be the round starting from C that is the same as β except that p_i also sends a message to p_k. Then $C\gamma$ is univalent and, by definition of β, all terminating executions in the class starting from $C\gamma$ decide v. Note that $C\gamma \overset{p_j}{\sim} C\beta$ for all processes $p_j \neq p_i, p_k$ that have not crashed in C. Consider any terminating execution in the class by these processes starting from $C\gamma$. By Lemma 2.1, the same sequence of events can occur starting from $C\beta$. This is impossible, since every execution in the class starting from $C\beta$ decides $1 - v$. ☐

This proof is from Macros Aguilera and Sam Toueg, "A simple bivalency proof that t-resilient consensus requires $t + 1$ rounds," *Information Processing Letters*, 1999 [3].

7.3 THE UNSOLVABILITY OF CONSENSUS IN ASYNCHRONOUS MESSAGE PASSING SYSTEMS

A similar proof can be used to prove that consensus is unsolvable in asynchronous message passing systems. Instead of crashing a process each round, it suffices to delay a process each round. Thus, the adversary never runs out of processes.

Theorem 7.3   *It is impossible to solve wait-free binary consensus in an asynchronous message passing system in which one process can crash.*

Proof. We restrict attention to a class $\mathscr{A}$ of almost synchronous executions, each of which can be viewed as a sequence of rounds. In each round, all or all but one of the processes each takes a step, in which it sends a message to every other process and then receives messages that have been sent to it. There are three types of rounds: In a *full* round, every process takes exactly one step in which it sends a message to every other and then receives all messages that have been sent to it, but not yet received, including those sent during the round by processes that were scheduled earlier. A *partial* round is the same as a full round, except that one process does not take a step. Finally, a p_i-*round* is like a full round, except that process p_i is not scheduled first and it does not receive the message sent to it during the round by the process scheduled immediately before it.

The proof of Lemma 2.7 applies to the class of executions $\mathscr{A}$, since an execution in this class in which some process takes no steps is a sequence of partial rounds. Thus, there is an initial configuration which is bivalent with respect to $\mathscr{A}$. It suffices to prove that, starting from any configuration, C, at the end of a round that is bivalent with respect to $\mathscr{A}$, there is a round in $\mathscr{A}$ which results in a configuration that is bivalent with respect to $\mathscr{A}$. To obtain a contradiction, suppose that every round in $\mathscr{A}$ results in a univalent configuration starting from C.

Since C is bivalent with respect to $\mathscr{A}$, there are two rounds, α_0 and α_1, such that all terminating executions in $\mathscr{A}$ starting from $C\alpha_0$ decide 0 and all terminating executions in $\mathscr{A}$ starting from $C\alpha_1$ decide 1.

If α_0 is a partial round, let α_0' be the full round obtained from α_0 by letting the one remaining process, p_i, take a step following α_0. Let β be any full round starting from $C\alpha_0$ that begins with a step by process p_i and let β' be the partial round obtained from α' by removing its first step. Then $\alpha_0\beta = \alpha_0'\beta'$. Since $C\alpha_0$ and $C\alpha_0'$ are both univalent and configuration $C\alpha_0\beta = C\alpha_0'\beta'$ is reachable from both, it follows that all terminating executions in $\mathscr{A}$ starting from $C\alpha_0'$ decide 0.

If α_0 is a p_i-round, let α_0' be the full round obtained from α_0 by letting p_i receive the message sent to it during the round by the process scheduled immediately before it. Since p_i sends all its messages before receiving any messages, $C\alpha_0$ and $C\alpha_0'$ are indistinguishable to all processes except p_i. Then any terminating execution of partial rounds starting from $C\alpha_0'$ in which p_i takes no steps must decide 0. Since $C\alpha_0'$ is univalent with respect to $\mathscr{A}$, all terminating executions in $\mathscr{A}$ starting from $C\alpha_0'$ decide 0.

Thus, without loss of generality, we may assume that α_0 is a full round, and, similarly, that α_1 is a full round. Since any permutation of $\{p_1, \ldots, p_n\}$ can be converted into any other by a sequence of transpositions, we may assume, without loss of generality, that α_0 and α_1 are identical, except that some process p_i is scheduled immediately before some other process p_j in α_0 and immediately after p_j in α_1. Let γ_0 be the p_j-round in which processes take steps in the same order as in α_0 and let γ_1 be the p_i-round in which processes take steps in the same order as in α_1. Then, as in the previous paragraph, all terminating executions in $\mathscr{A}$ starting from $C\gamma_0$ decide 0 and all terminating executions in $\mathscr{A}$ starting from $C\gamma_1$ decide 1. However, the histories γ_0 and γ_1 are indistinguishable to all processes and, thus, all terminating executions in $\mathscr{A}$ starting from $C\gamma_0$ and $C\gamma_1$ must decide the same value. This is a contradiction. $\square$

This lower bound was originally proved by Michael Fischer, Nancy Lynch, and Michael Paterson in their paper "Impossibility of Distributed Consensus with One Faulty Processor," *JACM*, 1985 [41]. The proof presented here was adapted from Yoram Moses and Sergio Rajsbaum, "A Layered Analysis of Consensus," *SIAM Journal on Computing*, 2002 [60]. Essentially, the same proof can also be used for shared memory models in which processes communicate using single-writer registers or a single-writer snapshot object.

7.4   THE SPACE COMPLEXITY OF CONSENSUS

From Section 7.1, we know that in an asynchronous shared memory model where processes only communicate via registers, wait-free consensus is unsolvable. However, consensus is solvable with weaker termination conditions. There are randomized algorithms which terminate in finite expected time. There are deterministic obstruction-free algorithms, in which a process terminates if it is given sufficiently many consecutive steps. The termination condition we use in this section, *nondeterministic solo termination*, is weaker than both of these. It requires that, from every configuration and for all processes, p, there is a finite solo execution by p in which p terminates.

Even though we are considering a weaker termination condition, the outputs of all executions must still satisfy the agreement and validity properties. To show that an algorithm is faulty, we construct an execution that decides both 0 and 1. For example, suppose there is a reachable configuration C in which all the registers are covered by a set of processes P and there is a solo history α by a process $q \notin P$ that decides 1 and can be performed starting from C. Consider the execution illustrated in Figure 7.1, in which the processes in P perform a block write β and, from the resulting configuration, a process $p \in P$ performs a solo history γ that decides 0. Then the execution of $\alpha\beta\gamma$ starting from C decides both 0 and 1.

The proof does not talk about probabilities, nor does it put any restrictions on the adversary, since the lower bound is proved for the *worst-case* space complexity of the algorithm, namely, the space used in *some* execution, regardless of its probability. This stands in contrast to the lower bound on the total step complexity (proved in the Section 7.5), which shows that, with high probability, an execution takes many steps.

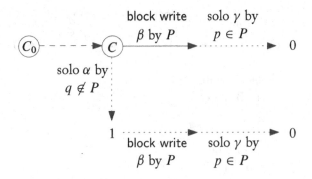

Figure 7.1: A simple situation where agreement can be violated.

We use a combination of valency and covering arguments to prove an $\Omega(\sqrt{n})$ lower bound on the number of registers used by any consensus algorithm that satisfies nondeterministic solo termination. Specifically, we show that, if the number of processes is sufficiently large relative to the number of registers, then it is possible to construct an execution that decides both 0 and 1. Starting from any bivalent configuration, we either construct an execution that decides both 0 and 1, or prove that it is possible to reach a bivalent configuration in which more registers are covered. This gives an upper bound on the number of processes (as a function of the number of registers) in any correct algorithm satisfying nondeterministic solo termination, which implies a lower bound on the number of registers (as a function of the number of processes). In particular, this lower bound applies to randomized algorithms and deterministic obstruction-free algorithms.

7.4.1 ANONYMOUS PROCESSES

We begin by proving the lower bound in a system of *anonymous* processes. This means that all processes are identical and they run the same code. If two such processes are in the same state, they apply the same primitive to the same object when they are next allocated a step and, if the results are the same (for example, they read the same value or they get the same outcome from a coin flip), then they go to the same state. Initially, all processes with the same input value will be in the same state. Although this model is quite restrictive, it provides important insight for the lower bound in the general case.

A *clone* of a process p in an execution is a process with the same input as p, which proceeds in lockstep with p, reading and writing the same values as p, until immediately before some write to a register. We only require that there exists an execution in which this process takes the same steps as process p, not that it takes the same steps as p in every execution. An adversary can have the clone apply that write in some extension of the execution to ensure that the value p reads from that register is the same as the value that p last wrote there. After applying its

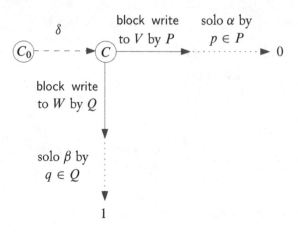

Figure 7.2: The situation in Lemma 7.4.

delayed write, a clone takes no further steps. Note that, until a clone does its delayed write, other processes, including p, are unaware of its existence. In other words, the execution with this clone and the execution without it are indistinguishable to the other processes. Although these executions are not technically the same and they result in different configurations, we will ignore these distinctions.

Let r denote the number of registers. The following lemma shows that, if there is a bivalent configuration in which there are sufficiently many processes available to be used as clones, then it is possible to construct an execution that decides both 0 and 1. The situation is illustrated in Figure 7.2.

Lemma 7.4   *Consider a reachable configuration C in which there is a set of processes P covering a set of registers V, a disjoint set of processes Q covering a (not necessarily disjoint) set of registers W, and at least $r^2 - r + (|V| + |W| - |V|^2 - |W|^2)/2$ processes that have taken no steps and are not in $P \cup Q$. Suppose that after the block write by P there is a solo execution with history α by a process $p \in P$ in which p decides 0 and after the block write by Q there is a solo execution with history β by a process $q \in Q$ in which q decides 1. Then there is an execution that decides both 0 and 1.*

Proof. The proof is by induction on (V, W), where pairs of sets are partially ordered by component-wise inclusion. Let δ be the history of an execution starting from an initial configuration and ending in configuration C, which exists since C is reachable.

The base case is when at least one of these two sets consists of all the registers. Suppose that $|W| = r$. The argument when $|V| = r$ is symmetric. Consider the execution, illustrated in Figure 7.3, consisting of δ, the block write to V by P, α, the block write to W by Q, and β. To the processes in P, this execution is indistinguishable from δ followed by the block write to V by P

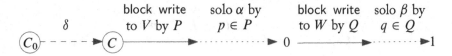

Figure 7.3: The case when $V \subseteq W$ and all writes during α are to registers in W.

and α, so p decides 0. To the processes in Q, this execution is indistinguishable from δ followed by the block write to W by Q and β, so q decides 1.

Now consider any pair (V, W) with $|V|, |W| \neq r$ and suppose that the claim is true for all $(V', W') \neq (V, W)$ such that $V \subseteq V'$ and $W \subseteq W'$. There are two cases.

Case 1. $V \subseteq W$ or $W \subseteq V$.

Suppose that $V \subseteq W$. The argument when $W \subseteq V$ is symmetric. If all writes that occur during α are to registers in W, then, as in the base case, the execution in Figure 7.3 decides both 0 and 1.

Otherwise, let α' be the longest prefix of α that only contains writes to registers in W, let $R \notin W$ be the register covered by p immediately after α', and let α'' be the remainder of α, following the write by p to R. Let C' be the configuration immediately after α', except that there is a clone covering each register in V, which was left behind when that register was last written to during α' or during the block write to V by P, if p doesn't write to that register during α'. The block write to V by the set, P', of these clones starting from configuration C' does not change the values of any registers, so starting from the resulting configuration, p can perform a write to R followed by the solo history α''. When the processes in Q perform a block write starting from C' instead of from C, the resulting configurations are indistinguishable to process q, so

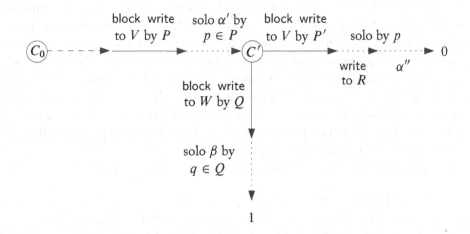

Figure 7.4: The case when $V \subseteq W$ and α contains a write to a register $R \notin W$.

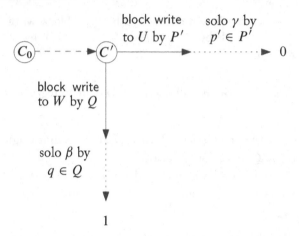

Figure 7.5: The case when $V \not\subseteq W$ and $W \not\subseteq V$.

the solo execution by q with history β still decides 1. Therefore, we have the situation depicted in Figure 7.4.

Let $V' = V \cup \{R\}$, so $|V'| = |V| + 1$. In C', the number of processes that have taken no steps and are not in $P' \cup Q$ is at least

$$r^2 - r + (|V| + |W| - |V|^2 - |W|^2)/2 - |V| = r^2 - r + (|V'| + |W| - |V'|^2 - |W|^2)/2.$$

By the induction hypothesis for (V', W), with C' instead of C and $P' \cup \{p\}$ instead of P, there is an execution that decides both 0 and 1.

Case 2. $V \not\subseteq W$ and $W \not\subseteq V$. Let $U = V \cup W$. Then $V, W \subsetneq U$. Consider any terminating execution starting from C that begins with a block write to U and continues with a terminating solo execution of a history γ by any one of these processes that covered a register in $U - (V \cup W)$. The existence of γ is guaranteed by nondeterministic solo termination. Without loss of generality, suppose that γ decides 0. Let C' be the configuration that is the same as C, except there is a clone of a process in Q covering each register in $W - V = U - V$, which was left behind when that register was last written to. Let P' consist of these clones plus the processes in P. Then P' is disjoint from Q. If the process performing γ is in P, let p' be that process. Otherwise, let p' be its clone in P'. This is illustrated in Figure 7.5.

In C', the number of processes that have taken no steps and are not in $P' \cup Q$ is at least

$$
\begin{aligned}
&r^2 - r + (|V| + |W| - |V|^2 - |W|^2)/2 - |W - V| \\
&= r^2 - r + (|U| - |W - V| + |W| - (|U| - |W - V|)^2 - |W|^2 - 2|W - V|)/2 \\
&= r^2 - r + (|U| + |W| - |U|^2 - |W|^2)/2 + |W - V| \cdot (|V| - |W - V|/2 - 3/2) \\
&\geq r^2 - r + (|U| + |W| - |U|^2 - |W|^2)/2,
\end{aligned}
$$

since $|V| \geq 1$ and $|W - V| \geq 1$. By the induction hypothesis for (U, W), with C' instead of C and P' instead of P, there is an execution that decides both 0 and 1. □

Using this lemma, we show that no consensus algorithm exists, if the number of anonymous processes is sufficiently large compared to the number of registers.

Theorem 7.5 *There is no consensus algorithm using r registers for $r^2 - r + 2$ or more processes that satisfies nondeterministic solo termination.*

Proof. Suppose there is such an algorithm. Let C_0 be an initial configuration in which p has input 0 and q has input 1. Nondeterministic solo termination implies that there is a solo execution from C_0 by p that decides 0. Let α be the history of that execution. Similarly, there is a solo history β by q that decides 1 and can be performed starting from C_0. If p doesn't write during α, then the execution starting from C_0 with history $\alpha\beta$ decides both 0 and 1. Similarly, if q doesn't write during β, then both 0 and 1 are decided in the execution starting from C_0 with history $\beta\alpha$. So, suppose that p first writes to R and q first writes to R'. Say that $\alpha = \alpha'\alpha''$, where α' is the longest prefix of α that contains no writes and $\beta = \beta'\beta''$, where β' is the longest prefix of β that contains no writes. Let $P = \{p\}$, $Q = \{q\}$, $V = \{R\}$, $W = \{R'\}$, and $C = C_0\alpha'\beta'$. In configuration C, the number of processes that have taken no steps and are not in $P \cup Q$ is at least $r^2 - r = r^2 - r + (|V| + |W| - |V|^2 - |W|^2)/2$. Therefore, by Lemma 7.4, there is an execution that decides both 0 and 1. This contradicts the correctness of the algorithm. □

7.4.2 THE GENERAL CASE

When processes are not anonymous, it is more difficult for the adversary to get multiple processes to cover the same register. Although the structure of the proof is the same as in the case of anonymous processes, there is more bookkeeping and combinatorics involved. The following notation is helpful. For any set of registers V, let $\overline{V}$ denote the set of registers not in V. Then $|\overline{V}| = r - |V|$, where r is the number of registers in the system.

The key to the lower bound is the following definition. It is the analogue of a block write followed by a terminating solo execution with added clones.

Definition 7.6 Let P be a set of processes and let V be a set of registers. An execution with history $\alpha = \alpha_1\alpha'$ starting from configuration C is *interruptible for P and V* if

(a) in C, there are at least $|\overline{V}| + 1$ processes in P covering every register in V,

(b) α_1 begins with a block write to V,

(c) all writes in α_1 are to registers in V,

(d) all steps of α are by processes in P,

(e) some process in P decides during α, and

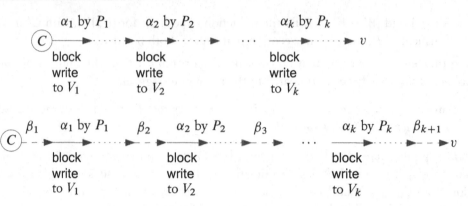

Figure 7.6: An interruptible execution starting from C (top) with steps by other processes inserted (bottom).

(f) either $\alpha = \alpha_1$ or there exist a set of processes $P' \subseteq P$ and a set of registers $V' \supsetneq V$ such that the execution of α' starting from configuration $C\alpha_1$ is interruptible for P' and V'.

Note that, if an execution is interruptible for P and V, it is also interruptible for P'' and V, for all $P'' \supseteq P$. It may be helpful to consider the following equivalent, noninductive definition: An execution with history α starting from configuration C is *interruptible for a set of processes P and a set of registers V* if α can be divided into one or more pieces $\alpha = \alpha_1 \cdots \alpha_k$ and there exist $V = V_1 \subsetneq V_2 \subsetneq \cdots \subsetneq V_k$ and $P = P_1 \supseteq P_2 \supseteq \cdots \supseteq P_k$ such that, for $i = 1, \ldots, k$,

(a) in configuration $C\alpha_1 \cdots \alpha_{i-1}$ (or configuration C, if $i = 1$) there are at least $|\overline{V_i}| + 1$ processes in P_i covering every register in V_i,

(b) α_i begins with a block write to a set of registers V_i,

(c) all writes in α_i are to registers in V_i,

(d) all steps of α_i are by processes in P_i, and

(e) some process in P_k decides during $\alpha = \alpha_1 \cdots \alpha_k$.

After each piece of an interruptible execution, there are more registers covered, but there may be fewer processes covering a particular register. This execution is interruptible in the sense that it is possible to insert certain steps by processes not in P between the pieces of α so that the resulting execution is indistinguishable from the original execution to the processes in P. Specifically, let $\beta_1, \ldots, \beta_k, \beta_{k+1}$ be histories of executions by processes not in P such that, for $i = 1, \ldots, k$, all writes in β_i are to registers in V_i. Then $\alpha \overset{P}{\sim} \beta_1 \alpha_1 \cdots \beta_k \alpha_k \beta_{k+1}$. These two executions are illustrated in Figure 7.6.

While it is straightforward to add clones to an execution when processes are anonymous, the existence of an interruptible execution for P and V starting from configuration C requires a careful proof, which depends on P being sufficiently large and, in configuration C, each register in V being covered by sufficiently many processes in P. We prove this in Lemma 7.8. Then, using this result, we prove Lemma 7.9, which is analogous to Lemma 7.4, and Theorem 7.10, which is analogous to Theorem 7.5.

A simplified version of Lemma 7.8 (with $Y = \phi$) can be used to show that, if $|P| > (r^2 - r + |V| - |V|^2)/2$ and, in configuration C, there are at least $|\overline{V}| + 1$ processes in P covering every register in V, then there is an interruptible execution for P and V starting from C. However, in the proof of the second case of Lemma 7.4, clones of processes in P that are covering registers in V are combined with clones of processes in Q covering registers in W to create a new execution. To facilitate this, we introduce the concept of reserving processes for a set of registers.

Definition 7.7   An interruptible execution with history $\alpha = \alpha_1 \alpha'$ for P and V starting at configuration C *reserves processes for* a set of registers Y if there are at least $|Y|$ processes not in P covering every register in $Y \cap V$ in configuration C and either $\alpha = \alpha_1$ or the execution of α' starting from $C\alpha_1$ is an interruptible execution for $P' \subseteq P$ and $V' \supsetneq V$ that reserves processes for Y.

Note that, if an execution reserves processes for Y and $Y' \subseteq Y$, then the execution also reserves processes for Y'.

Lemma 7.8   *Suppose that, in configuration C, there are at least $|\overline{V}| + 1$ processes in P covering every register in V and there are at least $|Y|$ processes not in P covering every register in $V \cap Y$. If $|P| > |Y| \cdot |Y \cap \overline{V}| + (r^2 - r + |V| - |V|^2)/2$, then there is an interruptible execution for P and V starting from C that reserves processes for Y.*

Proof. The proof is by induction on $|\overline{V}|$.

Let $\widehat{P} \subseteq P$ consist of $|\overline{V}|$ processes covering each register in V. Then $|P - \widehat{P}| = |P| - |\overline{V}| \cdot |V|$. Let α_1 be the history of an execution starting from C that begins with a block write to V by processes in $P - \widehat{P}$ and, one at a time, each process in $P - \widehat{P}$ takes steps until it is covering a register in $\overline{V}$ or it decides, whichever happens first. Nondeterministic solo termination guarantees the existence of such an execution.

If some process in P decides in α_1, then α_1 is the history of an interruptible execution for P and V that reserves processes for Y. In particular, if $|\overline{V}| = 0$, then every process in $P - \widehat{P}$ decides in α_1.

Now suppose $|\overline{V}| \geq 1$ and, in configuration $C\alpha_1$, every process in $P - \widehat{P}$ is covering a register in $\overline{V}$. For each register $R \in \overline{V}$, let $x'(R)$ denote the number of processes in $P - \widehat{P}$ covering R in configuration C'. Let $x(R) = x'(R) - |Y|$ if $R \in Y \cap \overline{V}$, let $x(R) = x'(R)$ if $R \in$

$\overline{Y} \cap \overline{V}$, and let $x_1 \le x_2 \le \cdots \le x_{|\overline{V}|}$ be a sorted list of the numbers $x(R)$, for $R \in \overline{V}$. Then

$$
\begin{aligned}
\sum_{i=1}^{|\overline{V}|} x_i &= \sum_{R \in \overline{V}} x'(R) - |Y| \cdot |Y \cap \overline{V}| \\
&= |P - \widehat{P}| - |Y| \cdot |Y \cap \overline{V}| \\
&= |P| - |\overline{V}| \cdot |V| - |Y| \cdot |\overline{V} \cap Y| \\
&> (r^2 - r + |V| - |V|^2)/2 - |\overline{V}| \cdot |V| \\
&= |\overline{V}|(|\overline{V}| - 1)/2.
\end{aligned}
$$

If $x_i \le i - 1$ for $i = 1, \ldots, |\overline{V}|$, then

$$
\sum_{i=1}^{|\overline{V}|} x_i \le \sum_{i=1}^{|\overline{V}|} (i - 1) = |\overline{V}|(|\overline{V}| - 1)/2.
$$

Hence, there exists $i \in \{1, \ldots, |\overline{V}|\}$ such that $x_i \ge i$. Since $x_{|\overline{V}|} \ge \cdots \ge x_i$, there is a set $S \subseteq \overline{V}$ of $|\overline{V}| - i + 1$ registers such that $x(R) \ge i$ for all $R \in S$. Let $V' = V \cup S$, so $|V'| = |V| + |S| = |V| + |\overline{V}| - i + 1 = r - i + 1$. Let P' be obtained from P by removing $|Y|$ processes covering each register in $Y \cap S$. Since only processes in P take steps in α_1, there are at least $|Y|$ processes not in P and, hence not in P', covering each register in $Y \cap V$. Thus, there are at least $|Y|$ processes not in P' covering each register in $Y \cap V'$.

There are $x'(R) - |Y| = x(R)$ processes in P' covering each register in $Y \cap S$ and $x'(R) = x(R)$ processes in P' covering each register in $\overline{Y} \cap S$. Thus, there are $x(R) \ge i = |V'| + 1$ processes in P' covering each register in S. There are also $|\overline{V}| \ge |V'| + 1$ processes in $\widehat{P} \subseteq P'$ covering each register in V. Hence, there are at least $|V'| + 1$ processes in P' covering each register in V'.

Since $|V'| > |V| \ge 1$ and $f(v) = v - v^2$ is a non-increasing function of the non-negative integers, it follows that

$$
\begin{aligned}
|P'| &= |P| - |Y| \cdot |Y \cap S| \\
&> |Y| \cdot |Y \cap \overline{V}| + (r^2 - r - |V|^2 + |V|)/2 - |Y| \cdot |Y \cap S| \\
&= |Y| \cdot |Y \cap \overline{V'}| + (r^2 - r - |V|^2 + |V|)/2 \\
&\ge |Y| \cdot |Y \cap \overline{V'}| + (r^2 - r - |V'|^2 + |V'|)/2
\end{aligned}
$$

So, by the induction hypothesis, there is an interruptible execution for P' and V starting from C' that reserves processes for Y. Let α' be the history of that execution. Then $\alpha_1 \alpha'$ is the history of an interruptible execution for P and V starting from C that reserves behind processes for Y.

□

The situation in the following lemma is illustrated in Figure 7.7, which is very similar to Figure 7.2. The proof of this result is also very similar to the proof of Lemma 7.4.

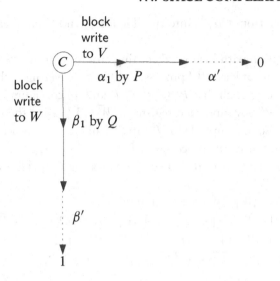

Figure 7.7: The situation in Lemma 7.9.

Lemma 7.9 *Let P and Q be disjoint sets of processes and let V and W be (not necessarily disjoint) sets of registers. Consider a configuration C from which there is an interruptible execution with history $\alpha = \alpha_1 \alpha'$ for P and V that decides 0 and reserves processes for $\overline{W}$ and an interruptible execution with history β for Q and W that decides 1 and reserves processes for $\overline{V}$. If*

$$|P| \geq |\overline{W}| \cdot |\overline{W} \cap \overline{V}| + (r^2 - r + |V| - |V|^2)/2 \quad and$$
$$|Q| \geq |\overline{V}| \cdot |\overline{V} \cap \overline{W}| + (r^2 - r + |W| - |W|^2)/2,$$

then there is an execution starting from C that decides both 0 and 1.

Proof. The proof is by induction on (V, W), as in the proof of Lemma 7.4.

The base case is when at least one of these two sets consists of all the registers. If $|W| = r$, then the execution with history $\alpha\beta$ starting from C decides both 0 and 1. Likewise, if $|V| = r$, the execution with history $\beta\alpha$ starting from C decides both 0 and 1.

Now consider any pair (V, W) with $|V|, |W| \neq r$ and suppose that the claim is true for all $(V', W') \neq (V, W)$ such that $V \subseteq V'$ and $W \subseteq W'$. There are two cases.

Case 1. $V \subseteq W$ or $W \subseteq V$.

Suppose that $V \subseteq W$. The argument when $W \subseteq V$ is symmetric. If all writes that occur during α are to registers in W, then $\alpha\beta$ starting from C decides both 0 and 1.

Otherwise, the execution with history α' starting from $C\alpha_1$ is interruptible for some $P' \subseteq P$ and $V' \supsetneq V$ and reserves processes for $\overline{W}$. Since all writes in α_1 are to registers in V and β begins with a block write to $W \supseteq V$, the executions with history β starting from C and $C\alpha_1$ are indistinguishable to processes in Q. Furthermore, $\overline{V'} \subseteq \overline{V}$. Therefore, the execution with history β starting from $C\alpha_1$ is interruptible for Q and W and leaves behind processes for $\overline{V'}$.

Since the execution with history α' starting from $C\alpha_1$ reserves processes for $\overline{W}$, in configuration $C\alpha_1$, there are at least $|\overline{W}|$ processes not in P' covering each register in $\overline{W} \cap V'$. Let P'' be a maximum size set such that $P' \subseteq P'' \subseteq P$ and, in configuration $C\alpha_1$, there are at least $|\overline{W}|$ processes not in P'' covering each register in $\overline{W} \cap V'$. Then the execution with history α' starting from $C\alpha_1$ is also interruptible for P'' and V' and reserves processes for $\overline{W}$. Furthermore, P'' and Q are disjoint. Since only processes in P take steps in α_1, there are at least $|\overline{W}|$ processes not in P covering each register in $\overline{W} \cap V$ in configuration $C\alpha_1$. Hence

$$\begin{aligned}
|P''| &\geq |P| - |\overline{W}| \cdot |\overline{W} \cap (V' - V)| \\
&\geq |\overline{W}| \cdot |\overline{W} \cap \overline{V}| + (r^2 - r + |V| - |V|^2)/2 - |\overline{W}| \cdot |\overline{W} \cap (V' - V)| \\
&= |\overline{W}| \cdot |\overline{W} \cap \overline{V'}| + (r^2 - r + |V| - |V|^2)/2 \\
&\geq |\overline{W}| \cdot |\overline{W} \cap \overline{V'}| + (r^2 - r + |V'| - |V'|^2)/2.
\end{aligned}$$

By the induction hypothesis applied to (V', W), there is an execution starting from $C\alpha_1$ that decides both 0 and 1. Let γ be the history of this execution. Then the execution with history $\alpha_1\gamma$ starting from C decides both 0 and 1.

Case 2. $V \not\subseteq W$ and $W \not\subseteq V$. Let $U = V \cup W$. Then $V, W \subsetneq U$, so $|\overline{V}|, |\overline{W}| \geq |\overline{U}| + 1$.

Consider configuration C. Since the execution with history α starting from C is interruptible for P and V and reserves processes for $\overline{W}$, there are at least $|\overline{V}| + 1$ processes in P covering each register in V and at least $|\overline{W}|$ processes not in P covering each register in $\overline{W} \cap V$. Let Q'' be a set consisting of $|\overline{W}|$ processes not in P covering each register in $\overline{W} \cap V = U - W$. Similarly, since β is interruptible for Q and W and reserves processes for $\overline{V}$, there are at least $|\overline{W}| + 1$ processes in Q covering each register in W and a set P'' consisting of $|\overline{V}|$ processes not in Q covering each register in $\overline{V} \cap W = U - V$. The processes in P'' and Q'' cover disjoint sets of registers, so $P'' \cap Q'' = \phi$. Let $P' = P \cup P''$ and $Q' = Q \cup Q''$. Since $P \cap Q = \phi$, $P \cap Q'' = \phi$, and $P'' \cap Q = \phi$, it follows that P' and Q' are disjoint.

There are at least $|\overline{V}| \geq |\overline{U}| + 1$ processes in P' covering each register in $V \cup (U - V) = U$ and there are at least $|\overline{W}|$ processes not in P' covering each register in $\overline{W} \cap V = \overline{W} \cap U$. Since

$$\begin{aligned}
|P'| \geq |P| &\geq |\overline{W}| \cdot |\overline{W} \cap \overline{V}| + (r^2 - r + |V| - |V|^2)/2 \\
&> |\overline{W}| \cdot |\overline{W} \cap \overline{U}| + (r^2 - r + |U| - |U|^2)/2,
\end{aligned}$$

Lemma 7.8 implies that there is an interruptible execution for P' and U starting from C that reserves processes for $\overline{W}$. Let α' be the history of this execution. Similarly, $|Q'| > |\overline{V}| \cdot |\overline{V} \cap \overline{U}| + (r^2 - r + |U| - |U|^2)/2$ and there is an execution with history β' starting from C that is interruptible for Q' and U and reserves processes for $\overline{V}$.

First suppose that α' decides 0. Since $\overline{U} \subseteq \overline{V}$, the execution with history β starting from C is interruptible for Q and W and reserves processes for $\overline{U}$. Then, by the induction hypothesis, there is an execution starting from C that decides both 0 and 1.

Similarly, if β' decides 1, there is an execution starting from C that decides both 0 and 1.

Otherwise, α' decides 1 and β' decides 0. Since $\overline{U} \subseteq \overline{V}, \overline{W}$, it follows that the execution with history α' starting from C is interruptible for P' and U and reserves processes for $\overline{U}$, the execution with history β' starting from C is interruptible for Q' and U and reserves processes for $\overline{U}$, and $|P'|, |Q'| > |\overline{U}| \cdot |\overline{U} \cap \overline{U}| + (r^2 - r + |U| - |U|^2)/2$. Hence, by the induction hypothesis, there is an execution starting from C that decides both 0 and 1. $\qquad\square$

Now we prove the main result, by showing that, if there are too many processes compared to the number of registers, then there is an execution in which both 0 and 1 are decided. Like the proof of Theorem 7.5, which is a simple application of Lemma 7.4, this result follows using a simple application of Lemma 7.9. However, it also needs Lemma 7.8 to set up the conditions for Lemma 7.9.

Theorem 7.10   *There is no consensus algorithm using r registers for $3r^2 - r + 2$ or more processes that satisfies nondeterministic solo termination.*

Proof. Suppose there is such an algorithm. Divide the processes into two sets, P and Q, with more than $(3r^2 - r)/2$ processes each. Let C_0 be an initial configuration in which each process in P has input 0 and each process in Q has input 1. Let $V = W = \phi$. Then $\overline{W} \cap V = \overline{V} \cap W = \phi$ and $|\overline{W}| \cdot |\overline{W} \cap \overline{V}| + (r^2 - r + |V| - |V|^2)/2 = |\overline{V}| \cdot |\overline{V} \cap \overline{W}| + (r^2 - r + |W| - |W|^2)/2 = (3r^2 - r)/2$. Lemma 7.8 implies that, starting from C_0, there is an interruptible execution for P and V that reserves processes for $\overline{W}$ and an interruptible execution for Q and W that reserves processes for $\overline{V}$. Since all processes in P have input 0, the former execution must decide 0. Similarly, the latter execution must decide 1. Then, by Lemma 7.9, there is an execution starting from C_0 that decides both 0 and 1. This contradicts the correctness of the algorithm. $\qquad\square$

These lower bounds, the use of clones, and the concept of nondeterministic solo termination first appeared in the paper "On the Space Complexity of Randomized Synchronization," by Faith Ellen Fich, Maurice Herlihy, and Nir Shavit, *Journal of the ACM*, 1998 [38]. They also extended these lower bounds to solving consensus using historyless objects.

7.5   A LOWER BOUND ON EXPECTED WORK FOR RANDOMIZED CONSENSUS

In a randomized consensus algorithm, each process p_i has an input value x_i and should decide on an output value y_i within a finite expected number of rounds. The outputs are required to satisfy both agreement and validity. In this section, we prove an $\Omega(n^2)$ lower bound on the expected *work* performed by any randomized consensus algorithm, that is, on the expected total number of steps taken by all processes.

Our model is the asynchronous message passing system, in which up to f processes might fail by crashing. As in Section 7.3, we restrict attention to a class of almost synchronous executions. These executions proceed in rounds. A round starts with processes performing all the local computation (including the coin flips) they wish to perform. If no process has decided, at least $n - f$ processes take a step, each sending at most one message to every other process and then each receiving all the messages that have been delivered to it. If exactly $n - f$ processes take a step in a given round, then all of their messages are delivered. If more processes take a step in that round, then there is at most one process such that one or more of the messages it sent are not delivered. If a message sent by process p to process q in round i is delivered to process q in round $j \geq i$, then all messages sent by process p to process q in previous rounds are delivered, in order, at or before round i. If a process does not take a step in a given round, it does no local computation in the next round. An adversary determines which processes take steps each round and which of their messages are delivered. After one or more processes have decided, the adversary is fault-free: each process that has not yet decided takes a step each round and all messages are delivered. Once all processes have decided, nothing happens during a round.

The $\Omega(n^2)$ lower bound on expected work is achieved by fixing an arbitrary randomized consensus algorithm and showing that there is a high probability of getting an n-round execution in which no process has decided. We do not exploit the length of executions with more than n rounds, nor steps that are taken by a process after some other process has decided. Therefore, the rest of this section considers only k-round executions, where $k \leq n$. A 0-round execution consists of an initial configuration.

Let α be an $(n - k)$-round execution of the algorithm, where $0 < k \leq n$. Since processes may flip coins, it is possible for several different configurations to arise when the processes (that took steps in round $n - k$, if $k < n$) perform their local computation in round $n - k + 1$. Let $\mathscr{C}(\alpha)$ denote the probability distribution over these possible configurations. Note that it is the product of a finite probability distribution for each process. The probability of C being the configuration that results from the local computation following α is denoted by

$$\underset{C \in \mathscr{C}(\alpha)}{\text{Prob } [C].}$$

At each configuration $C \in \mathscr{C}(\alpha)$, a one-round adversary a_1 deterministically decides which processes take steps and which messages are delivered during the round, after it has seen the result of all local computation (and coin flips) in the round. The resulting $(n - k + 1)$-round execution is denoted by $a_1(\alpha, C)$ and is called a *one-round extension of α from C under a_1*. The set of one-round extensions of α under a_1 is denoted by

$$\mathscr{E}_1(\alpha, a_1) = \{a_1(\alpha, C) \mid C \in \mathscr{C}(\alpha)\}$$

and the probability of $a_1(\alpha, C) \in \mathscr{E}_1(\alpha, a_1)$ is $\underset{C \in \mathscr{C}(\alpha)}{\text{Prob } [C].}$

An *r-round adversary* $a = a_1 \cdots a_r$ is a sequence of r one-round adversaries. In particular, the empty sequence is the only *zero-round adversary*. We define $\mathscr{E}_0(\alpha, \;)$ to be $\{\alpha\}$. For $1 < r \le k$, the set $\mathscr{E}_r(\alpha, a)$ of r-round extensions of α under adversary a is defined inductively. It consists of the one-round extensions of $\mathscr{E}_{r-1}(\alpha, a_1 \cdots a_{r-1})$ under a_r, so

$$\mathscr{E}_r(\alpha, a) = \{a_r(\alpha', C) \mid \text{ for some } \alpha' \in \mathscr{E}_{r-1}(\alpha, a_1 \cdots a_{r-1}) \text{ and some } C \in \mathscr{C}(\alpha')\}$$

and

$$\Prob_{\alpha'' \in \mathscr{E}_r(\alpha,a)} [\alpha'' = a_r(\alpha', C)] = \Prob_{\alpha' \in \mathscr{E}_{r-1}(\alpha,a_1,...,a_{r-1})} [\alpha'] \cdot \Prob_{C \in \mathscr{C}(\alpha')} [C].$$

The set $\mathscr{E}_k(\alpha, a)$ of all k-round extensions of an $(n-k)$-round execution α of the algorithm under a k-round adversary $a = a_1 \cdots a_k$ can be represented by a tree of height $2k$ with root α. For $0 < r \le k$, the set of nodes at depth $2r$ is $\mathscr{E}_r(\alpha, a_1 \cdots a_r)$, the set of children of node $\alpha' \in \mathscr{E}_{r-1}(\alpha, a_1 \cdots a_{r-1})$ is $\mathscr{C}(\alpha')$, and each child C of α' has exactly one child, $a_r(\alpha', C)$. An example of part of such a tree with $k = 4$ appears in Figure 7.8, with the executions $\alpha_0, \alpha_1, \alpha_2,$ and α_3 labeling the configurations at which they end.

An execution α *decides* a value $v \in \{0, 1\}$ if some process decides v during α. By agreement, if α decides v, it does not decide $\bar{v}$.

Definition 7.11 Let $0 \le \epsilon < 1$, let $v \in \{0, 1\}$, let $0 \le k \le n$, and let α be an $(n-k)$-round execution. A k-round adversary a is (ϵ, v)-*deciding from* α if

$$\Prob_{\alpha' \in \mathscr{E}_k(\alpha,a)} [\alpha' \text{ decides } v] \ge 1 - \epsilon.$$

In particular, if α is an n-round execution, the zero-round adversary is (ϵ, v)-deciding from α if and only if α decides v.

Definition 7.12 Univalent and bivalent executions. Let $0 \le \epsilon < 1$, let $v \in \{0, 1\}$, let $0 \le k \le n$, and let α be an $(n-k)$-round execution. Then α is

(ϵ, v)-*univalent* if it has a k-round (ϵ, v)-deciding adversary, but no k-round $(\epsilon, \bar{v})$-deciding adversary,

ϵ-*univalent* if it is either $(\epsilon, 0)$-univalent or $(\epsilon, 1)$-univalent, and

ϵ-*bivalent* if it has both a k-round $(\epsilon, 0)$-deciding adversary and a k-round $(\epsilon, 1)$-deciding adversary.

The agreement property implies that an n-round execution is not ϵ-bivalent and, hence, it is (ϵ, v)-univalent if and only if it decides v.

An adversary a is *p-free from* α if no extension of α under a contains a step by process p.

Definition 7.13 Nullvalent executions. Let $0 \leq \epsilon < 1$, let $0 \leq k \leq n$, let p be a process, and let α be an $(n - k)$-round execution. Then α is

ϵ-*nullvalent* for process p if every k-round p-free adversary starting from α is neither $(\epsilon, 0)$-deciding nor $(\epsilon, 1)$-deciding and

ϵ-*nullvalent* if it is ϵ-nullvalent for some process p.

In particular, an n-round execution is ϵ-nullvalent if it does not decide a value. Note that, if an execution is not ϵ-nullvalent, it is either ϵ-bivalent, $(\epsilon, 0)$-univalent, or $(\epsilon, 1)$-univalent. However, an ϵ-nullvalent execution with fewer than n rounds can also be ϵ-bivalent, $(\epsilon, 0)$-univalent, or $(\epsilon, 1)$-univalent. This is because, even if the p-free adversaries from α are neither $(\epsilon, 0)$-deciding nor $(\epsilon, 1)$-deciding for all processes p, other adversaries (which are not p-free) might be.

7.5.1 CHAIN ARGUMENTS

Chain arguments are used twice. The first of these is very similar to Lemma 2.7 and is analogous to showing that any deterministic consensus algorithm has a bivalent initial configuration.

Lemma 7.14 *For any $0 \leq \epsilon \leq 1$, every randomized consensus algorithm has a 0-round execution that is either ϵ-bivalent or ϵ-nullvalent.*

Proof. For $i = 0, \ldots, n$, let C_i denote the initial configuration in which the first i processes, $p_0, \ldots, p_{i-1}$, have input 1 and the rest have input 0. In other words, in configuration C_i,

$$x_j = \begin{cases} 1 & \text{for } j < i \\ 0 & \text{for } j \geq i. \end{cases}$$

Let α_i be the 0-round execution starting from C_i.

To obtain a contradiction, suppose that none of the executions $\alpha_0, \ldots, \alpha_n$ are ϵ-bivalent or ϵ-nullvalent. Then, for $i = 0, \ldots, n$, α_i is (ϵ, v_i)-univalent, for some $v_i \in \{0, 1\}$. By validity, $v_0 = 0$ and $v_n = 1$. Thus, there exists $j \in \{0, \ldots, n - 1\}$ such that $v_j = 0$ and $v_{j+1} = 1$. By Definition 7.12, α_j has no $(\epsilon, 1)$-deciding adversary. In particular, all p_j-free adversaries from α_j are not $(\epsilon, 1)$-deciding. Similarly, all p_j-free adversaries from α_{j+1} are not $(\epsilon, 0)$-deciding. However, the configurations at the end of executions α_j and α_{j+1} differ only in the state of process p_j, which takes no steps in any p_j-free execution. It follows that all p_j-free adversaries from α_j are not $(\epsilon, 0)$-deciding and all p_j-free adversaries from α_{j+1} are not $(\epsilon, 1)$-deciding. By Definition 7.13, α_j and α_{j+1} are ϵ-nullvalent. This is a contradiction. □

Now suppose there is an execution α that has both a one-round $(\epsilon, 0)$-univalent extension and a one-round $(\epsilon, 1)$-univalent extension. A somewhat more involved chain argument is used to show that α has a one-round extension that is either ϵ-bivalent or ϵ-nullvalent. As in the proof of Lemma 2.8, we first consider a chain of one-round extensions of α, where one fewer process participates in each successive execution in the chain, and then we consider a chain of one-round extensions of α, where one fewer message is delivered in each successive execution in the chain.

Lemma 7.15 *Let α be an $(n - k)$-round execution, where $0 < k \leq n$, and let $C \in \mathscr{C}(\alpha)$. Suppose there is a one-round adversary a^0 such that $a^0(\alpha, C)$ is $(\epsilon, 0)$-univalent and a one-round adversary a^1 such that $a^1(\alpha, C)$ is $(\epsilon, 1)$-univalent. Then there is a one-round adversary $a'' \in A$ such that $a''(\alpha, C)$ is ϵ-bivalent or ϵ-nullvalent.*

Proof. Let a be the one-round failure-free adversary from α. If $a(\alpha, C)$ is ϵ-bivalent or ϵ-nullvalent, let $a'' = a$. Otherwise, $a(\alpha, C)$ is ϵ-univalent. Without loss of generality, suppose that it is $(\epsilon, 0)$-univalent.

We begin by constructing a chain of $(n - k + 1)$-round executions starting from $a(\alpha, C)$, where the difference between each execution and the execution that precedes it in the chain is one process that doesn't participate in round $n - k + 1$. Let $\{p_{i_1}, \ldots, p_{i_t}\}$, where $0 \leq t \leq f$, be the set of processes that do not take steps in round $r + 1$ of $a^1(\alpha, C)$. Let $b_0 = a$. If $t > 0$, then, for $1 \leq h \leq t$, let b_h be obtained from b_{h-1} by not allowing p_{i_h} to take a step in round $n - k + 1$. If $b_h(\alpha, C)$ is ϵ-bivalent or ϵ-nullvalent for some $1 \leq h \leq t$, let $a'' = b_h$. Otherwise, $b_h(\alpha, C)$ is ϵ-univalent for all $1 \leq h \leq t$.

Next, we construct a chain of $(n - k + 1)$-round executions, where the difference between each execution and the execution that precedes it in the chain is one message that doesn't get delivered. The construction is slightly different depending on whether the previously constructed chain only contains $(\epsilon, 0)$-univalent executions or also contains an $(\epsilon, 1)$-univalent execution.

If $b_h(\alpha, C)$ is $(\epsilon, 0)$-univalent for all $0 \leq h \leq t$, let $b'_0 = b_t$. Since $a^1(\alpha, C)$ is $(\epsilon, 1)$-univalent and the same processes take steps in round $n - k + 1$ of $b_t(\alpha, C)$ and $a^1(\alpha, C)$, then, in round $n - k + 1$ of $a^1(\alpha, C)$, there is a process p_d that takes a step, but some of its messages are not delivered. Let $\{p_{j_1}, \ldots, p_{j_\ell}\}$ be the set of processes that take steps in round $n - k + 1$ of $a^1(\alpha, C)$, but do not receive the message sent by process p_d in that round. For $1 \leq m \leq \ell$, let b'_m be obtained from b'_{m-1} by not delivering the message sent by process p_d to process p_{j_m} in round $n - k + 1$. Note that $b'_\ell = a^1$.

Otherwise, there exists $1 \leq h \leq t$ such that $b_{h-1}(\alpha, C)$ is $(\epsilon, 0)$-univalent and $b_h(\alpha, C)$ is $(\epsilon, 1)$-univalent. In this case, let $b'_0 = b_{h-1}$ and let $d = i_h$. Let $\{p_{j_1}, \ldots, p_{j_{\ell-1}}\}$ be the set of processes that take steps in round $n - k + 1$ of $b_h(\alpha, C)$ and, for $1 \leq m \leq \ell - 1$, let b'_m be obtained from b'_{m-1} by not delivering the message sent by process p_d to process p_{j_m} in round $n - k + 1$. Also let $b'_\ell = b_k$ and $j_\ell = d$.

In both cases, for $1 \leq m \leq \ell$, executions $b'_{m-1}(\alpha, C)$ and $b'_m(\alpha, C)$ are indistinguishable to all processes except p_{j_m}. If $b'_m(\alpha, C)$ is ϵ-bivalent or ϵ-nullvalent for some $1 \leq m \leq \ell$, let $a'' = b'_m$. Otherwise, $b'_m(\alpha, C)$ is ϵ-univalent for all $1 \leq m \leq \ell$. Since $b'_0(\alpha, C) = a(\alpha, C)$ is $(\epsilon, 0)$-univalent and $b'_\ell(\alpha, C)$ is $(\epsilon, 1)$-univalent, there exists $1 \leq m \leq \ell$ such that $b'_{m-1}(\alpha, C)$ is $(\epsilon, 0)$-univalent and $b'_m(\alpha, C)$ is $(\epsilon, 1)$-univalent. By Definition 7.13, $b'_{m-1}(\alpha, C)$ has no $(\epsilon, 1)$-

deciding adversary and, hence, no $(\epsilon, 1)$-deciding p_{j_m}-free adversary. Similarly, $b'_m(\alpha, C)$ has no $(\epsilon, 0)$-deciding p_{j_m}-free adversary. Process p_{j_m} is the only process that has a different local history in the executions $b'_{m-1}(\alpha, C)$ and $b'_m(\alpha, C)$ and process p_{j_m} takes no steps in any extension generated by a p_{j_m}-free adversary. It follows that both these executions are ϵ-nullvalent and we let $a'' = b'_m$. □

7.5.2 NULLVALENT EXECUTIONS

We now describe how to handle nullvalent executions. This is where the main new ideas are needed. Informally, from a nullvalent execution, neither decision is highly likely. When no decision is made, indistinguishability doesn't lead to a contradiction. A different strategy is applied in this case: We show that, with high probability, the execution can be extended by one round and still remain nullvalent. This is done by applying a lemma about functions from products of probability distributions. Then we can repeat the strategy until the execution has n rounds.

Let $X_1, \ldots, X_{n-1}$ be probability distributions such that $\bot \notin X_i$ for $i = 1, \ldots, n-1$, let

$$G : (X_1 \cup \{\bot\}) \times \cdots \times (X_{n-1} \cup \{\bot\}) \longrightarrow \{0, 1, 2\}$$

be a three-valued function, and let $\vec{x} = (x_1, \ldots, x_{n-1}) \in X_1 \times \cdots \times X_{n-1}$. We say that $G(\vec{x})$ can be *forced to* $u \in \{0, 1, 2\}$ *by hiding at most t values* if there is a vector $\vec{x}' = (x'_1, \ldots, x'_{n-1}) \in (X_1 \cup \{\bot\}) \times \cdots \times (X_{n-1} \cup \{\bot\})$ with $G(\vec{x}') = u$ that can be obtained from $\vec{x}$ by changing at most t components to $\bot$.

The next lemma, which is stated without proof, says that, for one of the three possible outcomes, there is a large probability that a randomly chosen element of $X_1 \times \cdots \times X_{n-1}$ can be forced to this outcome by hiding a relatively small number of values.

Lemma 7.16 *There exist a constant $c > 0$ and an outcome $u \in \{0, 1, 2\}$ such that, for $t = c\sqrt{n \log n}$,*

$$\Pr_{\vec{x} \in X_1 \times \cdots \times X_{n-1}} [G(\vec{x}) \text{ can be forced to } u \text{ by hiding at most } t \text{ values}] > 1 - \frac{1}{n^3}.$$

We use this lemma to obtain a one-round extension of a nullvalent execution that is also nullvalent, albeit with a smaller value of ϵ. For the rest of this section, assume that $\epsilon > \frac{1}{n^3}$.

Lemma 7.17 *Let α be an $(n-k)$-round execution, where $0 < k \le n$. If α is ϵ-nullvalent for some process p then there is a one-round p-free adversary a such that*

$$\Pr_{\alpha' \in \mathcal{E}_1(\alpha, a)} [\alpha' \text{ is } (\epsilon - \tfrac{1}{n^3})\text{-nullvalent for } p] > 1 - \frac{1}{n^3}.$$

Proof. The probability distribution $\mathscr{C}(\alpha)$ is isomorphic to $\prod_{i=0}^{n-1} X_i$, where X_i is the probability distribution of the possible local states of process p_i, after performing its local computation including coin flips. (If this is not the first round, and the adversary did not let process p_i take a step in the previous round, then X_i contains a single state.) Without loss of generality, suppose that $p = p_0$. When restricting to p_0-free adversaries, the local state of process p_0 is irrelevant, so it suffices to consider the probability distribution $\prod_{i=1}^{n-1} X_i$. Throughout this subsection, we abuse notation and let $\mathscr{C}(\alpha)$ denote this probability distribution.

We define a three-valued function G on $\prod_{i=1}^{n-1}(X_i \cup \{\bot\})$, where $\bot$ in component i corresponds to an adversary not letting process p_i take a step during round $n - k + 1$. Formally, for any vector $C \in \mathscr{C}(\alpha) = \prod_{i=1}^{n-1} X_i$ and any vector $\hat{C} \in \prod_{i=1}^{n-1}(X_i \cup \{\bot\})$ obtained from C by hiding at most t values, let $a^{\hat{C}}$ be the one-round adversary that gives a step to every process p_i with $\hat{C}[i] \neq \bot$ and lets them receive all the messages that have been sent to them, but does not let any other process (i.e., p_0 or a process p_i such that $\hat{C}[i] = \bot$) take a step. In particular, a^C is the one-round adversary that lets each process, except p_0, take a step and receive all the messages that have been sent to it.

Define

$$
G(\hat{C}) = \begin{cases} 0 & \text{if } a^{\hat{C}}(\alpha, C) \text{ has an } (\epsilon - \frac{1}{n^3}, 0)\text{-deciding } (k-1)\text{-round } p_0\text{-free adversary,} \\ 1 & \text{if } a^{\hat{C}}(\alpha, C) \text{ has an } (\epsilon - \frac{1}{n^3}, 1)\text{-deciding } (k-1)\text{-round } p_0\text{-free adversary,} \\ & \text{but no } (\epsilon - \frac{1}{n^3}, 0)\text{-deciding } (k-1)\text{-round } p_0\text{-free adversary, and} \\ 2 & \text{otherwise.} \end{cases}
$$

Note that in the third case, $a^{\hat{C}}(\alpha, C)$ has neither an $(\epsilon - \frac{1}{n^3}, 0)$-deciding $(k-1)$-round p_0-free adversary nor an $(\epsilon - \frac{1}{n^3}, 0)$-deciding $(k-1)$-round p_0-free adversary, implying that $a^{\hat{C}}(\alpha, C)$ is $(\epsilon - \frac{1}{n^3})$-nullvalent for p_0. When $k = 1$, the definition can be expressed more simply:

$$
G(\hat{C}) = \begin{cases} 0 & \text{if } a^{\hat{C}}(\alpha, C) \text{ decides 0,} \\ 1 & \text{if } a^{\hat{C}}(\alpha, C) \text{ decides 1, and} \\ 2 & \text{otherwise.} \end{cases}
$$

By Lemma 7.16, there is $u \in \{0, 1, 2\}$ such that:

$$
\Pr_{\vec{x} \in \prod_{i=0}^{n-1} X_i} [G(\vec{x}) \text{ can be forced to } u \text{ by hiding at most } t \text{ values}] > 1 - \frac{1}{n^3}.
$$

Let $\mathscr{C}'(\alpha)$ be the subset of configurations $C \in \mathscr{C}(\alpha)$ for which there is a vector $\hat{C} \in \prod_{i=1}^{n-1}(X_i \cup \{\bot\})$ with $G(\hat{C}) = u$ that can be obtained from C by changing at most t components to $\bot$. Then

$$
\Pr_{C \in \mathscr{C}(\alpha)} [C \in \mathscr{C}'(\alpha)] > 1 - \frac{1}{n^3}.
$$

Let a be a one-round p_0-free adversary which is equal to $a^{\hat{C}}$ for every $C \in \mathscr{C}'(\alpha)$ and is equal to a^C for every other configuration in $\mathscr{C}(\alpha)$.

First, as a warmup, we consider the case $k = 1$. If u is 0 or 1, then $a(\alpha, C) = a^{\hat{C}}(\alpha, C)$ decides u for all $C \in \mathscr{C}'(\alpha)$, so

$$\operatorname*{Prob}_{C \in \mathscr{C}(\alpha)} [a(\alpha, C) \text{ decides } u] > 1 - \frac{1}{n^3}.$$

Thus a is a $(\frac{1}{n^3}, u)$-deciding p_0-free adversary from α. This contradicts the assumption that α is ϵ-nullvalent for p_0. Hence $u = 2$, $a(\alpha, C)$ does not decide for all $C \in \mathscr{C}'(\alpha)$, and a is a one-round p_0-free adversary such that

$$\operatorname*{Prob}_{\alpha' \in \mathscr{E}_1(\alpha, a)} [\alpha' \text{ is } (\epsilon - \tfrac{1}{n^3})\text{-nullvalent for } p_0] = \operatorname*{Prob}_{C \in \mathscr{C}'(\alpha)} [a^{\hat{C}}(\alpha, C) \text{ does not decide}] > 1 - \frac{1}{n^3}.$$

More generally, for $1 \leq k \leq n$, if u is 0 or 1, then $a(\alpha, C) = a^{\hat{C}}(\alpha, C)$ has an $(\epsilon - \frac{1}{n^3}, u)$-deciding $(k-1)$-round p_0-free adversary for each $C \in \mathscr{C}'(\alpha)$, so

$$\operatorname*{Prob}_{C \in \mathscr{C}(\alpha)} [a(\alpha, C) \text{ has an } (\epsilon - \tfrac{1}{n^3}, u)\text{-deciding } (k-1)\text{-round } p_0\text{-free adversary}] > 1 - \frac{1}{n^3}.$$

Let a' be a $(k-1)$-round p_0-free adversary that, for each $C \in \mathscr{C}'(\alpha)$, agrees with some $(\epsilon - \frac{1}{n^3}, u)$-deciding $(k-1)$-round p_0-free adversary b^C on all extensions of $a(\alpha, C)$. More formally, for all $C \in \mathscr{C}'(\alpha)$, all $0 \leq r \leq k-1$, all r-round extensions α'' of $a(\alpha, C)$, and all possible configurations $C' \in \mathscr{C}(\alpha'')$ that can arise when the processes perform their local computation at the end of α'', a' behaves the same as b^C at configuration C', i.e., $a'_r(\alpha'', C') = b^C_r(\alpha'', C')$. Then

$$\operatorname*{Prob}_{\alpha'' \in \mathscr{E}_k(\alpha, a \cdot a')} [\alpha'' \text{ decides } u] \geq \operatorname*{Prob}_{\alpha'' \in \mathscr{E}_{k-1}(a(\alpha, C), a')} [\alpha'' \text{ decides } u \mid C \in \mathscr{C}'(\alpha)] \cdot \operatorname*{Prob}_{C \in \mathscr{C}(\alpha)} [C \in \mathscr{C}'(\alpha)]$$

$$> \operatorname*{Prob}_{\alpha'' \in \mathscr{E}_{k-1}(a(\alpha, C), b^C)} [\alpha'' \text{ decides } u \mid C \in \mathscr{C}'(\alpha)] \cdot \left(1 - \frac{1}{n^3}\right)$$

$$\geq \left(1 - \left(\epsilon - \frac{1}{n^3}\right)\right) \cdot \left(1 - \frac{1}{n^3}\right)$$

$$= 1 - \epsilon + \frac{1}{n^3}\left(\epsilon - \frac{1}{n^3}\right) \geq 1 - \epsilon,$$

since b^C is an $(\epsilon - \frac{1}{n^3}, u)$-deciding $(k-1)$-round p_0-free adversary and $\epsilon > \frac{1}{n^3}$. Hence $a \cdot a'$ is an (ϵ, u)-deciding p_0-free adversary from α, contradicting the assumption that α is ϵ-nullvalent for p_0. Therefore, $u = 2$ and

$$\operatorname*{Prob}_{\alpha' \in \mathscr{E}_1(\alpha, a)} [a(\alpha, C) \text{ is } (\epsilon - \tfrac{1}{n^3})\text{-nullvalent for } p_0]$$

$$= \operatorname*{Prob}_{C \in \mathscr{C}(\alpha)} [a(\alpha, C) \text{ is } (\epsilon - \tfrac{1}{n^3})\text{-nullvalent for } p_0] > 1 - \frac{1}{n^3}.$$

$\square$

Now we can apply Lemma 7.17 repeatedly to construct an adversary for which the probability of deciding within a total of n rounds is small.

Lemma 7.18 *Let $0 \le k \le n$ and let α be an $(n-k)$-round execution. If α is ϵ-nullvalent for process p, then there is a k-round p-free adversary b such that*

$$\operatorname*{Prob}_{\alpha' \in \mathscr{E}_k(\alpha, b)} [\alpha' \text{ decides}] \le \frac{k}{n^3}.$$

Proof. The proof is by induction on k. If $k = 0$, then α is an n-round ϵ-nullvalent execution, so it does not decide. Hence

$$\operatorname*{Prob}_{\alpha' \in \mathscr{E}_0(\alpha, b)} [\alpha' \text{ decides}] = 0 = \frac{0}{n^3}.$$

Now, let $k > 0$ and suppose the claim is true for $k - 1$. By Lemma 7.17, there is a one-round p-free adversary a such that

$$\operatorname*{Prob}_{\alpha' \in \mathscr{E}_1(\alpha, a)} [\alpha' \text{ is } (\epsilon - \tfrac{1}{n^3})\text{-nullvalent for } p] > 1 - \frac{1}{n^3}.$$

Let $\mathscr{C}'(\alpha)$ be the subset of configurations $C \in \mathscr{C}(\alpha)$ for which $a(\alpha, C)$ is $(\epsilon - \tfrac{1}{n^3})$-nullvalent for p. Then

$$\operatorname*{Prob}_{C \in \mathscr{C}(\alpha)} [C \in \mathscr{C}'(\alpha)] \ge 1 - \frac{1}{n^3} \text{ and } \operatorname*{Prob}_{C \in \mathscr{C}(\alpha)} [C \notin \mathscr{C}'(\alpha)] \le \frac{1}{n^3}.$$

By the induction hypothesis, for each $C \in \mathscr{C}'(\alpha)$, there is a $(k-1)$-round p-free adversary b^C such that

$$\operatorname*{Prob}_{\alpha' \in \mathscr{E}_{k-1}(a(\alpha, C), b^C)} [\alpha' \text{ decides}] \le \frac{k-1}{n^3}.$$

Let b be a k-round p-free adversary that agrees with a, for each $C \in \mathscr{C}(\alpha)$, and agrees with b^C on all extensions of $a(\alpha, C)$, for each $C \in \mathscr{C}'(\alpha)$. Then

$$\Prob_{\alpha' \in \mathscr{E}_k(\alpha, b)} [\alpha' \text{ decides}] = \Prob_{\alpha' \in \mathscr{E}_k(\alpha, b)} [\alpha' \text{ decides} \mid C \notin \mathscr{C}'(\alpha)] \cdot \Prob_{C \in \mathscr{C}(\alpha)} [C \notin \mathscr{C}'(\alpha)]$$

$$+ \sum_{C \in \mathscr{C}'(\alpha)} \Prob_{\alpha' \in \mathscr{E}_{k-1}(a(\alpha,C), b^C)} [\alpha' \text{ decides}] \cdot \Prob_{C \in \mathscr{C}(\alpha)} [C]$$

$$\leq 1 \cdot \frac{1}{n^3} + \sum_{C \in \mathscr{C}'(\alpha)} \frac{k-1}{n^3} \cdot \Prob_{C \in \mathscr{C}(\alpha)} [C]$$

$$= \frac{1}{n^3} + \frac{k-1}{n^3} \cdot \sum_{C \in \mathscr{C}'(\alpha)} \Prob_{C \in \mathscr{C}(\alpha)} [C]$$

$$\leq \frac{1}{n^3} + \frac{k-1}{n^3} = \frac{k}{n^3}.$$

$\square$

7.5.3   BIVALENT EXECUTIONS

The next piece of the proof explicitly constructs an adversary starting from an ϵ-bivalent execution. If the execution can be extended to an ϵ-nullvalent execution, then Lemma 7.18 can be applied to obtain an n-round execution that does not decide. If the execution can be extended by one round to obtain an ϵ-bivalent execution, then induction can be applied. Therefore, most of the effort in this subsection goes to showing that there is only a negligible probability that neither is possible.

We define an n-round adversary, $b = b_1 \cdots b_n$ starting from any ϵ-bivalent initial configuration. The construction is illustrated in Figure 7.8. We consider each $(n - k)$-round execution α, starting from an ϵ-bivalent initial configuration, for $k = 1, \ldots, n$. If α has a proper prefix that is ϵ-nullvalent, then b will be defined on α and its extensions when the shortest such prefix of α is considered. So, it suffices to consider executions α that don't have a proper ϵ-nullvalent prefix.

Let $\mathscr{C}(\alpha)$ be the probability distribution over the possible different configurations that can arise following α when processes perform their local computations in round $n - k + 1$. We define:

$\mathscr{C}^N(\alpha) = \{C \in \mathscr{C}(\alpha) \mid a(\alpha, C) \text{ is } \epsilon\text{-nullvalent for some one-round adversary } a\}$,
$\mathscr{C}^B(\alpha) = \{C \in \mathscr{C}(\alpha) - \mathscr{C}^N(\alpha) \mid a(\alpha, C) \text{ is } \epsilon\text{-bivalent for some one-round adversary } a\}$,

and, for any $v \in \{0, 1\}$,

$\mathscr{C}^v(\alpha) = \{C \in \mathscr{C}(\alpha) - \mathscr{C}^N(\alpha) \mid a(\alpha, C) \text{ is } (\epsilon, v)\text{-univalent for all one-round adversaries } a\}$.

It follows from Lemma 7.15 that $\mathscr{C}(\alpha)$ is the disjoint union of $\mathscr{C}^N(\alpha)$, $\mathscr{C}^0(\alpha)$, $\mathscr{C}^1(\alpha)$, and $\mathscr{C}^B(\alpha)$.

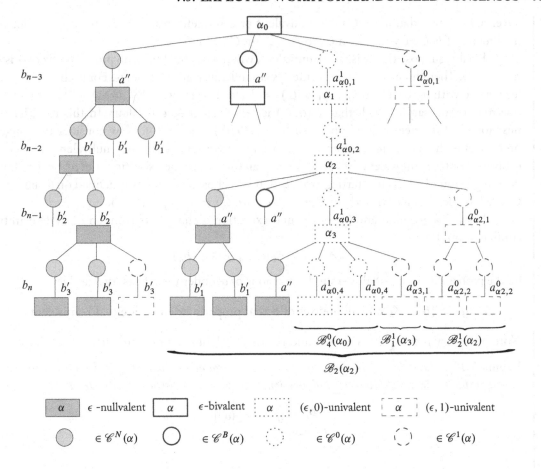

Figure 7.8: The construction of part of the adversary b from a bivalent configuration.

If α is ϵ-nullvalent (and no proper prefix of α is ϵ-nullvalent), then, by Lemma 7.18, there is a k-round adversary b' such that

$$\operatorname*{Prob}_{\alpha' \in \mathscr{E}_k(\alpha, b')} [\alpha' \text{ decides}] < k\epsilon. \tag{7.1}$$

Let b agree with b' on all extensions of α. More formally, for all r-round extensions α'' of α, where $0 \le r < k$, and all $C \in \mathscr{C}(\alpha'')$, let $b_{n-k+r+1}(\alpha'', C) = b'_{r+1}(\alpha'', C)$.

If α is ϵ-bivalent (and no proper prefix of α is ϵ-nullvalent), then there are $(\epsilon, 0)$-deciding and $(\epsilon, 1)$-deciding k-round adversaries, a_α^0 and a_α^1, from α. For each $C \in \mathscr{C}^0(\alpha)$, let b agree with a_α^1 on C, so $b_{n-k+1}(\alpha, C) = a_{\alpha,1}^1(\alpha, C)$. Similarly, for each $C \in \mathscr{C}^1(\alpha)$, let b agree with a_α^0 on C, so $b_{n-k+1}(\alpha, C) = a_{\alpha,1}^0(\alpha, C)$. For each $C \in \mathscr{C}^N(\alpha) \cup \mathscr{C}^B(\alpha)$ there is a one round adversary a'' such that $a''(\alpha, C)$ is ϵ-nullvalent or ϵ-bivalent, respectively. In this case, let the next round of b agree with a'' on C, so $b_{n-k+1}(\alpha, C) = a''(\alpha, C)$.

Finally, suppose that α is (ϵ, v)-univalent, where $v \in \{0, 1\}$ (and no proper prefix of α is ϵ-nullvalent). Then there is an (ϵ, v)-deciding k-round adversary a_α^v from α. For each $C \in \mathscr{C}^{\bar{v}}(\alpha)$, let b agree with a_α^v on C, so $b_{n-k+1}(\alpha, C) = a_{\alpha,1}^v(\alpha, C)$. For $C \in \mathscr{C}^N(\alpha) \cup \mathscr{C}^B(\alpha)$, there is a one round adversary a'' such that $a''(\alpha, C)$ is ϵ-nullvalent or ϵ-bivalent. In this case, let the next round of b agree with a'' on C, so $b_{n-k+1}(\alpha, C) = a''(\alpha, C)$. Now consider the longest prefix $\hat{\alpha}$ of α that is not (ϵ, v)-univalent. Since no proper prefix of α is ϵ-nullvalent, $\hat{\alpha}$ is either ϵ-bivalent or $(\epsilon, \bar{v})$-univalent. Suppose that $\hat{\alpha}$ is an $(n - r)$-round execution. Let $a_{\hat{\alpha}}^{\bar{v}}$ be the $(\epsilon, \bar{v})$-deciding r-round adversary starting from $\hat{\alpha}$ that was chosen when b was defined on $\hat{\alpha}$. For each $C \in \mathscr{C}^v(\alpha)$, let b agree with $a_{\hat{\alpha}}^{\bar{v}}$ on C, so $b_{n-k+1}(\alpha, C) = a_{\hat{\alpha}, r-k+1}^{\bar{v}}(\alpha, C)$.

For $1 \le k \le n$ and any $(n - k)$-round execution α that starts from an ϵ-bivalent initial configuration, let

$$\mathscr{B}_k(\alpha) = \mathscr{E}_k(\alpha, b_{n-k+1} \cdots b_n)$$

be the probability space of all k-round extensions of α under the adversary b and let

$$\mathscr{B}_k^v(\alpha) = \{\beta \in \mathscr{B}_k(\alpha) \mid \text{all prefixes of } \beta \text{ that properly extend } \alpha \text{ are } (\epsilon, v)\text{-univalent}\}.$$

Note that every $\beta \in \mathscr{B}_k^v(\alpha)$ is an n-round (ϵ, v)-univalent execution and, hence, decides v.

Lemma 7.19   *Let $1 \le k \le n$ and let α be an $(n - k)$-round ϵ-bivalent or $(\epsilon, \bar{v})$-univalent execution that starts from an ϵ-bivalent configuration and has no ϵ-nullvalent prefix. Then*

$$\Prob_{\beta \in \mathscr{B}_k(\alpha)} [\beta \in \mathscr{B}_k^v(\alpha)] \le \epsilon.$$

Proof. By definition of b, each $\beta \in \mathscr{B}_k^v(\alpha)$ has the same probability in $\mathscr{B}_k(\alpha)$ as it does in $\mathscr{E}_k(\alpha, a_{\hat{\alpha}}^{\bar{v}})$. Since $a_\alpha^{\bar{v}}$ is an $(\epsilon, \bar{v})$-deciding adversary starting from α, it follows that

$$\Prob_{\beta \in \mathscr{B}_k(\alpha)} [\beta \in \mathscr{B}_k^v(\alpha)] = \Prob_{\beta \in \mathscr{E}_k(\alpha, a_\alpha^{\bar{v}})} [\beta \in \mathscr{B}_k^v(\alpha)] \le \Prob_{\beta \in \mathscr{E}_k(\alpha, a_\alpha^{\bar{v}})} [\beta \text{ decides } v] \le \epsilon.$$

$\square$

Lemma 7.20   *Let $1 \le k \le n$ and let α be an $(n - k)$-round execution that starts from an ϵ-bivalent configuration and has no ϵ-nullvalent prefix.*

1. *If α is (ϵ, v)-univalent for $v \in \{0, 1\}$, then* $\Prob_{\beta \in \mathscr{B}_k(\alpha)} [\beta \text{ decides and } \beta \notin \mathscr{B}_k^v(\alpha)] \le (2k - 1)\epsilon.$

2. *If α is ϵ-bivalent, then* $\Prob_{\beta \in \mathscr{B}_k(\alpha)} [\beta \text{ decides}] \le 2k\epsilon.$

Proof. The proof is by induction on k.

First, suppose that $k = 1$. If $\beta \in \mathscr{B}_1(\alpha)$ decides 0, then β is an n-round $(\epsilon, 0)$-univalent execution and $\beta \in \mathscr{B}_1^0(\alpha)$. Similarly, if $\beta \in \mathscr{B}_1(\alpha)$ decides 1, then $\beta \in \mathscr{B}_1^1(\alpha)$. Hence, by Lemma 7.19, if α is (ϵ, v)-univalent, then

$$\Prob_{\beta \in \mathscr{B}_1(\alpha)} [\beta \text{ decides and } \beta \notin \mathscr{B}_k^v(\alpha)] = \Prob_{\beta \in \mathscr{B}_1(\alpha)} [\beta \in \mathscr{B}_1^{\bar{v}}(\alpha)] \le \epsilon$$

and, if α is ϵ-bivalent, then

$$\Prob_{\beta \in \mathscr{B}_1(\alpha)} [\beta \text{ decides}] = \Prob_{\beta \in \mathscr{B}_1(\alpha)} [\beta \in \mathscr{B}_1^0(\alpha)] + \Prob_{\beta \in \mathscr{B}_1(\alpha)} [\beta \in \mathscr{B}_1^1(\alpha)] \le \epsilon + \epsilon = 2\epsilon.$$

So, let $2 \le k \le n$ and assume the claim is true for $k - 1$. Let $C \in \mathscr{C}(\alpha) = \mathscr{C}^N(\alpha) \cup \mathscr{C}^B(\alpha) \cup \mathscr{C}^v(\alpha) \cup \mathscr{C}^{\bar{v}}(\alpha)$ and let $\alpha' = b_{n-k+1}(\alpha, C)$.
If $C \in \mathscr{C}^N(\alpha)$, then α' is ϵ-nullvalent, so, by (7.1) and the definitions of $\mathscr{B}_{k-1}(\alpha')$ and b,

$$\Prob_{\beta \in \mathscr{B}_{k-1}(\alpha')} [\beta \text{ decides and } \beta \notin \mathscr{B}_k^v(\alpha)] \le \Prob_{\beta \in \mathscr{B}_{k-1}(\alpha')} [\beta \text{ decides}] < (k-1)\epsilon. \qquad (7.2)$$

If $C \in \mathscr{C}^B(\alpha) \cup \mathscr{C}^v(\alpha) \cup \mathscr{C}^{\bar{v}}(\alpha)$, then $C \notin \mathscr{C}^N(\alpha)$, so α' is not ϵ-nullvalent. Since α has no ϵ-nullvalent prefix, neither does α'.
If $C \in \mathscr{C}^B(\alpha)$, then α' is ϵ-bivalent, so, by part 2 of the induction hypothesis,

$$\Prob_{\beta \in \mathscr{B}_{k-1}(\alpha')} [\beta \text{ decides and } \beta \notin \mathscr{B}_k^v(\alpha)] \le \Prob_{\beta \in \mathscr{B}_{k-1}(\alpha')} [\beta \text{ decides}] \le (2k-2)\epsilon. \qquad (7.3)$$

If $C \in \mathscr{C}^v(\alpha)$, then α' is (ϵ, v)-univalent, so, by the definition of $\mathscr{B}_k^v(\alpha)$ and part 1 of the induction hypothesis,

$$\Prob_{\beta \in \mathscr{B}_{k-1}(\alpha')} [\beta \text{ decides and } \beta \notin \mathscr{B}_k^v(\alpha)] = \Prob_{\beta \in \mathscr{B}_{k-1}(\alpha')} [\beta \text{ decides and } \beta \notin \mathscr{B}_{k-1}^v(\alpha')] \le (2k-3)\epsilon.$$
$$(7.4)$$

If $C \in \mathscr{C}^{\bar{v}}(\alpha)$, then α' is $(\epsilon, \bar{v})$-univalent, so

$$\Prob_{\beta \in \mathscr{B}_{k-1}(\alpha')} [\beta \text{ decides and } \beta \notin \mathscr{B}_k^v(\alpha)] \le \Prob_{\beta \in \mathscr{B}_{k-1}(\alpha')} [\beta \text{ decides}]$$
$$\le \Prob_{\beta \in \mathscr{B}_{k-1}(\alpha')} [\beta \text{ decides and } \beta \notin \mathscr{B}_{k-1}^{\bar{v}}(\alpha')] + \Prob_{\beta \in \mathscr{B}_{k-1}(\alpha')} [\beta \in \mathscr{B}_{k-1}^{\bar{v}}(\alpha')]$$

and, by part 1 of the induction hypothesis,

$$\Prob_{\beta \in \mathscr{B}_{k-1}(\alpha')} [\beta \text{ decides and } \beta \notin \mathscr{B}_{k-1}^{\bar{v}}(\alpha')] \le (2k-3)\epsilon. \qquad (7.5)$$

If α is (ϵ, v)-univalent, Lemma 7.19 implies that

$$\Pr_{\beta \in \mathscr{B}_k(\alpha)} [\beta \in \mathscr{B}_k^{\bar{v}}(\alpha)] \leq \epsilon,$$

so

$$\Pr_{\beta \in \mathscr{B}_k(\alpha)} [\beta \text{ decides and } \beta \notin \mathscr{B}_k^{v}(\alpha)]$$

$$= \sum_{C \in \mathscr{C}^N(\alpha)} \Pr_{\beta \in \mathscr{B}_{k-1}(b_{n-k+1}(\alpha,C))} [\beta \text{ decides and } \beta \notin \mathscr{B}_k^{v}(\alpha)] \cdot \Pr_{C \in \mathscr{C}(\alpha)} [C]$$

$$+ \sum_{C \in \mathscr{C}^B(\alpha)} \Pr_{\beta \in \mathscr{B}_{k-1}(b_{n-k+1}(\alpha,C))} [\beta \text{ decides and } \beta \notin \mathscr{B}_k^{v}(\alpha)] \cdot \Pr_{C \in \mathscr{C}(\alpha)} [C]$$

$$+ \sum_{C \in \mathscr{C}^v(\alpha)} \Pr_{\beta \in \mathscr{B}_{k-1}(b_{n-k+1}(\alpha,C))} [\beta \text{ decides and } \beta \notin \mathscr{B}_k^{v}(\alpha)] \cdot \Pr_{C \in \mathscr{C}(\alpha)} [C]$$

$$+ \sum_{C \in \mathscr{C}^{\bar{v}}(\alpha)} \Pr_{\beta \in \mathscr{B}_{k-1}(b_{n-k+1}(\alpha,C))} [\beta \text{ decides and } \beta \notin \mathscr{B}_{k-1}^{\bar{v}}(b_{n-k+1}(\alpha, C))] \cdot \Pr_{C \in \mathscr{C}(\alpha)} [C]$$

$$+ \sum_{C \in \mathscr{C}^{\bar{v}}(\alpha)} \Pr_{\beta \in \mathscr{B}_{k-1}(b_{n-k+1}(\alpha,C))} [\beta \in \mathscr{B}_{k-1}^{\bar{v}}(b_{n-k+1}(\alpha, C))] \cdot \Pr_{C \in \mathscr{C}(\alpha)} [C]$$

$$\leq \sum_{C \in \mathscr{C}^N(\alpha)} (k-1)\epsilon \Pr_{C \in \mathscr{C}(\alpha)} [C] \qquad \text{by (7.2)}$$

$$+ \sum_{C \in \mathscr{C}^B(\alpha)} (2k-2)\epsilon \Pr_{C \in \mathscr{C}(\alpha)} [C] \qquad \text{by (7.3)}$$

$$+ \sum_{C \in \mathscr{C}^v(\alpha)} (2k-3)\epsilon \Pr_{C \in \mathscr{C}(\alpha)} [C] \qquad \text{by (7.4)}$$

$$+ \sum_{C \in \mathscr{C}^{\bar{v}}(\alpha)} (2k-3)\epsilon \Pr_{C \in \mathscr{C}(\alpha)} [C] \qquad \text{by (7.5)}$$

$$+ \Pr_{\beta \in \mathscr{B}_k(\alpha)} [\beta \in \mathscr{B}_k^{\bar{v}}(\alpha)]$$

$$\leq (2k-2)\epsilon \cdot \sum_{C \in \mathscr{C}(\alpha)} \Pr_{C \in \mathscr{C}(\alpha)} [C] + \epsilon = (2k-2)\epsilon + \epsilon = (2k-1)\epsilon.$$

Likewise, if α is ϵ-bivalent, then

$$\Pr_{\beta \in \mathscr{B}_k(\alpha)} [\beta \in \mathscr{B}_k^0(\alpha)], \quad \Pr_{\beta \in \mathscr{B}_k(\alpha)} [\beta \in \mathscr{B}_k^1(\alpha)] \leq \epsilon,$$

by Lemma 7.19, and

$$\operatorname*{Prob}_{\beta \in \mathscr{B}_k(\alpha)} [\beta \text{ decides}]$$

$$= \sum_{C \in \mathscr{C}^N(\alpha)} \operatorname*{Prob}_{\beta \in \mathscr{B}_{k-1}(b_{n-k+1}(\alpha,C))} [\beta \text{ decides}] \cdot \operatorname*{Prob}_{C \in \mathscr{C}(\alpha)} [C]$$

$$+ \sum_{C \in \mathscr{C}^B(\alpha)} \operatorname*{Prob}_{\beta \in \mathscr{B}_{k-1}(b_{n-k+1}(\alpha,C))} [\beta \text{ decides}] \cdot \operatorname*{Prob}_{C \in \mathscr{C}(\alpha)} [C]$$

$$+ \sum_{C \in \mathscr{C}^0(\alpha)} \operatorname*{Prob}_{\beta \in \mathscr{B}_{k-1}(b_{n-k+1}(\alpha,C))} [\beta \text{ decides and } \beta \notin \mathscr{B}_k^0(\alpha)] \cdot \operatorname*{Prob}_{C \in \mathscr{C}(\alpha)} [C]$$

$$+ \sum_{C \in \mathscr{C}^0(\alpha)} \operatorname*{Prob}_{\beta \in \mathscr{B}_{k-1}(b_{n-k+1}(\alpha,C))} [\beta \in \mathscr{B}_k^0(\alpha)] \cdot \operatorname*{Prob}_{C \in \mathscr{C}(\alpha)} [C]$$

$$+ \sum_{C \in \mathscr{C}^1(\alpha)} \operatorname*{Prob}_{\beta \in \mathscr{B}_{k-1}(b_{n-k+1}(\alpha,C))} [\beta \text{ decides and } \beta \notin \mathscr{B}_k^1(\alpha)] \cdot \operatorname*{Prob}_{C \in \mathscr{C}(\alpha)} [C]$$

$$+ \sum_{C \in \mathscr{C}^1(\alpha)} \operatorname*{Prob}_{\beta \in \mathscr{B}_{k-1}(b_{n-k+1}(\alpha,C))} [\beta \in \mathscr{B}_k^1(\alpha)] \cdot \operatorname*{Prob}_{C \in \mathscr{C}(\alpha)} [C]$$

$$\leq \sum_{C \in \mathscr{C}^N(\alpha)} (k-1)\epsilon \operatorname*{Prob}_{C \in \mathscr{C}(\alpha)} [C] \qquad \text{by (7.2)}$$

$$+ \sum_{C \in \mathscr{C}^B(\alpha)} (2k-2)\epsilon \operatorname*{Prob}_{C \in \mathscr{C}(\alpha)} [C] \qquad \text{by (7.3)}$$

$$+ \sum_{C \in \mathscr{C}^0(\alpha)} (2k-3)\epsilon \operatorname*{Prob}_{C \in \mathscr{C}(\alpha)} [C] \qquad \text{by (7.4)}$$

$$+ \sum_{C \in \mathscr{C}^0(\alpha)} \operatorname*{Prob}_{\beta \in \mathscr{B}_{k-1}(b_{n-k+1}(\alpha,C))} [\beta \in \mathscr{B}_{k-1}^0(b_{n-k+1}(\alpha, C))] \cdot \operatorname*{Prob}_{C \in \mathscr{C}(\alpha)} [C]$$

$$+ \sum_{C \in \mathscr{C}_1(\alpha)} (2k-3)\epsilon \operatorname*{Prob}_{C \in \mathscr{C}(\alpha)} [C] \qquad \text{by (7.4)}$$

$$+ \sum_{C \in \mathscr{C}^1(\alpha)} \operatorname*{Prob}_{\beta \in \mathscr{B}_{k-1}(b_{n-k+1}(\alpha,C))} [\beta \in \mathscr{B}_{k-1}^1(b_{n-k+1}(\alpha, C))] \cdot \operatorname*{Prob}_{C \in \mathscr{C}(\alpha)} [C]$$

$$\leq (2k-2)\epsilon \cdot \sum_{C \in \mathscr{C}(\alpha)} \operatorname*{Prob}_{C \in \mathscr{C}(\alpha)} [C] + \operatorname*{Prob}_{\beta \in \mathscr{B}_k(\alpha)} [\beta \in \mathscr{B}_k^0(\alpha)] + \operatorname*{Prob}_{\beta \in \mathscr{B}_k(\alpha)} [\beta \in \mathscr{B}_k^1(\alpha)]$$

$$\leq (2k-2)\epsilon + \epsilon + \epsilon = 2k\epsilon.$$

$\square$

7.5.4   PUTTING THE PIECES TOGETHER

Theorem 7.21   *The expected total step complexity of any asynchronous algorithm for randomized consensus is $\Omega(n^2)$.*

Proof. Consider any randomized consensus algorithm. We show that there is an adversary b under which there is a high probability that the algorithm does not decide within n rounds. In each round of an execution that does not decide, at least $n - f$ processes take a step, where $f = 1 + c\sqrt{n \log n}$ and c is the constant from Lemma 7.16. This implies that the expected number of steps taken by the algorithm under this adversary is in $\Omega(n^2)$.

Let $\epsilon = \frac{1}{n^2}$. By Lemma 7.14, there is a 0-round execution α that is either ϵ-bivalent or ϵ-nullvalent.

If α is ϵ-nullvalent, then, by definition, it is ϵ-nullvalent for some process p. By Lemma 7.18 with $k = n$, there is an n-round adversary b such that the probability an n-round extension of α under b decides is at most $\frac{n}{n^3} = \frac{1}{n^2}$. Hence, under b, the expected number of steps taken by the algorithm is at least $n(n - f)(1 - \frac{1}{n^2}) \in \Omega(n^2)$.

If α is ϵ-bivalent, let b be the adversary defined in subsection 7.5.3. Then, by part 2 of Lemma 7.20 with $k = n$, the probability that an n-round extension of α under b decides is at most $2n\epsilon = \frac{2}{n}$. Hence, under b, the expected number of steps taken by the algorithm is at least $n(n - f)(1 - \frac{2}{n}) \in \Omega(n^2)$. □

The lower bound was proved by Hagit Attiya and Keren Censor in their paper "Tight Bounds for Asynchronous Randomized Consensus," *Journal of the ACM*, 2008 [11], which also includes a proof of Lemma 7.16. The idea of arguing about nullvalent executions through three-valued functions on products of probability distributions (Lemma 7.16 and Lemma 7.17) was suggested by Ziv Bar-Joseph and Michael Ben-Or in their paper, "A Tight Lower Bound for Randomized Synchronous Consensus," *PODC*, 1998 [23].

CHAPTER 8

Combinatorial Arguments

In this chapter, combinatorial and graph theoretic results are applied to obtain impossibility results. We begin, in Section 8.1, by proving that wait-free set consensus is unsolvable in an asynchronous shared memory system where processes communicate via registers. Then, in Section 8.2, we prove a lower bound on the number of steps required to perform an Update in a single-writer snapshot object implemented from single-writer registers. In both these proofs, counting is employed to show the existence of certain situations that an adversary can take advantage of to construct a bad execution.

Turán's theorem, discussed in Section 8.3, says that a graph without too many edges contains a relatively large independent set. It can be used to find a relatively large set of processes in an execution which have learned nothing about one another's inputs. In particular, it is used to obtain a lower bound on the step complexity of implementing a weak test&set object. In Section 8.4, a counting argument is used to show the existence of a relatively large subgraph of a bipartite graph with certain properties, which allows it to be used in a similar way to prove a lower bound on the step complexity of anonymous conflict detectors.

Yao's principle is a general tool for obtaining lower bounds on the worst case expected step complexity of randomized algorithms from lower bounds on the distributional complexity of deterministic algorithms. It is presented in Section 8.5 and applied in Section 8.6 to obtain a step complexity tradeoff for randomized implementations of a max register.

8.1 UNSOLVABILITY OF SET CONSENSUS

The k-*set consensus* problem is a variant of the consensus problem in which nonfaulty processes decide on at most k different values. Formally, each process p_i has a private input value x_i and, if it doesn't fail, it has to output a value y_i. The output values must satisfy the following two properties:

- k-*Agreement:* There are at most k different output values.

- *Validity:* Every output value is one of the input values.

Consensus is another name for 1-set consensus. It is trivial to solve n-set consensus for n processes: Each process can simply output its input value.

We consider an asynchronous shared memory system in which processes communicate using single-writer registers of unbounded size and any number of process crash failures are allowed. In this model, k-set consensus is impossible for $k < n$, that is, when the number of different output values must be smaller than the number of processes. It suffices to prove that $(n - 1)$-set consensus is impossible, since any algorithm for k-set consensus is also an algorithm for $(k + 1)$-set consensus.

Theorem 8.1   *There is no wait-free algorithm for n processes that solves $(n - 1)$-set consensus.*

The proof is by contradiction. Suppose there is a wait-free algorithm for n processes that solves $(n - 1)$-set consensus. It suffices that each process has one single-writer register, because the single-writer registers have unbounded size. We may also assume that when a process writes to its register, it writes its input and its current local history. An algorithm that does this is called a *full-information algorithm*.

Since we are not concerned with the step complexity of the algorithm, there is no loss of generality in assuming that each process starts with a write to its register and alternates between writing to its register and reading the registers of all $n - 1$ other processes, in order of their process identifiers. For our proof, it suffices to restrict attention to a class of special executions, which are induced by finite sequences of nonempty sets of processes, as follows: Given a sequence of nonempty sets of processes, $B_1, B_2, \ldots, B_r$, the execution proceeds in r rounds. In the ℓ'th round, each process in B_ℓ takes n steps. First, each process in B_ℓ, in increasing order of identifier, writes to its register. Then, each process in B_ℓ, in increasing order of identifier, reads the registers of all $n - 1$ other processes. For example, the sequence of operations in the three-round execution β induced by $\{p_0, p_1\}, \{p_1, p_2\}, \{p_3\}$ is

$$w_0 w_1 R_0 R_1 \,\big|\, w_1 w_2 R_1 R_2 \,\big|\, w_3 R_3.$$

Here w_i denotes a write by process p_i to its register and R_i denotes a sequence of $n - 1$ reads by process p_i, in which it reads the registers of all the other processes. The vertical bars separate the rounds.

If a process p_i reads the single-writer register of another process p_j in the ℓ'th round of an execution, it learns how many times p_j participated during the first ℓ rounds. This is the number of sets among $B_1, \ldots, B_\ell$ to which p_j belongs. It also learns the state of process p_j at the beginning of the last round in which p_j participated. For example, every process in B_1 learns which other processes belong to B_1 and every process in $B_2 - B_1$ learns which other processes belong to $B_1 \cap B_2$, $(B_1 - B_2) \cup (B_2 - B_1)$, and $\overline{B_1} \cap \overline{B_2}$. If B_1 and B_2 are disjoint, then a process in B_2 cannot determine whether another process is in $B_2 - B_1$ or $B_1 - B_2$, because the first time a process writes, it only writes its input. In this case, the executions induced by $B_1 \cup B_2$ and B_1, B_2 are indistinguishable to the processes in B_2. However, the processes in B_1 can distinguish between these two executions. More generally, because processes take steps in a fixed order within each round, the following result can be proved inductively.

Lemma 8.2 *Suppose β is the execution induced by $B_1, \ldots, B_r$ and β' is the execution induced by $B_1', \ldots, B_{r'}'$, both starting from the same configuration. If β and β' are indistinguishable to all processes, then $\beta = \beta'$, $r = r'$, and $B_i = B_i'$ for $i = 1, \ldots, r$.*

We are particularly interested in pairs of executions that are distinguishable by exactly one process. For example, the sequence of operations in the execution β_0 induced by $\{p_0\}, \{p_1\}, \{p_1, p_2\}, \{p_3\}$ is:

$$w_0 R_0 \,\Big|\, w_1 R_1 \,\Big|\, w_1 w_2 R_1 R_2 \,\Big|\, w_3 R_3$$

and the sequence of operations in the execution β_1 induced by $\{p_0, p_1\}, \{p_1\}, \{p_2\}, \{p_3\}$ is:

$$w_0 w_1 R_0 R_1 \,\Big|\, w_1 R_1 \,\Big|\, w_2 R_2 \,\Big|\, w_3 R_3.$$

Let $P = \{p_0, \ldots, p_{n-1}\}$ denote the set of all processes. Then β is indistinguishable from β_0 to all processes except p_0 (that is, $\beta_0 \overset{P-\{p_0\}}{\sim} \beta$ and $\beta_0 \overset{p_0}{\not\sim} \beta$) and β is indistinguishable from β_1 to all processes except p_1 (that is, $\beta_1 \overset{P-\{p_1\}}{\sim} \beta$ and $\beta_1 \overset{p_1}{\not\sim} \beta$).

To all processes except p_i, the execution induced by any finite sequence of sets is indistinguishable from the execution induced by that sequence with $\{p_i\}$ added to its end.

Observation 8.3 For every process p_i, if β and β' are the executions induced by the sequences $B_1, \ldots, B_r$ and $B_1, \ldots, B_r, \{p_i\}$, respectively, starting from the same configuration, then $\beta \overset{P-\{p_i\}}{\sim} \beta'$ and $\beta \overset{p_i}{\not\sim} \beta'$.

The next lemma shows that it is also possible to have two sequences of sets, neither of which ends in $\{p_i\}$, inducing executions that are indistinguishable to all processes except p_i.

Lemma 8.4 *If p_i participates in the execution β induced by $B_1, B_2, \ldots, B_r$ and $B_r \neq \{p_i\}$, then there is a unique sequence of sets $B_1', B_2', \ldots, B_{r'}'$ with $B_{r'}' \neq \{p_i\}$ which induces an execution β' starting from the same configuration, such that $\beta' \overset{P-\{p_i\}}{\sim} \beta$ and $\beta' \overset{p_i}{\not\sim} \beta$.*

Proof. Let $\ell = \max\{j \mid p_i \in B_j\}$ be the last round of β in which p_i participates. If $B_\ell \neq \{p_i\}$, split B_ℓ into two nonempty sets, the first of which contains only p_i and the second of which contains the rest of B_ℓ. Then $r' = r + 1$ and

$$
B_h' = \begin{cases}
B_h & \text{if } 1 \leq h < \ell \\
\{p_i\} & \text{if } h = \ell \\
B_\ell - \{p_i\} & \text{if } h = \ell + 1 \\
B_{h-1} & \text{if } \ell + 1 < h \leq r'.
\end{cases}
$$

Note that, if $\ell = r$, then $B_{r'}' = B_\ell - \{p_i\} \neq \{p_i\}$ and, if $\ell < r$, then $B_{r'}' = B_r \neq \{p_i\}$.

If $B_\ell = \{p_i\}$, then $\ell < r$ and $p_i \notin B_{\ell+1}$ (since ℓ is the last round in which p_i participates). In this case, merge B_ℓ with $B_{\ell+1}$, so $r' = r - 1$ and

$$B'_h = \begin{cases} B_h & \text{if } 1 \leq h < \ell \\ B_\ell \cup B_{\ell+1} & \text{if } h = \ell \\ B_{h+1} & \text{if } \ell + 1 \leq h \leq r'. \end{cases}$$

Since $B'_{r'} \supseteq B_r$ and $B_r \not\subseteq \{p_i\}$, it follows that $B'_{r'} \neq \{p_i\}$.

In both cases, $\beta' \overset{p_i}{\not\sim} \beta$. However, the induced executions β and β' are the same prior to round ℓ and they become distinguishable to process p_i only after it last writes to its single-writer register in round ℓ. The processes in $P - \{p_i\}$ that participate in round ℓ of the shorter of these two executions cannot tell the difference between it and round $\ell + 1$ of the longer execution. Since p_i takes no steps after round ℓ in either execution and the last $r - \ell$ rounds of these executions are the same, these executions remain indistinguishable to every other process. Thus, $\beta' \overset{P-\{p_i\}}{\sim} \beta$.

To prove uniqueness, consider any sequence of sets $B''_1, \ldots, B''_{r''}$ with $B''_{r''} \neq \{p_i\}$ which induces an execution β'' such that $\beta'' \overset{P-\{p_i\}}{\sim} \beta$ and $\beta'' \overset{p_i}{\not\sim} \beta$. Since $\beta \overset{P-\{p_i\}}{\sim} \beta'$, it follows that $\beta'' \overset{P-\{p_i\}}{\sim} \beta'$.

If a process writes a different number of times or sees a different number of writes by some other process in two executions, it will have a different state at the end of those executions. A process sees every write that occurs in the execution induced by a sequence of sets if and only if it is in the last block of the sequence. Since $\beta'' \overset{P-\{p_i\}}{\sim} \beta$, it follows that $B''_{r''} - \{p_i\} = B_r - \{p_i\} \neq \phi$ and every process participates in the same number of rounds in β and β''.

If p_i can distinguish between β and β'' prior to round ℓ, then it will write something different during round ℓ of β and during its last write in β'' and the processes in $B_r - \{p_i\}$ will have different states at the end of these executions. This is contrary to the assumption that $\beta'' \overset{P-\{p_i\}}{\sim} \beta$. Therefore, the first $\ell - 1$ rounds of β and β'' are indistinguishable to all processes. By Lemma 8.2, it follows that $B_1, \ldots, B_{\ell-1} = B''_1, \ldots, B''_{\ell-1}$. Furthermore, $p_i \in B''_\ell$.

Otherwise, any process in B''_ℓ will be able to distinguish β and β''. Since $\beta'' \overset{p_i}{\not\sim} \beta$, it follows that $B''_\ell \neq B_\ell$. Thus, any process in $B''_\ell \cap B_\ell$ will be able to distinguish β and β''. It follows that $B''_\ell \cap B_\ell = \{p_i\}$, since $\beta'' \overset{P-\{p_i\}}{\sim} \beta$.

First suppose that $B_\ell = \{p_i\}$. Then $\ell < r$. If $p_j \in B''_\ell - \{p_i\} - B_{\ell+1}$, then every step by every process that occurs after round $\ell - 1$ in β'' will see the value p_j writes in round ℓ. However, the steps by processes in round $\ell + 1$ of β will not see this value, contradicting the assumption that β and β'' are indistinguishable to these processes. Likewise, if $p_j \in B_{\ell+1} - B''_\ell$, then every step by every process other than p_i that occurs after round $\ell - 1$ in β will see the value p_j writes in round $\ell + 1$. But the steps by processes in round ℓ of β'' will not see this value, contradicting the assumption that $\beta'' \overset{P-\{p_i\}}{\sim} \beta$. Thus $B''_\ell = B_{\ell+1} \cup \{p_i\} = B'_\ell$.

Now suppose that $B_\ell \neq \{p_i\}$. Let $p_j \in B_\ell - \{p_i\}$. Then every step by every process that occurs after round $\ell - 1$ in β will see the value p_j writes in round ℓ. Since $p_j \notin B_\ell''$, any process in B_ℓ'' can distinguish between β and β''. This implies that $B_\ell'' = \{p_i\} = B_\ell'$.

Hence $B_1'', \ldots, B_\ell'' = B_1', \ldots, B_\ell'$. If $p_i \in B_h''$ for some $h > \ell$, then every process in $B_{r''}''$ could distinguish between β and β''. Therefore process p_i does not participate after round ℓ in either β'' or β'. Since $\beta'' \overset{P - \{p_i\}}{\sim} \beta'$, it follows from Lemma 8.2 that $r'' = r'$ and $B_1'', \ldots, B_{r''}'' = B_1', \ldots, B_{r'}'$. $\qquad\square$

We say that a process p_i is *seen in the ℓ'th round* of the execution induced by $B_1, B_2, \ldots, B_r$, if $p_i \in B_\ell$ and $\cup_{h=\ell}^{r} B_h \neq \{p_i\}$, i.e., there is some other process that participates in round ℓ or later. If a process p_i participates in the execution β induced by $B_1, B_2, \ldots, B_r$, but is not seen, we say that it is *unseen* in β. This means that p_i takes all its steps after all other participating processes have stopped taking steps, i.e., there exists $\ell \in \{1, \ldots, r\}$ such that $p_i \notin B_h$ for $1 \leq h < \ell$ and $B_h = \{p_i\}$ for $\ell \leq h \leq r$. At most one process is unseen in the execution induced by a sequence of sets of processes. For example, p_3 is unseen in β, β_1, and β_2.

An *m-process special execution* is an execution induced by a sequence of subsets of $\{p_0, \ldots, p_{m-1}\}$ such that, for $i = 0, \ldots, m - 1$, process p_i has input $x_i = i$ and outputs a value $y_i \in \{0, \ldots, m - 1\}$ in the last round in which it participates. Let $\mathcal{E}_m$ denote the set of all m-process special executions in which the output values are all different. In other words, $\{0, \ldots, m - 1\}$ is the set of values output by any execution in $\mathcal{E}_m$. Since the algorithm is deterministic and wait-free, $\mathcal{E}_m$ is finite.

If $\mathcal{E}_n \neq \phi$, then there is an n-process special execution in which n different values are decided. This violates $(n - 1)$-agreement, contradicting the assumption that the algorithm solves $(n - 1)$-set consensus. Hence, there is no wait-free algorithm for n processes that solves $(n - 1)$-set consensus. Thus, to complete the proof of Theorem 8.1, it suffices to prove that $|\mathcal{E}_n|$ is odd and, hence, nonzero.

Lemma 8.5 $|\mathcal{E}_m|$ *is odd, for* $1 \leq m \leq n$.

Proof. The proof is by induction. Since the algorithm is deterministic and wait-free, there is exactly one 1-process special execution. In this execution, p_0 outputs 0. Thus $|\mathcal{E}_1| = 1$, which is odd.

Let $1 \leq m \leq n - 1$ and assume that $|\mathcal{E}_m|$ is odd. Note that $\alpha \in \mathcal{E}_{m+1}$ if and only if α is an $(m + 1)$-process special execution, there is exactly one process that outputs m, and $\{0, \ldots, m - 1\}$ is the set of values output by the remaining m processes.

It is convenient to also consider the $(m + 1)$-process special executions in which the set of values output by $p_0, \ldots, p_m$ is $\{0, \ldots, m - 1\}$. Let $\mathcal{A}_{m+1}$ denote the set of pairs (α, p_i), where $i \in \{0, \ldots, m\}$, α is an $(m + 1)$-process special execution in which p_i participates, and $\{0, \ldots, m - 1\}$ is the set of values output by the remaining m processes. Let $\mathcal{A}_{m+1}'$ denote the set of pairs $(\alpha, p_i) \in \mathcal{A}_{m+1}$ such that p_i does not output m in α. Since $\mathcal{E}_{m+1} = \{\alpha \mid (\alpha, p_i) \in \mathcal{A}_{m+1}$ and p_i outputs m in α for some $i \in \{0, \ldots, m\}\}$, it follows that $|\mathcal{A}_{m+1}| = |\mathcal{A}_{m+1}'| + |\mathcal{E}_{m+1}|$.

Consider any pair $(\alpha, p_i) \in \mathcal{A}'_{m+1}$. By validity, p_i outputs a value $v \in \{0, \ldots, m-1\}$ in α. Since $\{0, \ldots, m-1\}$ is the set of values output by the remaining m processes, there is a unique process $p_j \in \{p_0, \ldots, p_m\} - \{p_i\}$ such that $y_j = v$. Thus $(\alpha, p_j) \in \mathcal{A}'_{m+1}$, but $(\alpha, p_k) \notin \mathcal{A}'_{m+1}$ for $k \neq i, j$. It follows that $\mathcal{A}'_{m+1}$ can be partitioned into groups of size two, so $|\mathcal{A}'_{m+1}|$ is even. It remains to prove that $|\mathcal{A}_{m+1}|$ is odd. There are three cases to consider.

First, consider the pairs $(\alpha, p_i) \in \mathcal{A}_{m+1}$ such that p_i is seen in α. Let β be the execution obtained from α by removing all rounds from the end of α in which only p_i participates. By Observation 8.3, $\alpha \overset{P-\{p_i\}}{\sim} \beta$. By Lemma 8.4, there is a unique execution β' such that the set of participants in its last round is not $\{p_i\}$, $\beta \overset{p_i}{\not\sim} \beta'$, and $\beta \overset{P-\{p_i\}}{\sim} \beta'$. Let α' be the $(m+1)$-process special execution obtained from β' by letting process p_i perform rounds by itself until it returns a value. Since α is an extension of β, α' is an extension of β' and p_i takes the same number of steps in β and β', it follows that $\alpha \overset{p_i}{\not\sim} \alpha'$. By Observation 8.3, $\beta' \overset{P-\{p_i\}}{\sim} \alpha'$. Hence $\alpha \overset{P-\{p_i\}}{\sim} \alpha'$ and $\{0, \ldots, m-1\}$ is the set of values output by the processes in $\{p_0, \ldots, p_m\} - \{p_i\}$. Thus $(\alpha', p_i) \in \mathcal{A}_{m+1}$. Since p_i is seen in α, it follows that p_i is seen in α', so $\overset{P-\{p_i\}}{\sim}$ partitions $\{(\alpha, p_i) \in \mathcal{A}_{m+1} \mid p_i \text{ is seen in } \alpha\}$ into equivalence classes of size at least two.

In fact, each of these equivalence classes has size exactly two. To see why, suppose $(\alpha_1, p_i), (\alpha_2, p_i), (\alpha_3, p_i) \in \mathcal{A}_{m+1}$, process p_i is seen in α_1, α_2, and α_3, and these three executions are indistinguishable to all processes in $P - \{p_i\}$. For $j = 1, 2, 3$, let β_j be the execution obtained from α_j by removing all rounds from the end of α_j in which only p_i participates. Note that p_i still participates in β_j, since p_i is seen in α_j. By Observation 8.3, β_1, β_2, and β_3 are indistinguishable to all processes in $P - \{p_i\}$. It follows from Lemma 8.4 that at least two of β_1, β_2, and β_3 are the same. Since the algorithm is deterministic, this implies that at least two of the $(m+1)$-process special executions α_1, α_2, and α_3 are the same. Hence, the cardinality of the set $\{(\alpha, p_i) \in \mathcal{A}_{m+1} \mid p_i \text{ is seen in } \alpha\}$ is even.

Next, consider the pairs $(\alpha, p_i) \in \mathcal{A}_{m+1}$ such that $p_i \neq p_m$ and p_i is unseen in α. Since $\{0, \ldots, m-1\}$ is the set of values output by the processes other than p_i, there exists $j \in \{0, \ldots, m\} - \{i\}$ such that $y_j = i$. Let α' be obtained from α by deleting all steps by p_i. By Observation 8.3, $\alpha' \overset{P-\{p_i\}}{\sim} \alpha$, so $\alpha \overset{p_j}{\sim} \alpha'$. Let β be obtained from α' by changing the value of x_i from i to another value. Since p_i takes no steps in α', it follows that $\alpha' \overset{p_j}{\sim} \beta$. Hence, process p_j also outputs i in β. However, this violates validity. Thus, there are no pairs $(\alpha, p_i) \in \mathcal{A}_{m+1}$ with $p_i \neq p_m$ in which p_i is unseen in α.

Finally, consider the pairs $(\alpha, p_m) \in \mathcal{A}_{m+1}$ such that p_m is unseen in α. Let α' be obtained from α by deleting all steps by p_m. By Observation 8.3, $\alpha' \overset{P-\{p_m\}}{\sim} \alpha$, so α' is an m-process special execution in which $\{0, \ldots, m-1\}$ is the set of values output. Hence, $\alpha' \in \mathcal{E}_m$. Similarly, from any execution $\alpha' \in \mathcal{E}_m$, we can construct a pair $(\alpha, p_m) \in \mathcal{A}_{m+1}$ such that p_m is unseen in α, by letting process p_m perform rounds by itself until it returns a value, starting after processes $p_0, \ldots, p_{m-1}$ have all produced their output values. Because the algorithm is deterministic and wait-free, α is unique. Thus $\mathcal{E}_m$ is isomorphic to $\{(\alpha, p_m) \in \mathcal{A}_{m+1} \mid p_m$ is unseen in $\alpha\}$. By the induction hypothesis, $|\mathcal{E}_m|$ is odd. Thus, $|\mathcal{A}_{m+1}|$ is odd. It follows that $|\mathcal{E}_{m+1}|$ is odd, which proves the inductive step. $\qquad\qquad\qquad\qquad\qquad\qquad\qquad\qquad\qquad\qquad\qquad\qquad\qquad\qquad\qquad\quad$ $\square$

Lemma 8.4 is from Hagit Attiya and Sergio Rajsbaum's paper "The Combinatorial Structure of Wait-free Solvable Tasks," *SIAM Journal on Computing*, 2002 [20]. Lemma 8.5 is from "Counting-Based Impossibility Proofs for Renaming and Set Agreement," by Hagit Attiya and Ami Paz, which appeared at *DISC*, 2012 [18]. Theorem 8.1 has appeared in a number of papers, including "Generalized FLP Impossibility Result for t-resilient Asynchronous Computations," by Borowsky and Gafni [26], "Wait-free k-set Agreement is Impossible: the Topology of Public Knowledge," by Saks and Zaharoglou [62], and "The Asynchronous Computability Theorem for t-resilient Tasks," by Herlihy and Shavit [49], all of which originally appeared in *STOC*, 1993.

8.2   A LOWER BOUND ON UPDATE TIME FOR A SINGLE-WRITER SNAPSHOT

We consider the wait-free implementation of an n-component single-writer snapshot object, defined in Section 5.6, and prove that, in the worst case, an Update performs $\Omega(n)$ steps. However, instead of n processes that can perform both Scan and Update, we'll assume that processes $p_0, \ldots, p_{n-1}$ only perform Update and there n additional processes, $q_0, \ldots, q_{n-1}$, that only perform Scan. We'll call the former *updaters* and the latter *scanners*. Alternatively, we could have $n/2$ updaters and $n/2$ scanners and the lower bound would decrease by a factor of 2.

The model we consider is asynchronous shared memory system in which processes communicate using single-writer registers (of unbounded size).

The proof shows that, if every Update takes less than $n/12 - 1$ steps, it is possible to construct an infinite execution in which some Scan takes an infinite number of steps. The execution will be formed as the limit of a sequence of finite executions of increasing length, where each execution is a prefix of the next execution in the sequence. This sequence of finite executions will be constructed inductively. The finite executions we construct will have a special form:

Definition 8.6   A *flippable execution* is a finite execution with history

$$U_0 s_1 U_1 s_2 \cdots s_k U_k$$

such that

- it starts from an initial configuration C_0 in which all components have value 0,

- U_j is a solo history of an Update in which a process changes its component to have value one more than it had before, for $j = 0, \ldots, k$,

- consecutive Updates are performed by different processes,

- s_j is a single step of a Scan, for $j = 1, \ldots, k$

- for $j = 1, \ldots, k$, the execution with history

$$U_0 s_1 U_1 \ldots s_{j-1} U_{j-1} s_j U_j s_{j+1} \ldots s_k U_k \text{ starting from } C_0$$

is indistinguishable (to all processes) from the flipped execution with history

$$U_0 s_1 U_1 \ldots s_{j-1} U_j U_{j-1} s_j s_{j+1} \ldots s_k U_k \text{ starting from } C_0$$

in which U_j is performed before $U_{j-1} s_j$ instead of after $U_{j-1} s_j$.

This definition is illustrated in Figure 8.1.

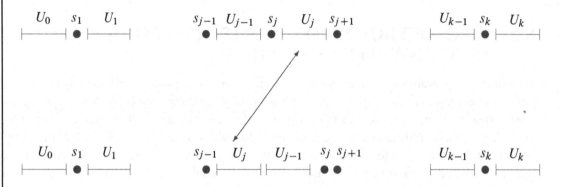

Figure 8.1: A flippable execution and the flipped execution E_j.

The lower bound will even apply to an implementation of a single-writer snapshot object which is only correct when Updates do not overlap one another. This is because we are restricting attention to flippable executions. Moreover, it will give a lower bound on the worst case number of steps taken by Update in solo executions. In general, this might be less than the number of steps taken in executions in which Updates overlap.

First, we show that the Scans being performed in a flippable execution cannot be linearized anywhere and, hence, cannot have terminated.

Lemma 8.7 *No Scan in a flippable execution has terminated.*

Proof. Let $E = U_0 s_1 U_1 \ldots s_k U_k$ be the history of a flippable execution starting from configuration C_0. To obtain a contradiction, suppose that process q_i has completed a Scan by the end of E.

Since the Updates do not overlap, they are linearized in the order $U_0, U_1, \ldots, U_k$. Since the scanner q_i takes no steps during the Updates U_0 and U_k, the Scan by q_i begins after U_0 and finishes before U_k. Thus, the linearization point of this Scan must occur after the linearization point of U_0 and before the linearization point of U_k. This implies that the linearization point of this Scan occurs between the linearization points of U_{j-1} and U_j, for some $j \in \{1, \ldots, k\}$.

Consider the flipped execution with history $E_j = U_0 s_1 U_1 \ldots s_{j-1} U_j U_{j-1} s_j s_{j+1} \ldots s_k U_k$ starting from C_0. The executions with histories E and E_j are indistinguishable to every process, so q_i returns the same result for its Scan in both executions. The Updates U_{j-1} and U_j are performed by two different processes, p and p'. Let v and v' be the values of these two Updates.

Where is the Scan by q_i linearized in an execution with history E_j? Since q_i returns v and $v' - 1$ in the components for p and p', respectively, it must be linearized after U_{j-1}, but before U_j. But this is impossible, since U_j occurs before U_{j-1} in E_j. $\square$

This argument doesn't work if the number of possible values a component can have is finite. For example, consider a binary snapshot object, in which each component is either 0 or 1. Then the natural definition of a flippable execution is one in which each Update flips the value of its component from 0 to 1 or from 1 to 0. Suppose $k > 2^n$. In this case, by the pigeonhole principle, the snapshot has the same n-bit value between two different pairs of consecutive Updates. If the Scan by q_i in the original execution returns this value, then the Scan by q_i can be linearized at either point. In the flipped execution, the value of the snapshot object is changed at only one of these points, so the other point can still be used. The important thing to remember is that, even if two executions are indistinguishable to all processes, the linearizations of the operations in those executions are not necessarily the same.

Next, we show how to inductively construct a flippable execution so that it can be repeatedly extended. The key idea is to choose the process to do each successive Update U_j so that its single-writer register is not read during the previous and next Updates, U_{j-1} and U_{j+1}, nor during the steps s_j and s_{j+1} of the Scans that precede and follow it. Furthermore, the single-writer registers of the processes that perform the steps s_j and s_{j+1} cannot be read by the process that is chosen to perform U_j. A counting argument shows that all of this is possible.

It is helpful to use a matrix to keep track of who reads what registers. For any configuration C, and every value v, let B_C denote the $n \times 2n$ Boolean matrix whose rows are indexed by the updaters $p_0, \ldots, p_{n-1}$, whose columns are indexed by all the processes $p_0, \ldots, p_{n-1}, q_0, \ldots, q_{n-1}$, and whose entries $B_C[p, q]$ are 1 if and only if either $p = q$ or a solo execution of the Update by process p starting from configuration C reads from q's single-writer register. We say that a column of B_C is *light* if at most $n/4$ of its entries are 1.

Lemma 8.8   *Suppose that, starting from configuration C, every updater takes at most $n/12 - 1$ steps to perform a solo execution of Update in which it increments the value of its component. Then B_C has more than $5n/3$ light columns.*

Proof. Since each updater, p_i, performs at most $n/12 - 1$ steps in its solo execution of Update starting from configuration C, it reads from at most $n/12 - 1$ different single-writer registers. Furthermore $B_C[p_i, p_i] = 1$. Hence, at most $n/12$ entries in each row of B_C are 1 and the number of 1's in B_C is at most $n^2/12$.

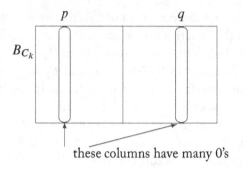

these columns have many 0's

Figure 8.2: The Matrix B_{C_k}.

Let ℓ be the number of light columns in B_C. Then the number of 1's in B_C is greater than $(2n - \ell)n/4$. This implies that $n^2/12 > (2n - \ell)n/4$ or, equivalently, $\ell > 5n/3$. $\square$

We now prove the main technical lemma, which shows the existence of a flippable execution, but with one additional property that makes the construction proceed more easily.

Lemma 8.9 *Suppose that every solo execution of* Update *takes at most $n/12 - 1$ steps starting from any configuration where there are no pending* Updates. *Then, for all $k \geq 0$, there is a flippable execution with history $U_0 s_1 U_1 \ldots s_k U_k$ such that column p of B_{C_k} is light, where p is the process that performs the last* Update *and C_k is the configuration from which it begins that* Update.

Proof. The proof is by induction on k.

First consider the base case, $k = 0$. By Lemma 8.8, there are at least $5n/3$ light columns in B_{C_0}. Thus, more than $2n/3$ of the columns indexed by the processes $p_0, \ldots, p_{n-1}$ are light. Let p be one such process and let U_0 be the history of a solo execution of an Update starting from C_0 by p that sets its component to 1.

For the induction step, let $k \geq 0$ and suppose the claim is true for k. Then there is a flippable execution with history $U_0 s_1 U_1 \ldots s_k U_k$ such that column p of B_{C_k} is light, where p is the process that performs the last Update and C_k is the configuration from which it begins that Update.

By Lemma 8.8, there are at least $5n/3$ light columns in B_{C_k}. Thus, more than $2n/3$ of the columns indexed by the processes $q_0, \ldots, q_{n-1}$ are light. Let q be one such process, let s_{k+1} be the next step by process q starting from the end of the flippable execution and let C_{k+1} be the resulting configuration.

Consider the matrices B_{C_k} and $B_{C_{k+1}}$. We want to choose an updater p' with the following properties:

1. Column p' of $B_{C_{k+1}}$ is light.

2. $B_{C_k}[p', p] = 0$.

3. $B_{C_k}[p', q] = 0$.

4. $B_{C_k}[p, p'] = 0$.

5. s_{k+1} is not a read of the single-writer register of p'.

Property 1 ensures that the additional condition in the inductive claim will be satisfied. Properties 2 and 3 ensure that p' can't tell whether its next Update occurs before or after $U_k s_{k+1}$. Properties 4 and 5 ensure that p and q can't tell whether their operations occur before or after the next Update by p'. In particular, property 4 ensures that $p \neq p'$.

By Lemma 8.8, there are at most $n/3$ choices for column p' that don't satisfy property 1. Since columns p and q of B_{C_k} are light, each contains at most $n/4$ entries that are 1. Therefore, there are at most $n/4$ choices for row p' that don't satisfy property 2 and at most $n/4$ choices that don't satisfy property 3.

Process p performs at most $n/12 - 1$ steps in its solo execution of Update starting from configuration C_k, so it reads from at most $n/12 - 1$ different single-writer registers. Hence, at most $n/12$ entries in row p of B_{C_k} are 1. Thus, there are at most $n/12$ choices for column p' that don't satisfy property 4. There is at most 1 choice for column p' that doesn't satisfy property 5, since s_{k+1} is a single step.

Therefore, there are at least $n - n/3 - n/4 - n/4 - n/12 - 1 = n/12 - 1$ choices for column p' that satisfy all 5 properties. Let U_{k+1} be the Update by one such p' in which it increments the value of its component.

It remains to prove that the execution with history $E' = U_0 s_1 U_1 \ldots s_{k+1} U_{k+1}$ starting from C_0 is flippable. By the induction hypothesis, for $j = 1, \ldots, k$, the execution with history

$$E = U_0 s_1 U_1 \ldots s_{j-1} U_{j-1} s_j U_j s_{j+1} \ldots s_k U_k \text{ starting from } C_0$$

is indistinguishable (to all processes) from the execution with history

$$E_j = U_0 s_1 U_1 \ldots s_{j-1} U_j U_{j-1} s_j s_{j+1} \ldots s_k U_k \text{ starting from } C_0.$$

Notice that the only difference between these two executions is that U_j and $U_{j-1} s_j$ are performed in the opposite order. In particular, configuration $C_0 E$ is identical to configuration $C_0 E_j$. Hence the executions with histories $E' = E s_{k+1} U_{k+1}$ and $E_j s_{k+1} U_{k+1}$ starting from C_0 are indistinguishable to all processes.

Now let E_{k+1} be the execution with history $U_0 s_1 U_1 \ldots U_{k-1} s_k U_{k+1} U_k s_{k+1}$ starting from C_0. This differs from the execution with history $E' = E s_{k+1} U_{k+1} = U_0 s_1 U_1 \ldots U_{k-1} s_k U_k s_{k+1} U_{k+1}$ in the order in which U_{k+1} and $U_k s_{k+1}$ are performed. By properties 2 and 3, these two executions are indistinguishable to p', since p' does not read from the single-writer registers of p or q during U_{k+1}. By properties 4 and 5, these two executions are indistinguishable to p and q, since neither reads the single-writer register of p' during $U_k s_{k+1}$. No other processes take any steps in $U_k s_{k+1} U_{k+1}$. Thus the executions with histories E_{k+1} and $Es_{k+1}U_{k+1}$ starting from C_0 are indistinguishable to all processes and the claim holds for $k + 1$. $\qquad\square$

Theorem 8.10 *In any wait-free implementation of an n-component single-writer snapshot object using only single-writer registers, the worst case number of steps to perform an Update is in* $\Omega(n)$.

Proof. Suppose there is such an implementation in which Updates take at most $n/12 - 1$ steps. By Lemmas 8.7 and 8.9, there is a sequence of executions in which each is a prefix of the next, no scanner has completed a Scan, and the total number of steps taken by scanners is strictly increasing. Hence, there is an infinite execution in which no process completes a Scan and at least one scanner takes an infinite number of steps. This contradicts the assumption that the implementation is wait-free. $\qquad\square$

This lower bound was originally proved by Amos Israeli and Assaf Shirazi in their paper, "The time complexity of updating snapshot memories," *Information Processing Letters*, 1998 [51]. Our presentation follows a more general result for multi-writer snapshot objects proved by Hagit Attiya, Faith Ellen, and Panagiota Fatourou in their paper, "The Complexity of Updating Snapshot Objects," *Journal of Parallel and Distributed Computing*, 2011 [12]. A similar technique was used by Hagit Attiya, Eshcar Hillel, and Alessia Milani in their paper, "Inherent Limitations on Disjoint-access Parallel Implementations of Transactional Memory," *Theory of Computer Systems*, 2011 [15], to prove lower bounds for transactional memory implementations.

8.3 A LOWER BOUND ON THE SOLO STEP COMPLEXITY OF WEAK TEST&SET USING TURÁN'S THEOREM

Some objects limit the number of processes that can access them. For example, a single-writer register can be accessed by only one process. More generally, the *contention* of an object is the maximum, over all reachable configurations, C, of the number of processes that are poised to perform nontrivial operations on the object in configuration C. We consider a synchronous shared memory model containing any types of objects with contention at most w. Processes can crash, but only at the beginning of an execution.

We prove a lower bound on the number of steps taken in a solo execution, i.e., when all but one of the processes crash before taking any steps. To do so, we consider executions which may involve multiple processes, but which are indistinguishable from solo executions to every nonfaulty process. For any set of processes Q, we define a *Q-independent execution* to be an execution in which only processes in Q take steps and each process in Q only accesses objects that have not been modified by any other processes (in Q). In particular, a solo execution by process p is a $\{p\}$-independent execution. Also, an empty execution is Q-solo for any set of processes Q. Furthermore, if all the steps of some process $p \in Q$ are removed from a Q-independent execution, then the resulting execution is $(Q - \{p\})$-independent and both executions are indistinguishable to all of the processes in $Q - \{p\}$.

We say that a problem is *solo-conflicting* if no algorithm that solves it has a Q-independent execution in which more than one process terminates. An example of such a problem is presented later in the section.

Lemma 8.12 shows how an adversary can construct Q-independent executions of algorithms that solve solo-conflicting problems. It uses the following result from graph theory, proved by Paul Turán in 1941, to find a set of processes that do not acquire any information about one another during a round.

Theorem 8.11   *Any graph $G = (V, E)$ has an independent set of size at least $\frac{|V|^2}{|V|+2|E|}$.*

Lemma 8.12   *Any n-process algorithm for a solo-conflicting problem using objects with contention at most w has a t-round Q_t-independent execution with $|Q_t| \geq n/(w + 2)^t$, for every non-negative integer $t < \log_{w+2} n$.*

Proof. The proof is by induction on t. When $t = 0$, the empty execution, α_0, is a 0 round Q_0-independent execution, where Q_0 is the set of all n processes. So, suppose that $t > 0$.

For the induction hypothesis, assume there is a $(t-1)$-round Q_{t-1}-independent execution, α_{t-1}, where $|Q_{t-1}| \geq n/(w + 2)^{t-1}$. Let C be the configuration at the end of α_{t-1}. Since the problem is solo-conflicting, at most one process in Q_{t-1} has terminated in C. For each process in Q_{t-1} which hasn't terminated, consider the operation it is poised to perform in C.

Let $G = (Q_{t-1}, E)$ be an undirected graph where $\{p_i, p_j\} \in E$ if and only if either

- p_i and p_j are both poised to perform a nontrivial operation on the same object in C or

- one of them is poised to access an object in C that was modified by the other process during α_{t-1}.

For each process poised to perform a nontrivial operation, there are at most $w - 1$ other processes poised to perform a nontrivial operation on the same object, since the contention of every object is at most w. This counts each edge of the first type twice, once for each of its end points. Thus, there are at most $|Q_{t-1}|(w - 1)/2$ such edges.

Since α_{t-1} is a Q_{t-1}-independent execution, each object is modified by at most one process during α_{t-1}. In C, each of the processes in Q_{t-1} is poised to access at most one of these objects. Thus, there are most $|Q_{t-1}|$ edges of the second type.

Hence, $|E| \leq |Q_{t-1}|(w - 1)/2 + |Q_{t-1}| = |Q_{t-1}|(w + 1)/2$. By Turán's Theorem, there is an independent set Q_t in G such that

$$|Q_t| \geq \frac{|Q_{t-1}|^2}{|Q_{t-1}| + 2|E|} \geq \frac{|Q_{t-1}|^2}{|Q_{t-1}| + |Q_{t-1}|(w + 1)} = \frac{|Q_{t-1}|}{w + 2} \geq \frac{n}{(w + 2)^t}.$$

Let α'_t be the $t - 1$ round execution obtained from α_{t-1} by removing all steps of all processes in $Q_{t-1} - Q_t$. Let α_t be an execution obtained by extending α'_t with the next step of each process in Q_t, where, in the last round, all trivial operations precede all nontrivial operations.

Since $|Q_t| > 1$ and at most one process in $Q_{t-1} \supseteq Q_t$ has terminated in configuration C, it follows that α_t has one more round than α'_t.

By the induction hypothesis, each access in α'_t is to an object that has not been modified by any other process. By construction, each access in the last round of α_t has this property. Thus α_t is a t-round Q_t-independent execution. $\qquad\square$

A *weak test&set* object supports a single operation, weak test&set, which can either *succeed* or *fail*. In every execution, at most one weak test&set operation on each object succeeds. A weak test&set operation must succeed if no other weak test&set operations on the same object begin until after it has completed. In particular, in a solo execution, a process that terminates must succeed.

The implementation of a weak test&set object is an example of a solo-conflicting problem: Any process that terminates in a Q-independent execution must succeed, since it is indistinguishable from a solo execution to that process. Hence, at most one process terminates in any Q-independent execution.

The following result is a simple corollary of Lemma 8.12.

Theorem 8.13   *Any implementation of an n-process weak test&set object from objects with contention at most w has a solo execution of a* weak test&set *operation with $\Omega(\frac{\log n}{\log(w+2)})$ steps.*

Proof. Consider any implementation of a weak test&set object that uses only objects with contention at most w. Let $t = \lceil \log_{w+2} n \rceil - 1$. By Lemma 8.12, this implementation has a t-round Q_t-independent execution, where $|Q_t| \geq n/(w+2)^t \geq 2$. Hence, there is a solo execution of a weak test&set operation that takes at least $t \in \Omega(\frac{\log n}{\log(w+2)})$ steps. $\qquad\square$

A proof of Turán's Theorem 8.11 can be found in *Proofs from THE BOOK*, 1998 [4]. A somewhat weaker version of Theorem 8.13 appears in Hagit Attiya, Faith Ellen Fich, and Yaniv Kaplan, "Lower Bounds for Adaptive Collect and Related Objects," *PODC,* 2004 [13]. For $w > 1$, they also give a weak test&set implementation with $O(\log n/\log w)$ step complexity in asynchronous shared memory using $O(n/w)$ registers with contention at most w. Thus, the step complexity and solo-step complexity of implementing weak test&set are the same to within a constant factor and they do not improve when more powerful base objects are available.

8.4   ANONYMOUS CONFLICT DETECTORS

In the m-valued conflict detector problem, each process p_i has an input value $v_i \in \{1, \ldots, m\}$ and, if nonfaulty, must output a Boolean value b_i that satisfies the following properties:

- If all the inputs are the same, all the outputs are false.

- If $v_i \neq v_j$, then at least one of b_i and b_j is true.

Algorithms that solve this problem are components of many randomized consensus algorithms. (See, for example, the paper, "A Modular Approach to Shared-Memory Consensus, with Applications to the Probabilistic-Write Model," by James Aspnes [8], which appeared in *PODC*, 2010.)

The model we consider is asynchronous shared memory, where processes are anonymous and only communicate using registers.

Theorem 8.14 *Any wait-free algorithm that solves the m-valued conflict detector problem for n anonymous processes has* $\Omega(\min(n, \log m / \log \log m))$ *step complexity.*

Consider any wait-free algorithm for the problem. We will prove that it has a solo execution that contains $\Omega(\min(n, \log m / \log \log m))$ steps.

For each $v \in \{1, \ldots, m\}$ and each positive integer k, let $E_k(v)$ denote the solo execution by a process with input v, if it has length at most k, or the first k steps of that execution, if it does not terminate within k steps.

Suppose that there is a subset $V_k \subseteq \{1, \ldots, m\}$ of size at least 2 such that, for all distinct $v, w \in V_k$ and all $1 \leq i \leq k$, if p reads register R in step i of $E_k(v)$ and p does not write to R before step i of $E_k(v)$, then q does not write to R before step i of $E_k(w)$. We show that an adversary can construct an execution E' that is indistinguishable from $E_k(v)$ to a process p performing $E_k(v)$ and indistinguishable from $E_k(w)$ to another process q, performing $E_k(w)$ for any distinct $v, w \in V_k$.

Starting with $E_k(v)$ performed by process p, we construct an execution $E_k^*(v)$ that also includes steps by at most $k - 1$ clones of p. Specifically, $E_k^*(v)$ consists of a sequence of rounds in which p and some of its clones each takes one step. In round i, process p performs its i'th step. For each step of $E_k(v)$ in which p reads from a register, R, to which it has previously written, there is a clone of p which is scheduled to perform the same step as p in every round up to, but not including p's last write to R prior to the read. This clone delays its next step until immediately before the read and then takes no further steps. Note that the last step of this clone rewrites the value that is already in R, so $E_k(v)$ and $E_k^*(v)$ are indistinguishable to p.

We interleave $E_k^*(v)$ and $E_k^*(w)$ to create the desired execution E'. Specifically, E' consists of a sequence of rounds in which p, q, and their clones each take at most one step. If p writes to register R in step i of $E_k(v)$, then p and all of its clones that take steps in round i of $E_k^*(v)$ write to R at the end of round i of E'. If p reads register R in step i of $E_k(v)$, but has written to R earlier, then there is a clone of p whose last step in $E_k^*(v)$ is a write to R immediately before step i by process p. In this case, this clone writes to R in the middle of round i of E', immediately followed by the reads of R by p and those of its clones that read R in round i of $E_k^*(v)$. Thus they all read the same value that they read in round i of $E_k^*(v)$. Finally, if p reads from register R in step i of $E_k(v)$ and does not write to R before step i of $E_k(v)$, then p and all of its clones that take steps in round i of $E_k^*(v)$ read R at the beginning of round i of E'. Note that, since $v, w \in V_k$, it follows that q does not write to R before step i of $E_k(w)$, nor does any

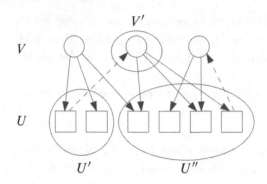

Figure 8.3: The construction in the proof of Lemma 8.15.

of its clones. Therefore, p and its clones read the initial value of R in round i of E', just as they do in $E_k^*(v)$. The steps of process q and its clones in round i of E' are defined analogously.

If $k \leq n/2$, then there are at most n processes taking steps in E'. Hence execution E' can be constructed.

Note that $E_k(v)$ and E' are indistinguishable to p. Since $E_k(v)$ is a solo execution, if p returns during $E_k(v)$, it returns false, since it is possible that all the inputs are the same. Thus p also returns false in E'. Similarly, if q returns during $E_k(w)$, it also returns false in E'. Since p and q cannot both return false in E', it follows that either p or q must perform more than k steps.

To prove our lower bound, it remains to prove the existence of the set V_k, for some $k \in \Omega(\log m/\log\log m)$. This is an easy consequence of the following result.

Lemma 8.15   *For all $k \geq 1$, there is a subset $V_k \subseteq \{1, \ldots, m\}$ of size at least $m/(e + 2)^{k-1}(k - 1)!$ such that, for all distinct $v, w \in V_k$ and all $1 \leq i \leq k$, if p reads register R in step i of $E_k(v)$ and does not write to R before step i of $E_k(v)$, then q does not write to R before step i of $E_k(w)$.*

Proof. The proof is by induction on k. The claim is vacuously true for $V_1 = \{1, \ldots, m\}$. So, suppose the claim is true for some $k \geq 1$.

Construct a directed bipartite graph with vertex set $V_k \times U$, where $U = \cup\{U_k(v) \mid v \in V_k\}$ and $U_k(v)$ is the set of all registers written to in $E_k(v)$. For each $v \in V_k$, there is an edge from v to each register in $U_k(v)$ and, if step $k + 1$ of $E_{k+1}(v)$ is the read of a register $R \in U - U_k(v)$, there is also an edge from R to v. Note that, in this graph, each $v \in V_k$ has outdegree at most k and indegree at most 1. Also, there are no cycles of length 2.

Randomly partition U into two parts, U' and U'', where each register $R \in U$ is in U' independently with probability $1/(k + 1)$. Let $V' = \{v \in V_k \mid$ there is no edge from v to U' and no edge from U'' to $v\}$. This is illustrated in Figure 8.3.

For each $v \in V_k$, if there is an edge from R to v in the graph, then $\mathrm{Prob}\,[R \notin U''] = 1/(k + 1)$. Also, $|U_k(v)| \leq k$ and, for each $R \in U_k(v)$, $\mathrm{Prob}\,[R \notin U'] = 1 - 1/(k + 1)$. Therefore,

$$\text{Prob}\left[v \in V'\right] \geq \frac{1}{k+1}\left(1 - \frac{1}{k+1}\right)^k = \frac{1}{k}\left(1 - \frac{1}{k+1}\right)^{k+1} > 1/(e+2)k.$$

Thus the expected size of V' is at least $|V_k|/(e+2)k \geq m/(e+2)^k k!$. Hence, there exist a partition of U into U' and U'' and a subset $V_{k+1} \subseteq V_k$ of size at least $m/(e+2)^k k!$ such that each vertex $v \in V_{k+1}$ has no edge to any vertex in U' and no edge from any vertex in U''.

Consider distinct $v, w \in V_{k+1} \subseteq V_k$. The first k steps of $E_k(v)$ and $E_{k+1}(v)$ are the same and the first k steps of $E_k(w)$ and $E_{k+1}(w)$ are the same. Hence, if p reads register R in step i of $E_{k+1}(v)$ and does not write to R before step i of $E_{k+1}(v)$, where $1 \leq i \leq k$, then q does not write to R before step i of $E_{k+1}(w)$. If p reads register R in step $k+1$ of $E_{k+1}(v)$ and does not write to R before step $k+1$ of $E_{k+1}(v)$, there is an edge from R to v in the graph. Hence, by definition of V_{k+1}, $R \notin U''$, so $R \in U'$ and there is no edge from w to R. This means that q does not write to R during $E_k(w)$ and, hence, before step $k+1$ of $E_{k+1}(w)$. Thus the claim is true for $k+1$.   □

The proofs of Lemma 8.15 and Theorem 8.14 are due to James Aspnes, Faith Ellen, and Nati Linial. A different proof of Theorem 8.14 appears in "Tight Bounds for Adopt-Commit Objects," by James Aspnes and Faith Ellen, *Theory of Computing Systems*, 2013 [10]. That paper gives two algorithms for the m-valued conflict detector problem, one with $O(n)$ step complexity and another with $O(\log m / \log \log m)$ step complexity. Thus, the lower bound is asymptotically tight. It also presents nearly matching upper and lower bounds for this problem without the restriction of anonymity.

8.5   YAO'S PRINCIPLE

Given any deterministic algorithm D, an adversary can produce an execution by specifying the inputs each process receives and the order in which the processes take steps.

Consider any complexity measure that assigns a cost $c(D,\sigma)$ to an execution produced by an adversary σ applied to a deterministic algorithm D. Then the *worst case complexity* of D for a set of adversaries S is

$$\max_{\sigma \in S} c(D, \sigma).$$

For any probability distribution over a set of adversaries S, the *average case complexity* of a deterministic algorithm D is

$$\mathop{\mathrm{E}}_{\sigma \in S} [c(D, \sigma)].$$

This is also called the *distributional complexity* of the algorithm D. The *distributional complexity of a problem* is the distributional complexity of the best algorithm that solves the problem, i.e.,

$$\min_D \mathop{\mathrm{E}}_{\sigma \in S} [c(D, \sigma)],$$

where the minimum is taken over all deterministic algorithms D that solve the problem.

For a randomized algorithm, an adversary defines a set of executions, rather than a single execution. The execution that results depends on the outcomes of the coin tosses that each process performs. Thus, a randomized algorithm A can be viewed as a probability distribution over deterministic algorithms $A[\rho]$, where ρ denotes the sequences of coin toss outcomes, one for each process. For example, if each process performs at most r coin tosses, then ρ is distributed uniformly over $(\{0, 1\}^r)^n$.

Given an adversary σ, the *expected cost* of a randomized algorithm A is

$$\operatorname*{E}_{\rho} [c(A[\rho], \sigma)]$$

and its *worst case expected complexity* for a set of adversaries S is

$$\max_{\sigma \in S} \operatorname*{E}_{\rho} [c(A[\rho], \sigma)].$$

The *worst case expected complexity of a problem* for a set of adversaries S is the worst case expected complexity of the best algorithm that solves it, i.e.,

$$\min_{A} \max_{\sigma \in S} \operatorname*{E}_{\rho} [c(A[\rho], \sigma)],$$

where the minimum is taken over all randomized algorithms A that solve the problem.

We restrict attention to *oblivious adversaries*, which choose the inputs each process receives and the order in which processes take steps before the execution begins. Therefore, they do not depend on the outcomes of the coin tosses performed by the processes during the execution of the algorithm. Note that lower bounds proved for oblivious adversaries also apply for more powerful adversaries.

Yao's principle says that the worst case expected complexity of a problem for a set of oblivious adversaries S is bounded below by its distributional complexity, for any probability distribution over S.

Lemma 8.16   For any probability distribution over a set of oblivious adversaries S, $\min_{A} \max_{\sigma \in S} \operatorname*{E}_{\rho} [c(A[\rho], \sigma)] \geq \min_{D} \operatorname*{E}_{\sigma \in S} [c(D, \sigma)]$, where A is chosen from a set of randomized algorithms, D is chosen from the set of all deterministic algorithms obtained from randomized algorithms in this set by fixing the outcomes of their coin tosses, and ρ is chosen from the possible sequences of coin toss outcomes.

Proof. Consider any randomized algorithm A from the set. Then

$$\max_{\sigma \in S} \operatorname*{E}_{\rho} [c(A[\rho], \sigma)] \geq \operatorname*{E}_{\sigma \in S} \operatorname*{E}_{\rho} [c(A[\rho], \sigma)] = \operatorname*{E}_{\rho} \operatorname*{E}_{\sigma \in S} [c(A[\rho], \sigma)] \geq \min_{\rho} \operatorname*{E}_{\sigma \in S} [c(A[\rho], \sigma)].$$

The order of the expectations can be interchanged because all the adversaries are oblivious. Since $A[\rho]$ is a deterministic algorithm for each choice of ρ,

$$\max_{\sigma \in S} \mathop{\mathrm{E}}_{\rho} [c(A[\rho], \sigma)] \geq \min_{\rho} \mathop{\mathrm{E}}_{\sigma \in S} [c(A[\rho], \sigma)] \geq \min_{D} \mathop{\mathrm{E}}_{\sigma \in S} [c(D, \sigma)].$$

Finally, since A is an arbitrary randomized algorithm from the set,

$$\min_{A} \max_{\sigma \in S} \mathop{\mathrm{E}}_{\rho} [c(A[\rho], \sigma)] \geq \min_{D} \mathop{\mathrm{E}}_{\sigma \in S} [c(D, \sigma)].$$

$\square$

Thus, a lower bound on the worst case expected complexity of a problem against a set of oblivious adversaries, S, can be obtained by (carefully) choosing a probability distribution over S and deriving a lower bound on the distributional complexity of the problem under that distribution.

Yao's principle was first presented for the decision tree model in Andrew Yao's paper "Probabilistic Computations: Toward a Unified Measure of Complexity," *FOCS,* 1977 [66]. It is possible to obtain versions of Yao's principle for distributed algorithms against more general adversaries, but care is needed. See, for example, the papers "New Lower Bound Techniques for Distributed Leader Finding and Other Problems on Rings of Processors," by Hans Bodlaender, which appeared in *Theoretical Computer Science,* 1991 [25], "Average and Randomized Complexity of Distributed Problems," by Nechama Allenberg-Navony, Alon Itai, and Shlomo Moran, which appeared in *SIAM Journal on Computing,* 1996 [5], and "A Tight RMR Lower Bound for Randomized Mutual Exclusion," by George Giakkoupis and Philipp Woelfel, which appeared in *STOC,* 2012 [44].

8.6 EXPECTED STEP COMPLEXITY OF RANDOMIZED IMPLEMENTATIONS OF A MAX REGISTER

A *max register* allows processes to read the largest value ever written to the register, rather than the last value written there. Max registers were used in efficient implementations of several other objects, including counters and atomic snapshots, which are accessed a bounded number of times. Formally, a max register supports two operations,

- ReadMax, which returns the current value of the object, and

- WriteMax(v), which sets the value of the object to be the maximum of its current value and v.

Consider the asynchronous shared memory model, where processes communicate using registers. We use Yao's principle (Lemma 8.16) to derive a lower bound for the expected step complexity of randomized implementations of a max register against oblivious adversaries. The input to an implementation is the sequence of operations each process performs.

We begin by considering a set of adversaries in which process p_0 is allocated no steps and, for $i = 1, \ldots, n-1$, process p_i performs a single WriteMax(i) operation and is allocated at most w steps. For $k_1, \ldots, k_{n-2} \in \{0, \ldots, w-1\}$ and $i \in \{1, \ldots, n-1\}$, let $\sigma'(k_1, \ldots, k_{n-2}, 0)$ denote the adversary that allocates no steps to any process and let $\sigma'(k_1, \ldots, k_{n-2}, i)$ denote the adversary that allocates k_j steps to process p_j, for $j = 1, \ldots, i-1$, followed by w steps to process i, followed by one more step to process p_j for $j = i-1, \ldots, 1$. A process does nothing when it is allocated a step after it has finished its operation.

Let D be an arbitrary deterministic implementation of a max register such that WriteMax has worst case step complexity w. Fix $k_1, \ldots, k_{n-2} \in \{0, \ldots, w-1\}$ and consider the sequence of steps α_i' that occur when D is performed starting from its initial configuration C_0 using the adversary $\sigma'(k_1, \ldots, k_{n-2}, i)$, for $i = 0, \ldots, n-1$. Then

$$
\begin{aligned}
\alpha_0' &= \\
\alpha_1' &= \beta_1 \\
\alpha_2' &= \beta_1' \beta_2 \delta_1 \\
\alpha_3' &= \beta_1' \beta_2' \beta_3 \delta_2 \delta_1,
\end{aligned}
$$

$$\vdots$$

$$\alpha_i' = \beta_1' \beta_2' \cdots \beta_{i-1}' \beta_i \delta_{i-1} \cdots \delta_2 \delta_1,$$

$$\vdots$$

$$\text{and } \alpha_{n-1}' = \beta_1' \beta_2' \cdots \beta_{n-2}' \beta_{n-1} \delta_{n-1} \cdots \delta_2 \delta_1.$$

Here β_i is a sequence of at most w consecutive steps by process p_i in which it completes WriteMax(i). If β_i consists of at most k_i steps, then $\beta_i' = \beta_i$ and δ_i is empty. Otherwise, β_i' is the prefix of β_i consisting of k_i steps and δ_i consists of the next step by process p_i. In general, β_i depends on the values of $k_1, \ldots, k_{i-1}$ and β_i' and δ_i also depend on the value of k_i, but none of them depend on the values of $k_{j+1}, \ldots, k_{n-2}$. Note that, if δ_i is a read, it might return different values when $\alpha_{i+1}', \ldots, \alpha_{n-1}'$ are performed starting from C_0.

Let $v_R(i)$ denote the value of register R in configuration $C_0 \alpha_i'$. In particular, $v_R(0)$ is the initial value of register R and, if δ_i is a write to R, then $v_R(i+1) = \cdots = v_R(n-1)$. Let $V_R = \#\{v_R(i) \mid 0 \le i \le n-1\}$ denote the number of different values in register R at the end of these n executions. If none of $\beta_1, \ldots, \beta_{n-1}$ write to R, then $V_R = 1$.

Suppose that $v_R(i) \notin \{v_R(0), \ldots, v_R(i-1)\}$. Then $\delta_1, \ldots, \delta_{i-2}$ are not writes to R. One possibility is that δ_{i-1} is a write to R. Another possibility is that β_i contains a write to R. Otherwise, $\beta_1' \cdots \beta_{i-1}'$ contains a write to R, since $v_R(i) \ne v_R(0)$. In this case, let $f(i) = \max\{j \in \{1, \ldots, i-1\} \mid \beta_j' \text{ contains a write to } R\}$. Then $v_R(i)$ is the value written by the last write to R in $\beta_{f(i)}'$ and, for $f(i) \le j \le i-1$, $v_R(i) \ne v_R(j)$ implies that β_j contains a write to R after $\beta_j' \delta_j$. For example, suppose R is initially 0, suppose β_1' writes the value 10 to R, δ_1 is not a write to R, and β_1 writes the value 20 to R after δ_1, suppose β_2 writes the value 30 to R, but does not write to R during $\beta_2'\delta_2$, and suppose β_3 contain no writes to R. Then $v_R(0) = 0$, $v_R(1) = 20$, $v_R(2) = 30$, $v_R(3) = 10$, and $f(3) = 1$.

If $V_R > d$, then there exist process indices $0 < i_1 < \cdots < i_d \leq n - 1$ such that $v_R(i_u) \notin \{v_R(0), \ldots, v_R(i_u - 1)\}$, for $1 \leq u \leq d$. Since $v_R(i_d) \neq v_R(i_d - 1)$, it follows that $\delta_1, \delta_2, \ldots, \delta_{i_d-2}$ are not writes to R. Furthermore, for $1 \leq u \leq d - 1$, if β_{i_u} does not contain a write to R, then $\beta_{f(i_u)}$ contains a write to R. Thus, at least $(d-2)/2 = d/2 - 1$ of the sequences of steps $\beta_1, \beta_2, \ldots, \beta_{i_d-2}$ contain a write to R.

The following lemma shows it is unlikely that a register can contain many different values at the ends of the different sequences of steps $\alpha_0', \ldots, \alpha_{n-1}'$. The idea is that, if a process p_i writes to the register when it is allocated w steps, then, with probability at least $1/w$, process p_i will cover the register after the adversary first allocates steps to p_i and the register will contain the same value at the ends of $\alpha_{i+1}', \ldots, \alpha_{n-1}'$.

Lemma 8.17 *For every register R, if $k_1, \ldots, k_{n-2}$ are chosen independently and uniformly from $\{0, \ldots, w-1\}$, then, for any positive integer $d \leq n$, $\mathrm{Prob}\,[V_R > d] \leq (1 - 1/w)^{d/2-1}$.*

Proof. We prove by backwards induction on m that, for all $0 \leq m \leq n - 2$, for all $0 \leq c \leq n - m - 2$, and for all choices of $k_1, \ldots, k_m \in \{0, \ldots, w-1\}$, if $k_{m+1}, \ldots, k_{n-2}$ are chosen independently and uniformly from $\{0, \ldots, w-1\}$, then

$$\mathrm{Prob}\left[\begin{array}{l} \text{for some } i \in \{0, \ldots, n-1\}, \text{ none of } \delta_1, \ldots, \delta_i \\ \text{are writes to } R \text{ and at least } c \text{ of the sequences} \\ \beta_{m+1}, \ldots, \beta_i \text{ contain a write to } R \end{array}\right] \leq (1 - 1/w)^c.$$

If $c = 0$, then choosing $i = 0$ vacuously satisfies the condition, so the probability is $1 = (1 - 1/w)^c$. In particular, if $m = n - 2$, then $c = 0$, so the claim is true.

Now let $m < n - 2$ and suppose the claim holds for $m + 1$. Fix $k_1, \ldots, k_m \in \{0, \ldots, w-1\}$. This defines $\beta_1, \ldots, \beta_{m+1}$ and $\delta_1, \ldots, \delta_m$. Let $0 < c \leq n - m - 2$.

First, suppose that β_{m+1} does not contain a write to R. Then for each choice of $k_{m+1} \in \{0, \ldots, w-1\}$, δ_{m+1} is not a write to R and, by the induction hypothesis, if $k_{m+2}, \ldots, k_{n-2}$ are chosen independently and uniformly from $\{0, \ldots, w-1\}$, then

$$\mathrm{Prob}\left[\begin{array}{l} \text{for some } i \in \{0, \ldots, n-1\}, \text{ none of } \delta_1, \ldots, \delta_i \\ \text{are writes to } R \text{ and at least } c \text{ of the sequences} \\ \beta_{m+2}, \ldots, \beta_i \text{ contain a write to } R \end{array}\right] \leq (1 - 1/w)^c.$$

Hence, if $k_{m+1}, \ldots, k_{n-2}$ are chosen independently and uniformly from $\{0, \ldots, w-1\}$, then the claim also holds for m.

Now suppose that β_{m+1} does contain a write to R. Let

$$K = \{k \in \{0, \ldots, w-1\} \mid \delta_{m+1} \text{ is a write to } R \text{ when } k_{m+1} = k\}.$$

Since β_{m+1} depends on the choices of $k_1, \ldots, k_m$, so does K. If k_{m+1} is chosen uniformly from $\{0, \ldots, w-1\}$, then $\mathrm{Prob}\,[k_{m+1} \in K] \geq 1/w$. Since $c > 0$, if at least c of the sequences

$\beta_{m+1}, \ldots, \beta_i$ contain a write to R, then $i \geq m + 1$. Hence, for each $k \in K$, δ_{m+1} is a write to R when $k_{m+1} = k$, so

$$\text{Prob} \left[\begin{array}{c} \text{for some } i \in \{0, \ldots, n-1\}, \text{ none of } \delta_1, \ldots, \delta_i \\ \text{are writes to } R \text{ and at least } c \text{ of the sequences} \\ \beta_{m+1}, \ldots, \beta_i \text{ contain a write to } R \end{array} \middle| k_{m+1} = k \right] = 0.$$

Fix $k_{m+1} = k \notin K$. Recall that $k_1, \ldots, k_m$ have already been fixed. If $k_{m+2}, \ldots, k_{n-2}$ are chosen independently and uniformly from $\{0, \ldots, w - 1\}$, then, by the induction hypothesis,

$$\text{Prob} \left[\begin{array}{c} \text{for some } i \in \{0, \ldots, n-1\}, \text{ none of } \delta_1, \ldots, \delta_i \\ \text{are writes to } R \text{ and at least } c - 1 \text{ of the sequences} \\ \beta_{m+2}, \ldots, \beta_i \text{ contain a write to } R \end{array} \right] \leq (1 - 1/w)^{c-1}.$$

Since β_{m+1} does contain a write to R, at least c of the sequences $\beta_{m+1}, \ldots, \beta_i$ contain a write to R if and only if at least $c - 1$ of the sequences $\beta_{m+2}, \ldots, \beta_i$ contain a write to R. Thus

$$\text{Prob} \left[\begin{array}{c} \text{for some } i \in \{0, \ldots, n-1\}, \text{ none of } \delta_1, \ldots, \delta_i \\ \text{are writes to } R \text{ and at least } c \text{ of the sequences} \\ \beta_{m+1}, \ldots, \beta_i \text{ contain a write to } R \end{array} \right] \leq (1 - 1/w)^{c-1}.$$

Hence, if k_{m+1} is also chosen independently and uniformly from $\{0, \ldots, w - 1\}$, then

$$\text{Prob} \left[\begin{array}{c} \text{for some } i \in \{0, \ldots, n-1\}, \text{ none of } \delta_1, \ldots, \delta_i \\ \text{are writes to } R \text{ and at least } c \text{ of the sequences} \\ \beta_{m+1}, \ldots, \beta_i \text{ contain a write to } R \end{array} \middle| k_{m+1} = k \right] \leq (1 - 1/w)^{c-1}.$$

It follows that, when $k_{m+1}, k_{m+2}, \ldots, k_{n-2}$ are chosen independently and uniformly from $\{0, \ldots, w - 1\}$,

$$\text{Prob}\left[\begin{array}{l}\text{for some } i \in \{0,\ldots,n-1\}, \text{ none of } \delta_1,\ldots,\delta_i \\ \text{are writes to } R \text{ and at least } c \text{ of the sequences} \\ \beta_{m+1},\ldots,\beta_i \text{ contain a write to } R\end{array}\right]$$

$$= \sum_{k=0}^{w-1} \text{Prob}\left[\begin{array}{l}\text{for some } i \in \{0,\ldots,n-1\}, \text{ none of} \\ \delta_1,\ldots,\delta_i \text{ are writes to } R \text{ and at least} \\ c \text{ of the sequences } \beta_{m+1},\ldots,\beta_i \\ \text{contain a write to } R\end{array}\middle| k_{m+1}=k\right] \cdot \text{Prob}\left[k_{m+1}=k\right]$$

$$= \sum_{k \notin K} \text{Prob}\left[\begin{array}{l}\text{for some } i \in \{0,\ldots,n-1\}, \text{ none of} \\ \delta_1,\ldots,\delta_i \text{ are writes to } R \text{ and at least} \\ c \text{ of the sequences } \beta_{m+1},\ldots,\beta_i \\ \text{contain a write to } R\end{array}\middle| k_{m+1}=k\right] \cdot \text{Prob}\left[k_{m+1}=k\right]$$

$$\leq \sum_{k \notin K} (1-1/w)^{c-1} \text{Prob}\left[k_{m+1}=k\right]$$
$$= (1-1/w)^{c-1} \text{Prob}\left[k_{m+1} \notin K\right]$$
$$\leq (1-1/w)^{c}.$$

This proves the claim for m.

By induction, when $m = 0$ and $c = d/2 - 1$, if $k_1,\ldots,k_{n-2}$ are chosen independently and uniformly from $\{0,\ldots,w-1\}$, then

$$\text{Prob}\left[V_R > d\right] \leq \left[\begin{array}{l}\text{for some } i \in \{0,\ldots,n-1\}, \text{ none of } \delta_1,\ldots,\delta_i \\ \text{are writes to } R \text{ and at least } d/2-1 \text{ of the} \\ \text{sequences } \beta_1,\ldots,\beta_i \text{ contain a write to } R\end{array}\right] \leq (1-1/w)^{d/2-1}.$$

$\square$

For each oblivious adversary $\sigma'(k_1,\ldots,k_{n-2},i)$, with $k_1,\ldots,k_{n-2} \in \{0,\ldots,w-1\}$ and $i \in \{0,\ldots,n-1\}$, let $\sigma(k_1,\ldots,k_{n-2},i) = \sigma'(k_1,\ldots,k_{n-2},i)\rho$ be the oblivious adversary that allocates steps to a single ReadMax operation by process p_0 following the steps it allocates to other processes performing WriteMax operations. When the deterministic implementation D is performed starting from its initial configuration C_0 using the adversary $\sigma(k_1,\ldots,k_{n-2},i)$, an instance of WriteMax(i) is completed (by the steps of β_i) and no instances of WriteMax(i') are invoked, for $0 < i < i' \leq n-1$, so p_0 must return i. If $i = 0$, then no instance of WriteMax are invoked, so p_0 must return 0.

For each choice of $k_1,\ldots,k_{n-2}$, the executions of ReadMax starting from C_0 using the adversaries $\sigma(k_1,\ldots,k_{n-2},0),\ldots,\sigma(k_1,\ldots,k_{n-2},n-1)$ can be described by a decision tree. Each node in the tree represents a read by p_0 from some register R, and its children represent the next step of p_0, depending on the value read from R. If $V_R \leq d$, then the branching factor at each node of this tree is at most d and, for any integer $r \geq 0$, the decision tree has at most d^r leaves at depth r or less. Since p_0 has n different return values, the tree has at least n leaves, of which at least $n - d^r$ are at depth greater than r, and, hence, the average depth of the leaves in this tree is greater than $r(n - d^r)/n$. Let $r = \log_d (n/2)$. Then the average step complexity of ReadMax for an adversary chosen uniformly from $\{\sigma(k_1, \ldots, k_{n-2}, 0), \ldots, \sigma(k_1, \ldots, k_{n-2}, n - 1)\})$ is greater than $r(n - d^r)/n = r/2$. From Lemma 8.17,

$$\text{Prob}\,[V_R > d] \leq (1 - 1/w)^{d/2-1} \leq e^{-(d/2-1)/w},$$

so

$$\text{Prob}\,[V_R \leq d] \geq 1 - e^{-(d/2-1)/w}.$$

It follows that the average step complexity of ReadMax for an adversary chosen uniformly from $\{\sigma(k_1, \ldots, k_{n-2}, i) \mid k_1, \ldots, k_{n-2} \in \{0, \ldots, w - 1\}, i \in \{0, \ldots, n - 1\}\}$ is greater than

$$\text{Prob}\,[V_R > d] \cdot 0 + \text{Prob}\,[V_R \leq d] \cdot r/2 \geq \left(1 - e^{-(d/2-1)/w}\right) \log_d (n/2)/2.$$

Setting $d = 2 + 2w \ln n$ gives a lower bound of $(1 - 1/n) \log(n/2)/2 \log(2 + 2w \ln n) \in \Omega((\log n)/\log(w \log n))$.

Among all deterministic implementations such that WriteMax has worst case step complexity at most w, the implementation D was chosen arbitrarily. Thus, this is a lower bound on the distributional step complexity of ReadMax and, hence, by Yao's principle, on the worst case expected step complexity of ReadMax, for all randomized implementations such that WriteMax has worst case step complexity at most w. This holds against the set of adversaries

$$\{\sigma(k_1, \ldots, k_{n-2}, i) \mid k_1, \ldots, k_{n-2} \in \{0, \ldots, w - 1\}, i \in \{0, \ldots, n - 1\}\}$$

and, more generally, against the set of all oblivious adversaries.

Theorem 8.18   *For any randomized implementation of a max register that can be accessed by n processes and for which the worst case step complexity of* WriteMax *is at most w, the worst case expected step complexity of* ReadMax *against an oblivious adversary is in $\Omega((\log n)/\log(w \log n))$.*

When w is polylogarithmic in n, the worst case expected step complexity of ReadMax is in $\Omega(\log n/\log \log n)$. When w is polynomial in n, the worst case expected step complexity of ReadMax is in $\Omega(1)$.

The $\Omega((\log n)/\log(w \log n))$ lower bound on the worst case expected step complexity of ReadMax can be extended to randomized implementations of a max register for which the worst case expected step complexity of WriteMax is at most w, even when a ReadMax operation can return an incorrect result with low probability. This result is from the paper "Polylogarithmic concurrent data structures from monotone circuits," by James Aspnes, Hagit Attiya, and Keren Censor-Hillel, *Journal of the ACM*, 2012 [9]. This paper also contains a deterministic implementation of a max register in which the worst case step complexities of ReadMax and WriteMax are both in $O(\log n)$, when at most n operations are performed, and a randomized implementation of a max register in which the worst case step complexity of WriteMax is in $O(n^3)$, the worst case step complexity of ReadMax is in $O(1)$, and ReadMax returns an incorrect result with probability $O(1/n)$.

CHAPTER 9

Reductions and Simulations

Reductions and simulations are useful for converting impossibility results from one problem to another or from one model to another. A *reduction* shows how to solve a problem P in a model M, assuming the existence of a solution to another problem P' in a (possibly different) model M'. From this, it follows that if P cannot be solved in M, then P' cannot be solved in M'. A *simulation* shows how the processes of a model M can perform the steps of (a class of) algorithms in another model M'. This implies that if there is no solution to a problem P in model M, there is no solution to P in model M'.

We begin with a very simple example of a reduction. Suppose M is a model with $n = cn'$ processes and M' is a model with n' processes that communicate with one another in the same way. If $k \geq ck'$, then k-set consensus in M can be reduced to k'-set consensus in M'. The idea is that the n processes in M are partitioned into c groups of n' processes each. Given an instance of k-set consensus, each group separately solves k'-set consensus, where each processes uses its input from the instance of k-set consensus as its input for k'-set consensus and uses its output from k'-set consensus as its output for the instance of k-set consensus. The processes in each group output at most k' different values. Hence, the total number of different output values is at most $ck' \leq k$, so k-agreement is satisfied. Validity and termination follow from the validity and termination of k'-set consensus. Thus, if there is no wait-free algorithm for k-set consensus in M, there is no wait-free algorithm for k'-set consensus in M'.

An *implementation* of an object $\mathcal{O}$ in a shared memory model M is an example of a simulation. It consists of a representation of the object using base objects of M and algorithms for each process to simulate the operations supported by object $\mathcal{O}$. The *execution interval* of an operation in an execution of this implementation is the portion of the execution from when the operation begins until the operation ends. For example, see Section 3.2.

An execution of an implementation of $\mathcal{O}$ is *admissible* if each process performs a (possibly empty) sequence of operations on $\mathcal{O}$ and begins an operation only when the previous operation in its sequence has completed. This means that no two operations on $\mathcal{O}$ by the same process have overlapping execution intervals. An admissible execution is *sequential* if no two operations on $\mathcal{O}$ have overlapping execution intervals.

An implementation of object $\mathcal{O}$ is *linearizable* if, for every admissible execution E, there is a sequential execution E' in which

- each process performs the same sequence of operations on $\mathcal{O}$ in E' as in E, except possibly the last operation in E, if it is not completed,

- the response returned by each operation on $\mathcal{O}$ in E is the same as in E', and

- every pair of operations on $\mathcal{O}$ whose execution intervals do not overlap in E have the same relative order in E'.

An important property of linearizable implementations is that they compose.

Lemma 9.1 *If there is a linearizable implementation of an object $\mathcal{O}$ in M' using a set B of base objects and there is a linearizable implementation in M of all the objects in B, then there is also a linearizable implementation of $\mathcal{O}$ in M.*

An implementation is *wait-free* if all of its algorithms are wait-free. Thus, in every admissible execution of a wait-free implementation, every operation by every nonfaulty process completes within a finite number of its own steps, no matter how the steps of the processes are scheduled and which other processes crash. Likewise, an implementation *tolerates f process crashes*, if, in every admissible execution in which at most f processes crash, every operation by every nonfaulty process eventually completes. Note that the composition of implementations that are wait-free (or tolerate f process crashes) is also wait-free (or tolerates f process crashes).

One can also use a simulation, given in the following lemma, to get space complexity lower bound in any shared memory model.

Lemma 9.2 *If there is a linearizable implementation of an object $\mathcal{O}$ using m' instances of object $\mathcal{O}'$ that is (randomized) wait-free (or tolerates f process crashes) and there is a solution to a problem P using m instances of object $\mathcal{O}$ that is (randomized) wait-free (or tolerates f process crashes), then there is a solution to problem P using $m'm$ instances of object $\mathcal{O}'$ that is (randomized) wait-free (or tolerates f process crashes).*

James Aspnes, in his paper "Time and Space Efficient Randomized Consensus," which appears in *PODC,* 1990 [7], showed that randomized consensus can be solved using $O(1)$ bounded counters. If there is a (randomized) wait-free implementation of a bounded counter using $o(\sqrt{n})$ registers, then Lemma 9.2 implies that there is a randomized wait-free solution to consensus using $o(\sqrt{n})$ registers, which contradicts Theorem 7.10, the $\Omega(\sqrt{n})$ lower bound on the number of registers needed for solving randomized consensus. Thus, we have the following result.

Corollary 9.3 $\Omega(\sqrt{n})$ *registers are needed for any (randomized) wait-free implementation of a bounded counter shared by n processes.*

When using a simulation, one should be careful to ensure that its cost is asymptotically smaller than the lower bound you are trying to obtain. For expected time complexity lower bounds on randomized implementations, composability is not straightforward and subtle issues can arise. See, for example, the paper "Linearizable Implementations do not Suffice for Randomized Distributed Computation," by Wojciech Golab, Lisa Higham, and Philipp Woelfel, in *STOC,* 2011 [45].

9.1   SIMULATIONS WITH DIFFERENT NUMBERS OF PROCESSES

In this section, we consider simulations of one asynchronous shared memory model by another with a different number of processes. Recall that the consensus number of an object is the maximum number of processes for which wait-free consensus can be solved in an asynchronous system in which processes communicate using only copies of the object and registers. (See Section 7.1.)

An easy observation is that a wait-free implementation of an object shared by n processes is also a wait-free implementation shared by fewer processes. This leads to the following impossibility result.

Lemma 9.4   *If there is a wait-free linearizable implementation of an object $\mathcal{O}'$ with consensus number c' in a model with $n > c$ processes using only registers and instances of objects with consensus number at most c, then $c \geq c'$.*

Proof.   Let B be a set of objects with consensus number at most c, let $\mathcal{O}'$ be an object with consensus number c', and suppose there is a wait-free linearizable implementation of $\mathcal{O}'$ in a model with $n > c$ processes using only registers and objects in B. Because this implementation is wait-free, it also works if there are only $n' = \min\{n, c'\} \leq n$ processes.

Since $\mathcal{O}'$ has consensus number c', there is a consensus algorithm for c' processes and, hence, for $n' \leq c'$ processes, using only registers and instances of $\mathcal{O}'$. Simulate this algorithm by replacing each instance of $\mathcal{O}'$ with an implementation from registers and instances of objects in B. This simulation solves consensus for n' processes using only registers and objects with consensus number at most c, so $n' \leq c$. This implies $n' < n$ and, thus, $n' = c'$. Hence $c' \leq c$. □

The availability of additional processes is not a problem if the number of processes that can crash does not increase.

Lemma 9.5   *Let M' be a model with $f + 1$ processes and let M be a model with $n > f$ processes and one register, R, in addition to the objects in M'. Furthermore, suppose that, in any execution of M, at most f processes can crash. If there is no solution to consensus in M, then there is no wait-free algorithm for consensus in M'.*

Proof.   Suppose there is a wait-free algorithm for consensus in M'. This algorithm can be simulated in M. Specifically, each process in M' is simulated by a different process in M. Just before returning, it writes its output value to R. The initial value of R is not a valid output. The remaining $n - f - 1$ processes in M repeatedly read R until it contains a value different from its initial value.

Since at most f processes crash in any execution, at least one of the processes performing the simulation does not crash. All such processes eventually complete the simulation and write the same output value to R. All of the $n - f - 1$ remaining processes that do not crash will eventually read this value and return it. Thus, there is a solution to consensus in M. $\square$

More generally, an algorithm can be simulated by any number of processes if the number of processes that can crash does not change, using extra registers and test&set objects. The idea is that every simulated process is simulated by every simulating process, rather than by just one simulating process.

A test&set object has two possible values, 0 and 1, and supports two operations, test&set, which returns the value of the object and sets it to 1, and reset, which resets the value of the object to 0. If test&set returns 0, we say that it *succeeds*. If it returns 1, we say it *fails*.

Theorem 9.6   *Let M' be a model with $n > f$ processes. Let M be a model with $f + 1$ processes that has n test&set objects and n registers in addition to the objects in M'. If there is no wait-free algorithm for k-set consensus in M, then there is no algorithm for k-set consensus in M' that tolerates f process crashes.*

Proof. Suppose there is an algorithm for k-set consensus in M' that tolerates f process crashes. The algorithm can be simulated in M as follows. Associated with each process q'_j in M', there is one test&set object, T_j, which is initially 0, and one register, R_j which will contain a state of the process. Initially R_j contains $\perp$, which is not a valid state. Every object that is in M' has the same initial value in M as it has in M'.

Each process p_i in M tries to choose the input for each process q'_j in M' and simulate the successive steps of its algorithm. It begins by performing test&set on T_j. If it is unsuccessful, it continues on to the next process in M' in round-robin order. If it is successful, it reads R_j. If R_j contains $\perp$, process p_i writes the initial state of process q'_j into R_j, using its own input as the input to q'_j. Then process p_i resets T_j and continues to the next process in M'. If $R_j \neq \perp$, then R_j contains the current state of q'_j. If process q'_j is about to return a value v, process p_i resets T_j to 0 and returns v. Otherwise, p_i performs the next step on behalf of q'_j, writes the resulting state of q'_j into R_j, resets T_j, and continues on to the next process in M'.

Each step that is performed on behalf of a process in M' is linearized when it is performed during the execution in M. The test&set object T_j associated with process q'_j is used as a lock to prevent any step of q'_j from being performed more than once. If a process in M crashes when it holds this lock, no further steps of process q'_j are simulated. In other words, process q'_j crashes in the simulated execution. If at most f of the $f + 1$ processes in M crash, then at most f simulated processes crash in the simulated execution. Since the k-set consensus algorithm being simulated tolerates f process crashes, the simulated outputs satisfy k-agreement and validity. Hence, the simulated algorithm solves k-set consensus in M. $\square$

In their paper, "A Completeness Theorem for a Class of Synchronization Objects," *PODC*, 1993 [2], Afek, Weisberger, and Weisman gave a wait-free, linearizable implementation of a test&set object using registers and any objects with consensus number at least two. Combining this fact with Theorem 9.6 for $k = 1$ and Lemma 9.2 implies the following result.

Corollary 9.7   *There is no solution to consensus that tolerates $f \geq 2$ process crashes in a system of $n > f$ processes using only objects with consensus number at most f.*

In particular, there is no algorithm for consensus in a system of $n \geq 3$ processes that tolerates two process crashes using only registers and test&set objects, fetch&add objects, swap objects, stacks, or queues. There is also no algorithm for consensus in a system of $n \geq 2m - 1$ processes that tolerates $2m - 2$ process crashes using only registers and m-assignment objects, for $m \geq 2$.

Theorem 9.6 and Corollary 9.7 are from Tushar Deepak Chandra, Vassos Hadzilacos, Prasad Jayanti, and Sam Toueg's paper, "Generalized Irreducibility of Consensus and the Equivalence of t-Resilient and Wait-Free Implementations of Consensus," *SIAM Journal on Computing*, 2005 [31]. However, the corollary is false when $f = 1$. In their paper "On the Power of Shared Object Types to Implement One-Resilient Consensus," *Distributed Computing*, 2000 [57], Wai-Kau Lo and Vassos Hadzilacos designed a deterministic object, which, together with five registers, can be used by three processes to get a solution to consensus that tolerates one process crash. They also proved that wait-free consensus for two processes cannot be solved using only instances of this object and registers.

9.2   THE BG SIMULATION

The BG simulation uses an approach similar to the proof of Theorem 9.6 for simulating an algorithm by a smaller number of processes, while still tolerating the same number of process crashes. However, it assumes that processes only communicate using single-writer registers.

Instead of using a test&set object as a lock to ensure that each step of each simulated process is performed at most once, it uses an object, called *safe election*, that can be implemented from single-writer registers. It supports two operations, nominate and elect. Each nonfaulty process first performs nominate and then repeatedly performs elect until it gets a result other than $\perp$. The identifier of a process that has completed nominate can also be returned by elect. We will show that, in any execution of safe election, all instances of elect that don't return $\perp$ return the same identifier. We will also show that, if no process crashes while performing nominate, then all processes that do not crash (while repeatedly performing elect) eventually get a result other than $\perp$ from elect.

The implementation of safe election that appears in Figure 9.1 uses one single-writer register $S[i]$ for each process p_i. These are all initialized to 0. In nominate, process p_i writes 1 to $S[i]$ and then reads the other registers. If any of them contains the value 2, it writes 0 to $S[i]$; otherwise, it writes 2. In elect, a process reads the registers in order until it sees a nonzero value. If it reads the value 1, it returns $\perp$. If it reads 2 from register $S[\ell]$, it returns the value ℓ, indicating that process p_ℓ has been elected.

```
nominate                                      elect
S[i] ← 1                                       for ℓ ← 0 to n − 1 do
for j ∈ {0, ..., n − 1} − {i} do                   s ← S[ℓ]
    if S[j] = 2                                    if s = 1 then return(⊥)
    then S[i] ← 0                                  if s = 2 then return(ℓ)
        return
S[i] ← 2
return
```

Figure 9.1: Safe election, code for process p_i.

From the code, it follows that no process completes nominate until some register contains the value 2. Furthermore, once a register contains the value 2, it never changes value. Thus, if a process does not crash while performing elect, one of the tests will be successful and the process will return with ⊥ or with a process id. A process has 1 in its register only when it is performing nominate. Therefore, if no process crashes while performing nominate, then, eventually, no register contains 1. Any instance of elect that starts after this point will not return ⊥.

Consider any execution of safe election in which each process begins by performing nominate and thereafter only performs elect. Let p_j be the process with smallest index that writes 2 to its register. Then no process returns any value smaller than j from elect. Let C be the first configuration in which some register contains 2. Any process that starts nominate after configuration C will read 2 from some register and, hence, will not write 2 to its own register. Therefore, in configuration C, register $S[j]$ contains 1 or 2. Since no process starts elect until after C, every call of elect returns either ⊥ or j. Thus, all processes that return from elect with a value other than ⊥ return the same value.

Let M' be an asynchronous shared memory model in which n processes communicate using single-writer registers. It suffices to assume each process q'_j in M' has exactly one single-writer register R'_j to which it can write, since multiple single-writer registers with the same writer can be combined into one single-writer register having multiple fields.

Suppose there is a solution to k-set consensus in M' that tolerates f process crashes, where $k \leq f < n$. We will show how to obtain a wait-free simulation of this algorithm in an asynchronous shared memory model M with $f + 1$ processes that communicate using single-writer registers.

As in the simulation in the proof of Theorem 9.6, each process p_i in M tries to choose the input for each process q'_j in M' and simulate the successive steps of its algorithm. A separate set of n single-writer registers, $\{S[j, t, i] \mid i = 0, ..., n − 1\}$, is used to perform safe election for the t'th simulated step of process q'_j.

If a process p_i crashes while it is performing multiple instances of nominate, it could cause the simulations of those processes to block. To prevent this from happening, once process p_i begins to perform nominate, it completes it before doing anything else. Since the worst-case step complexity of nominate is $n + 1$, this cannot prevent p_i from simulating other processes in M'.

A process p_i might continually perform elect with result $\perp$ in some instance of safe election, because some other process has crashed or will eventually crash. To ensure it continues to make progress, process p_i might have to perform many instances of safe election concurrently. However, if process p_i crashes after being elected to perform the next steps of many simulated processes, but before it performs them, the simulations of all those processes will be blocked. Instead, to simulate the t'th step of process q'_j, each process p_i performs this step and records the resulting state of q'_j (including the contents of R'_j) in a single-writer register $R[j, t, i]$ before performing the t'th instance of safe election for process q'_j. Then, even if the elected process crashes while it is performing elect, the remaining processes in M can continue with the simulation of process q'_j.

Suppose that, during an execution of the instance of safe election for the t'th step of process q'_j, a process is elected that changes the simulated value of R'_j from v to v'. Later, it is possible that another (slow) process crashes while performing nominate in the same instance of safe election. Then any process that performs elect afterwards will return $\perp$ and, hence, is blocked from finding out which process was elected. This can make it impossible to linearize the simulated execution, since one process could simulate reading v' from R'_j and, later, another process could simulate reading v from R'_j. To prevent this from happening, there is an n-component single-writer snapshot object A_j for each process q'_j in M'. (Note that there is a wait-free, linearizable implementation of a single-writer snapshot object from single-writer registers [1].) We may assume that, initially, each component of A_j contains $\perp$. Immediately after a process p_i returns with id ℓ from elect in the t'th instance of safe election for process q'_j, it updates component i of the snapshot object A_j with the value (t, ℓ). A simulating process can then scan A_j to determine the last step of process q'_j that has been simulated and which simulating process was elected for that step.

A process p_i simulating a process q'_j first does a scan of A_j. If it sees that A_j has never been updated, it writes the initial state of process q'_j to register $R[j, 0, i]$ (including the initial value of R'_j) using its own input as the input to process q'_j. Then it performs nominate and one call to elect in the instance of safe election for the initialization of process q'_j using the set of registers $\{S[j, 0, i] \mid i = 0, \ldots, n - 1\}$. If $\perp$ is returned, it temporarily stops simulating q'_j and starts or continues simulating the next process in M', in round-robin order. If p_i ever returns from elect with a value $\ell \neq \perp$ in this instance of safe election, it then updates component i of the snapshot object A_j with the pair $(0, \ell)$ to finish its simulation of the initialization of process q'_j.

If process p_i sees that A_j has been updated at least once, it finds the pair (t, ℓ) contained in its components with the largest value of t. Then it reads the state of process q'_j after its t'th step, as recorded in $R[j, t, \ell]$ by the process p_ℓ elected for this step. If the next step of process q'_j is to return value v, then process p_i returns value v and performs no further steps in the simulation. If the next step of process q'_j is a WRITE, process p_i determines the resulting state of process q'_j and writes this state (including the value written by process q'_j) to register $R[j, t + 1, i]$. If the next step of process q'_j is a READ of the single-writer register R'_r of process q'_r, process p_i scans the snapshot object A_r. From this, p_i determines t_h, the number of steps of process q'_r that have been simulated, and which process, p_h, was elected in the instance of safe election for the last of these steps. Then process p_i reads $R[r, t_h, h]$ and, from it, determines the simulated contents of R'_r at the end of step t_h. Finally, process p_i determines the resulting state of process q'_j and writes this state to $R[j, t + 1, i]$. For both READs and WRITEs, process p_i next performs nominate and one call to elect in the instance of safe election for step $k + 1$ by process q'_j, using the set of registers $\{S[j, t + 1, i] \mid i = 0, \ldots, n - 1\}$. If $\perp$ is returned, it temporarily stops simulating q'_j and starts or continues simulating the next process in M', in round-robin order. If p_i ever returns from elect with a value $\ell \neq \perp$ in this instance of safe election, it then updates component i of the snapshot object A_j with the pair $(k + 1, \ell)$ as its final piece of the simulation of step $k + 1$ by process q'_j.

After finishing the simulation of the initialization of process q'_j or a step by process q'_j, process p_i scans A_j and starts simulating another step of process q'_j.

Each READ that is performed on behalf of a process q'_j in M' is linearized when the process elected for that step last did its (atomic) scan of A_j prior to being elected. If step t of a simulated process is a WRITE, it is linearized the first time any process updates the snapshot object A_j with a pair (t, ℓ). Note that all processes that finish this instance of safe election return from elect with the same value, namely the index of the process elected for this step.

If a process in M crashes while it is performing nominate as part of its simulation of step t by process q'_j, it can only block further steps of process q'_j from being simulated. Thus, if at least one process (in M) does not crash, then at most f simulated processes crash in the simulated execution. Since the k-set consensus algorithm being simulated tolerates f process crashes, the simulated outputs satisfy k-agreement and validity. Hence, the simulated algorithm solves k-set consensus in M.

Thus, we have shown the following result.

Theorem 9.8 *Let M and M' be asynchronous shared memory models in which processes communicate using single-writer registers. Suppose M has $f + 1$ processes and M' has $n > f \geq k$ processes. If there is no wait-free solution to k-set consensus in M, then there is no solution to k-set consensus in M' that tolerates f process crashes.*

Corollary 9.9 *There is no solution to k-set consensus for $n > f \geq k$ processes that tolerates f process crashes in an asynchronous shared memory model in which processes communicate using single-writer registers.*

Proof. Suppose there is a solution to k-set consensus in M' that tolerates f process crashes. Since any algorithm for k-set consensus is also an algorithm for f-set consensus, it follows from Theorem 9.8 that there is a wait-free algorithm for $f + 1$ processes that solves f-set consensus using only single-writer registers. This contradicts Theorem 8.1. ☐

The BG simulation was presented by Elizabeth Borowsky and Eli Gafni, in their paper, "Generalized FLP Impossibility Result for t-resilient Asynchronous Computations," *STOC,* 1993 [26]. Its proof of correctness appears in "The BG Distributed Simulation Algorithm," by Elizabeth Borowsky, Eli Gafni, Nancy Lynch, and Sergio Rajsbaum, *Distributed Computing,* 2001 [27]. Our proof uses a more modular safe election object.

9.3   ROUND-BY-ROUND SIMULATIONS

Round-by-round simulations are used to derive a lower bound on the number of rounds to solve a problem in a synchronous message-passing model M from the impossibility of that problem in an asynchronous shared-memory model M' with the same number of processes, in which processes communicate using registers. Specifically, they show how to simulate any f-round execution in model M, in which at most one process crashes each round, using model M', in which at most one process crashes.

We consider a synchronous broadcast model M. In each round, a process sends the same message to all processes, receives messages from all processes that have not crashed, and possibly receives some messages from the processes that crashed during the round.

This model can simulate a model in which a process can send different messages to different processes in the same round by broadcasting the concatenation of all the messages and their intended recipients in the round. This does not change the number of rounds of communication.

The round by round simulation will use a simple approximate agreement object, which can solve the approximate agreement problem defined in Section 2.3, with $\epsilon = \frac{1}{2}$ and each input in $\{0, 1\}$. This object supports one operation, propose(v), where $v \in \{0, 1\}$, which returns a value in $\{0, \frac{1}{2}, 1\}$ such that, in every execution, the return values satisfy validity and $\frac{1}{2}$-agreement. Thus, if all inputs to propose are the same, then this is the only value that is returned. Furthermore, there is no execution in which 0 and 1 are both returned.

The implementation in Figure 9.2 uses two registers, R_0 and R_1, both initially 0. If the input value of a process is 0, it writes 1 to R_0; otherwise it writes 1 to R_1. Then it reads the other register. If the other register is still 0, then the process outputs its input value; otherwise, it outputs $\frac{1}{2}$. If all processes have the same input value v, they only write to R_v and, hence, they can only read 0 from R_{1-v}. Thus, the only value they output is v. Otherwise, some process has input 0 and some other process has input 1. This ensures validity, since the only possible output values are 0, 1, and $\frac{1}{2}$.

$$\text{propose}(x)$$
$$R_x \leftarrow \text{write } 1$$
$$\text{if } R_{1-x} = 0 \text{ then return } x$$
$$\text{else return } \tfrac{1}{2}$$

Figure 9.2: Approximate agreement object, code for process p_i.

Suppose register R_v is the first register that is written to in some execution. Then every process with input value $1 - v$ will read 1 from R_v and will output $\tfrac{1}{2}$. Hence, only values in $\{v, \tfrac{1}{2}\}$ are output and they are within $\tfrac{1}{2}$ of one another. Thus, $\tfrac{1}{2}$-agreement is ensured.

Theorem 9.10   *Any n-process consensus algorithm in model M that tolerates $f < n$ process crashes requires more than f rounds.*

Proof. Suppose there is an algorithm for n-process consensus in model M that tolerates $f < n$ process crashes and requires at most f rounds. We will simulate an execution of this algorithm in the asynchronous shared memory model M' with at most one process crash. Since consensus is unsolvable in M', we get a contradiction.

Each process q_i of M' simulates a different process p_i of M, using its own input as the input to p_i. The processes simulate the rounds of the algorithm in order. Since one process in M' can crash, processes must finish the simulation of a round when at least $n - 1$ processes have participated in it.

The idea is that if some process q_i is slow to participate in round r or it crashes before announcing the message p_i broadcast in round r, other processes will propose that process p_i is faulty. If the processes agree that p_i is faulty, they will stop simulating it. However, it is not necessary that the simulating processes agree in the same round. It suffices that some processes think agreement is reached in one round and the remainder think it is reached in the subsequent round. This simulates the situation in which process p_i fails during the round after sending messages to the second set of processes.

Each process, q_i locally maintains a set *faulty*$_i$ of processes in M that it proposes to be faulty. Initially, this set is empty. Once a process identifier is added to this set, it is never removed.

For each round, there is a shared array of single-writer registers, $B_r[0..n-1]$, all of whose entries are initially empty, and a shared array $A_r[0..n-1]$ of approximate agreement objects, each in its initial state.

At the beginning of the simulation of round $r \geq 1$, the message that process p_i broadcasts in round r is written into $B_r[i]$ by process q_i, unless process q_i agreed that process p_i was faulty in an earlier round. Then process q_i repeatedly performs collect on B_r until it has seen a view with n nonempty components or it has twice seen a view with $n - 1$ nonempty components. If q_i does not fail, one of these will happen eventually, since at most one process fails.

For all $j \in \{0, \ldots, n-1\}$, if $j \in faulty_i$ or process q_i sees that $B_r[j]$ is empty, then process q_i performs propose(0) on $A_r[j]$; otherwise it performs propose(1) on $A_r[j]$. If the approximate agreement object returns 0 to process q_i, then q_i agrees that process p_j has crashed, adds j to $faulty_i$, and, if $j \neq i$, does not simulate the receipt of a message from process p_j to process p_i. If it returns 1 or $\frac{1}{2}$ to process q_i, then at least one process saw that $B_r[j]$ was nonempty, so process q_i can read $B_r[j]$ to simulate the receipt of a message from process p_j to process p_i. When $\frac{1}{2}$ is returned, process q_i also adds j to $faulty_i$.

If $A_r[j]$ returns 0 to any process, then it returns either 0 or $\frac{1}{2}$ to every process, so every process q_i will add j to $faulty_i$. Hence, in all subsequent rounds, r', no process will perform propose(1) on $A_{r'}[j]$ and, by validity, $A_{r'}[j]$ will return 0 to every process. Thus, each process will agree that process p_i is faulty in either round r or round $r+1$.

Note that every process that sees $n-1$ nonempty components in its last collect of B_r sees the same empty component. Thus, at most one process is added to $\cup_{i=0}^{n-1} faulty_i$ each round. Since every simulated process that has failed is in $\cup_{i=0}^{n-1} faulty_i$, at most r simulated processes fail during the simulation of the first r rounds. $\qquad \square$

The use of a simulation to prove the lower bound on the number of rounds was originally suggested by Eli Gafni, in "Round-by-round Fault Detectors: Unifying Synchrony and Asynchrony," *PODC*, 1998 [42]. Our proof is somewhat simpler, using standard approximate agreement, instead of the specialized consensus object Gafni used.

9.4 UNCOMPUTABILITY OF CONSENSUS NUMBER

In sequential computation, a common way to prove that a problem is undecidable is to give a reduction to it from a problem already known to be undecidable, such as the halting problem. We can use the same technique for showing the uncomputability of distributed computing problems. Here is one example.

Theorem 9.11 *There is no algorithm that, given the sequential specifications of an object, decides whether its consensus number is 1.*

Proof. To obtain a contradiction, suppose there is such an algorithm. We will use it to solve the halting problem for one-tape Turing machines with initially blank tape.

Given a deterministic Turing machine M, let $\mathcal{C}$ be the set of all configurations of M and let C_0 be the configuration when M is in its initial state and its tape is blank. Define the object $\mathcal{O}$ whose value set is $\mathcal{C} \times \{true, false\}$, whose initial value is $(C_0, false)$, and which supports one operation, next. This operation takes no input and returns a value in $\{0, 1, 2\}$. When $\mathcal{O}$ has value $(C, flag)$, next behaves as follows:

- If $flag = false$ and C is not a final configuration of M, then next returns 0 and the new value of $\mathcal{O}$ is $(C', false)$, where C' is the configuration that results when M takes one step starting from configuration C.

- If $flag = false$ and C is a final configuration of M, then next returns 1 and the new value of $\mathcal{O}$ is $(C, true)$.

- If $flag = true$, next returns 2 and the value of $\mathcal{O}$ remains unchanged.

Suppose that M halts starting from configuration C_0. Then the algorithm in Figure 9.3 solves wait-free consensus for two processes using object $\mathcal{O}$ and two single-writer registers, R_0 and R_1.

$$R_i \leftarrow x_i$$
$$\text{repeat } u \leftarrow \text{next until } u \neq 0$$
$$\text{if } u = 1 \text{ then return } x_i$$
$$\text{else return } R_{1-i}$$

Figure 9.3: Two-process wait-free consensus, code for process p_i with input x_i.

The value decided in any execution of this algorithm is the input value of the process that first performs next after $\mathcal{O}$'s first component is a final configuration. In this case, the consensus number of $\mathcal{O}$ is at least 2.

Now suppose that M does not halt starting from configuration C_0. Then next always returns 0. If there was an algorithm that solved wait-free consensus for two processes using only registers and copies of object $\mathcal{O}$, then there would also be an algorithm that solved wait-free consensus for two processes using only registers: simply replace each occurrence of next by the constant 0. But this is impossible. Therefore, the consensus number of $\mathcal{O}$ is 1.

Therefore M halts starting from configuration C_0 if and only if the consensus number of $\mathcal{O}$ is not 1. Since the halting problem is undecidable, it follow that deciding whether $\mathcal{O}$ has consensus number 1 is also undecidable. □

It follows that there is no algorithm to compute the consensus number of an object. This result is from "Some Results on the Impossibility, Universality, and Decidability of Consensus," by Prasad Jayanti and Sam Toueg, which appeared in *WDAG*, 1992 [54]. However, Eric Ruppert, in his paper, "Determining Consensus Numbers," *SIAM Journal on Computing*, 2000 [61], shows that, for certain classes of objects, for example, deterministic objects with finite value sets that support only read-modify-write primitives, there is an algorithm that decides whether a given object has consensus number at least n.

Bibliography

[1] Yehuda Afek, Hagit Attiya, Danny Dolev, Eli Gafni, Michael Merritt, and Nir Shavit. Atomic snapshots of shared memory. *Journal of the ACM*, 40(4):873–890, 1993. DOI: 10.1145/153724.153741. 129

[2] Yehuda Afek, Eytan Weisberger, and Hanan Weisman. A completeness theorem for a class of synchronization objects. In *Proceedings of the Twelfth Annual ACM Symposium on Principles of Distributed Computing*, pages 159–170, 1993. DOI: 10.1145/164051.164071. 126

[3] Marcos Kawazoe Aguilera and Sam Toueg. A simple bivalency proof that t-resilient consensus requires $t + 1$ rounds. *Information Processing Letters*, 71(3-4):155–158, 1999. DOI: 10.1016/S0020-0190(99)00100-3. 68

[4] Martin Aigner and Günter M. Ziegler, *Proofs from THE BOOK*, Springer-Verlag, 1998. DOI: 10.1007/978-3-642-00856-6 110

[5] Nechama Allenberg-Navony, Alon Itai, and Shlomo Moran. Average and randomized complexity of distributed problems. *SIAM Journal on Computing*, 25(6):1254–1267, 1996. DOI: 10.1137/S0097539793252432. 115

[6] Eshrat Arjomandi, Michael J. Fischer, and Nancy A. Lynch. Efficiency of synchronous versus asynchronous distributed systems. *Journal of the ACM*, 30(3):449–456, 1983. DOI: 10.1145/2402.322387. 15

[7] James Aspnes. Time-and space-efficient randomized consensus. *Journal of Algorithms*, 14(3):414–431, 1993. DOI: 10.1006/jagm.1993.1022. 124

[8] James Aspnes. A modular approach to shared-memory consensus, with applications to the probabilistic-write model. *Distributed Computing*, 25(2):179–188, 2012. DOI: 10.1007/s00446-011-0134-8. 111

[9] James Aspnes, Hagit Attiya, and Keren Censor-Hillel. Polylogarithmic concurrent data structures from monotone circuits. *Journal of the ACM*, 59(1), 2012. DOI: 10.1145/2108242.2108244. 120

[10] Jim Aspnes and Faith Ellen. Tight bounds for adopt-commit objects. *Theory of Computing Systems*, to appear, 2013. DOI: 10.1007/s00224-013-9448-1. 113

[11] Hagit Attiya and Keren Censor. Tight bounds for asynchronous randomized consensus. *Journal of the ACM*, 55(5):20, 2008. DOI: 10.1145/1411509.1411510. 96

[12] Hagit Attiya, Faith Ellen, and Panagiota Fatourou. The complexity of updating snapshot objects. *Journal of Parallel and Distributed Computing*, 71(12):1570–1577, 2011. DOI: 10.1016/j.jpdc.2011.08.002. 108

[13] Hagit Attiya, Faith Ellen Fich, and Yaniv Kaplan. Lower bounds for adaptive collect and related objects. In *Proceedings of the Twenty-Third Annual ACM Symposium on Principles of Distributed Computing*, pages 60–69, 2004. DOI: 10.1145/1011767.1011777. 110

[14] Hagit Attiya and Danny Hendler. Time and space lower bounds for implementations using k-CAS. *IEEE Transactions on Parallel and Distributed Systems*, 21(2):162–173, 2010. DOI: 10.1109/TPDS.2009.60. 40

[15] Hagit Attiya, Eshcar Hillel, and Alessia Milani. Inherent limitations on disjoint-access parallel implementations of transactional memory. *Theory of Computing Systems*, 49(2):698–719, 2011. DOI: 10.1007/s00224-010-9304-5. 108

[16] Hagit Attiya, Nancy A. Lynch, and Nir Shavit. Are wait-free algorithms fast? *Journal of the ACM*, 41(4):725–763, 1994. DOI: 10.1145/179812.179902. 37

[17] Hagit Attiya and Marios Mavronicolas. Efficiency of semisynchronous versus asynchronous networks. *Mathematical Systems Theory*, 27(6):547–571, 1994. DOI: 10.1007/BF01191625. 15

[18] Hagit Attiya and Ami Paz. Counting-based impossibility proofs for renaming and set agreement. In *Proceedings of Twenty-Sixth International Symposium on Distributed Computing*, pages 356–370, 2012. DOI: 10.1007/978-3-642-33651-5_25. 103

[19] Hagit Attiya and Ophir Rachman. Atomic snapshots in $O(n \log n)$ operations. *SIAM Journal on Computing*, 27(2):319–340, 1998. DOI: 10.1137/S0097539795279463. 61

[20] Hagit Attiya and Sergio Rajsbaum. The combinatorial structure of wait-free solvable tasks. *SIAM Journal on Computing*, 31(4):1286–1313, 2002. DOI: 10.1137/S0097539797330689. 103

[21] Hagit Attiya and Jennifer L. Welch. Sequential consistency versus linearizability. *ACM Transactions on Computer Systems*, 12(2):91–122, 1994. DOI: 10.1145/176575.176576. 22

[22] Hagit Attiya and Jennifer L. Welch. *Distributed Computing: Fundamentals, Simulations, and Advanced Topics, second edition*. Wiley-Interscience, 2004. DOI: 10.1002/0471478210. 2

[23] Ziv Bar-Joseph and Michael Ben-Or. A tight lower bound for randomized synchronous consensus. In *Proceedings of the Seventeenth Annual ACM Symposium on Principles of Distributed Computing*, pages 193–199, 1998. DOI: 10.1145/277697.277733. 96

[24] Paul Beame. Limits on the power of concurrent-write parallel machines. *Information and Computation*, 76(1):13–28, 1988. DOI: 10.1016/0890-5401(88)90040-5. 41

[25] Hans L. Bodlaender. New lower bound techniques for distributed leader finding and other problems on rings of processors. *Theoretical Computer Science*, 81(2):237–256, 1991. DOI: 10.1016/0304-3975(91)90193-6. 115

[26] Elizabeth Borowsky and Eli Gafni. Generalized FLP impossibility result for *t*-resilient asynchronous computations. In *Proceedings of the Twenty-Fifth Annual ACM Symposium on Theory of Computing*, pages 91–100, 1993. DOI: 10.1145/167088.167119. 103, 131

[27] Elizabeth Borowsky, Eli Gafni, Nancy Lynch, and Sergio Rajsbaum. The BG distributed simulation algorithm. *Distributed Computing*, 14(3):127–146, 2001. DOI: 10.1007/PL00008933. 131

[28] Alex Brodsky and Faith Ellen Fich. Efficient synchronous snapshots. In *Proceedings of the Twenty-Third Annual ACM Symposium on Principles of Distributed Computing*, pages 70–79, 2004. DOI: 10.1145/1011767.1011778. 42

[29] James E. Burns, Paul Jackson, Nancy A. Lynch, Michael J. Fischer, and Gary L. Peterson. Data requirements for implementation of n-process mutual exclusion using a single shared variable. *Journal of the ACM*, 29(1):183–205, 1982. DOI: 10.1145/322290.322302. 7

[30] James E. Burns and Nancy A. Lynch. Bounds on shared memory for mutual exclusion. *Information and Computation*, 107(2):171–184, 1993. DOI: 10.1006/inco.1993.1065. 44

[31] Tushar Deepak Chandra, Vassos Hadzilacos, Prasad Jayanti, and Sam Toueg. Generalized irreducibility of consensus and the equivalence of t-resilient and wait-free implementations of consensus. *SIAM Journal on Computing*, 34(2):333–357, 2005. DOI: 10.1137/S0097539798344367. 127

[32] Soma Chaudhuri, Rainer Gawlick, and Nancy A. Lynch. Designing algorithms for distributed systems with partially synchronized clocks. In *Proceedings of the Twelfth Annual ACM Symposium on Principles of Distributed Computing*, pages 121–132, 1993. DOI: 10.1145/164051.164068. 22

[33] Stephen Cook, Cynthia Dwork, and Rüdiger Reischuk. Upper and lower time bounds for parallel random access machines without simultaneous writes. *SIAM Journal on Computing*, 15(1):87–97, 1986. DOI: 10.1137/0215006. 36

[34] Cynthia Dwork and Yoram Moses. Knowledge and common knowledge in a byzantine environment: Crash failures. *Information and Computation*, 88(2):156–186, 1990. DOI: 10.1016/0890-5401(90)90014-9. 13

[35] Faith Ellen, Panagiota Fatourou, and Eric Ruppert. Time lower bounds for implementations of multi-writer snapshots. *Journal of the ACM*, 54(6), 2007. DOI: 10.1145/1314690.1314694. 61

[36] Faith Ellen, Panagiota Fatourou, and Eric Ruppert. The space complexity of unbounded timestamps. *Distributed Computing*, 21(2):103–115, 2008. DOI: 10.1007/s00446-008-0060-6. 52

[37] Faith Ellen, Danny Hendler, and Nir Shavit. On the inherent sequentiality of concurrent objects. *SIAM Journal on Computing*, 41(3):519–536, 2012. DOI: 10.1137/08072646X. 64

[38] Faith Fich, Maurice Herlihy, and Nir Shavit. On the space complexity of randomized synchronization. *Journal of the ACM*, 45(5):843–862, 1998. DOI: 10.1145/290179.290183. 81

[39] Faith Fich and Eric Ruppert. Hundreds of impossibility results for distributed computing, *Distributed Computing*, 16(2-3):121–163, 2003. DOI: 10.1007/s00446-003-0091-y. 2

[40] Michael J. Fischer, Nancy A. Lynch, and Michael Merritt. Easy impossibility proofs for distributed consensus problems. *Distributed Computing*, 1(1):26–39, 1986. DOI: 10.1007/BF01843568. 29, 32

[41] Michael J. Fischer, Nancy A. Lynch, and Michael S. Paterson. Impossibility of distributed consensus with one faulty process. *Journal of the ACM*, 32(2):374–382, 1985. DOI: 10.1145/3149.214121. 13, 65, 70

[42] Eli Gafni. Round-by-round fault detectors: Unifying synchrony and asynchrony. In *Proceedings of the Seventeenth Annual ACM Symposium on Principles of Distributed Computing*, pages 143–152, 1998. DOI: 10.1145/277697.277724. 133

[43] Juan A. Garay and Yoram Moses. Fully polynomial byzantine agreement for $n > 3t$ processors in $t + 1$ rounds. *SIAM Journal on Computing*, 27(1):247–290, 1998. DOI: 10.1137/S0097539794265232. 29

[44] George Giakkoupis and Philipp Woelfel. A tight RMR lower bound for randomized mutual exclusion. In *Proceedings of the Forty-Fourth Annual ACM Symposium on Theory of Computing*, pages 983–1001, 2012. DOI: 10.1145/2213977.2214066. 115

[45] Wojciech Golab, Lisa Higham, and Philipp Woelfel. Linearizable implementations do not suffice for randomized distributed computation. In *Proceedings of the Forty-Third Annual ACM Symposium on Theory of Computing*, pages 373–382, 2011. DOI: 10.1145/1993636.1993687. 124

[46] Maryam Helmi, Lisa Higham, Eduardo Pacheco, and Philipp Woelfel. The space complexity of long-lived and one-shot timestamp implementations. In *Proceedings of the Thirtieh Annual ACM Symposium on Principles of Distributed Computing*, pages 139–148, 2011. DOI: 10.1145/1993806.1993826. 52

[47] Maurice Herlihy. Wait-free synchronization. *ACM Transactions on Programming Languages and Systems*, 13(1):124–149, 1991. DOI: 10.1145/114005.102808. 67

[48] Maurice Herlihy, Dmitry Kozlov, and Sergio Rajsbaum. *Distributed Computing Through Combinatorial Topology*. Morgan Kaufmann, 2013. 2

[49] Maurice Herlihy and Nir Shavit. The topological structure of asynchronous computability. *Journal of the ACM*, 46(6):858–923, 1999. DOI: 10.1145/331524.331529. 103

[50] Amos Israeli, Amnon Shaham, and Asaf Shirazi. Linear-time snapshot implementations in unbalanced systems. *Mathematical Systems Theory*, 28(5):469–486, 1995. DOI: 10.1007/BF01185868. 61

[51] Amos Israeli and Asaf Shirazi. The time complexity of updating snapshot memories. *Information Processing Letters*, 65(1):33–40, 1998. DOI: 10.1016/S0020-0190(97)00189-0. 108

[52] Prasad Jayanti. A time complexity lower bound for randomized implementations of some shared objects. In *Proceedings of the Seventeenth Annual ACM Symposium on Principles of Distributed Computing*, pages 201–210, 1998. DOI: 10.1145/277697.277735. 41

[53] Prasad Jayanti, King Tan, and Sam Toueg. Time and space lower bounds for nonblocking implementations. *SIAM Journal on Computing*, 30(2):438–456, 2000. DOI: 10.1137/S0097539797317299. 55

[54] Prasad Jayanti and Sam Toueg. Some results on the impossibility, universality, and decidability of consensus. In *Proceedings of the Sixth International Workshop on Distributed Algorithms*, pages 69–84, 1992. DOI: 10.1007/3-540-56188-9_5. 134

[55] Leslie Lamport. A new solution of Dijkstra's concurrent programming problem. *Communications of the ACM*, 17(4):453–455, 1974. DOI: 10.1145/361082.361093. 49

[56] Richard J. Lipton and Jonathan S. Sandberg. PRAM: A scalable shared memory. Technical report, Princeton University, 1988. 6

[57] Wai-Kau Lo and Vassos Hadzilacos. On the power of shared object types to implement one-resilient consensus. *Distributed Computing*, 13(4):219–238, 2000. DOI: 10.1007/PL00008920. 127

[58] Jennifer Lundelius and Nancy A. Lynch. An upper and lower bound for clock synchronization. *Information and Control*, 62(2):190–204, 1984. DOI: 10.1016/S0019-9958(84)80033-9. 24

[59] Nancy A. Lynch. A hundred impossibility proofs for distributed computing. In *Proceedings of the Eighth Annual ACM Symposium on Principles of Distributed Computing*, pages 1–28, 1989. DOI: 10.1145/72981.72982. 2

[60] Yoram Moses and Sergio Rajsbaum. A layered analysis of consensus. *SIAM Journal on Computing*, 31(4):989–1021, 2002. DOI: 10.1137/S0097539799364006. 70

[61] Eric Ruppert. Determining consensus numbers. *SIAM Journal on Computing*, 30(4):1156–1168, 2000. DOI: 10.1137/S0097539797329439. 134

[62] Michael Saks and Fotios Zaharoglou. Wait-free k-set agreement is impossible: The topology of public knowledge. *SIAM Journal on Computing*, 29(5):1449–1483, 2000. DOI: 10.1137/S0097539796307698. 103

[63] Erik Schenk. Faster approximate agreement with multi-writer registers. In *Proceedings of the Thirty-Six Annual IEEE Symposium on Foundations of Computer Science*, pages 714–723, 1995. DOI: 10.1109/SFCS.1995.492673. 8

[64] T. K. Srikanth and Sam Toueg. Optimal clock synchronization. *Journal of the ACM*, 34(3):626–645, 1987. DOI: 10.1145/28869.28876. 26, 32

[65] Paul Vitanyi and Baruch Awerbuch. Atomic shared register access by asynchronous hardware. In *Proceedings of the Twenty-Seventh Annual IEEE Symposium on Foundations of Computer Science*, pages 233–243, 1986. DOI: 10.1109/SFCS.1986.11. 9

[66] Andrew Chi-Chih Yao. Probabilistic computations: Toward a unified measure of complexity. In *Proceedings of the Eighteenth Annual IEEE Symposium on Foundations of Computer Science*, pages 222–227, 1977. DOI: 10.1109/SFCS.1977.24. 115

Authors' Biographies

HAGIT ATTIYA

Hagit Attiya is a Professor in the Department of Computer Science at the Technion–Israel Institute of Technology. She received her Ph.D. from the Hebrew University of Jerusalem in 1987 and was a post-doctoral research associate at the Laboratory for Computer Science at MIT until 1990. Her research spans various topics of distributed computing and she is particularly interested in how the theoretical principles affect the design of distributed and concurrent systems. She co-authored the book *Distributed Computing: Fundamentals, Simulations, and Advanced Topics*, published by Wiley. In 1997, Hagit served as the chair of the program committee for PODC, and she is currently the editor-in-chief of the journal *Distributed Computing*.

FAITH ELLEN

Faith Ellen is a Professor in the Department of Computer Science at the University of Toronto. She received her Ph.D. from the University of California at Berkeley in 1986 and was an Assistant Professor in the Computer Science Department at the University of Washington in Seattle from 1983 to 1986. Her research spans the theory of distributed computing, complexity theory, and data structures and she is primarily interested in understanding how parameters of various models affect their computational power. Faith was the vice-chair of SIGACT from 1997 to 2001 and the chair of the steering committee for PODC from 2006 to 2009. In 2003, she served as the chair of the program committee for DISC.

Index

Printed in the United States
by Baker & Taylor Publisher Services